MIKE KER[R]

FOUR FUNERALS, NO MARRIAGE

A MEMOIR

MIKE KEREN

Four Funerals, No Marriage

A memoir

Woodhall Press
Norwalk, CT

woodhall press

Woodhall Press, 81 Old Saugatuck Road, Norwalk, CT 06855
WoodhallPress.com

Cover design: Andrea Orlic
Layout artist: Amie McCracken

Library of Congress Cataloging-in-Publication Data available
ISBN 978-1-949116-67-0 (paper: alk paper)
ISBN 978-1-949116-68-7 (electronic)
First Edition

Distributed by Independent Publishers Group
(800) 888-4741
Printed in the United States of America

Author's Note on Memoir

Memoir, according to etymonline.com, an etymology website, from the Latin "memoria (to remember)," meaning a person's written account of his or her life. This book is my memoir, an account of the almost three years that my life was consumed with care giving responsibilities as my parents and in-laws faced their end of life. As a psychologist, I know that memory can be a tricky thing. It is impacted by our emotional reactions, time, and many other factors. This book is an account of that time as I remember it. Others, including those written about herein, are welcome to write and publish their own accounts of their memories of the process. Those years were a very salient time in my life and thus I was inspired to put them to paper, to share the moments of humor, love, and frustration along the way. It was a journey of discovery, where a sense of duty often evolved into love, and my feelings of love supported my sense of duty.

As a psychologist, I also realize that the doctor-patient relationship is a vital part of healthcare and of healing. My experiences of my relationships with the varied doctors, nurses, and other providers we worked with may be different than the experiences of others who worked with the same doctors, etc. Doctors I may have idolized and viewed as heroes, others may have disliked and vice versa. For that reason, I have chosen to change the names of all the doctors and nurses referenced in this account, and I have not given the names of the hospitals I wrote about.

To Joan Marie and Jim Johnson
And
Gloria and Arthur Keren
who gave me the honor to care for them and help them to finish their lives with dignity.

CONTENTS

PART
ONE

1

THE EYES OF OEDIPUS

Preparing to place the leads for an EKG, the nurse looked at me across Mom's hospital bed, suggesting that I leave the room. I returned a warm and reassuring smile, stating, "Oh, Mom was a stripper back in the day. She raised me in the dressing rooms at the clubs. I've seen it all." Mom's monitor went berserk, as she couldn't restrain her laughing fit at this. Of course, Mom was never a stripper (at least not that I knew) but that was the warped sense of humor Mom and I shared.

Since we had arrived at the ER a few hours before, the nurses and techs had been poking and prodding her. Most asked me to leave the room if they had to expose flesh. My mother would protest, "He came out of me, I'm not worried about him seeing me."

There'd be a shrug, maybe a giggle, and the test or procedure would proceed. I would make an effort to turn my head, not just because I hated watching needles, blood draws, and procedures, but because despite Mom's comfort with my seeing her, I did not feel the need to have that experience. Tom, my partner, would always leave the room, although Mom encouraged him to stay as well. I had never realized she was a frustrated exhibitionist. Throughout the tests and pokes, she would grip my hand with ever-increasing pressure, betraying her fear and showing confidence in my ability to protect her.

Whether or not the nurse believed Mom had been a stripper, the story certainly put her at ease. Where previous nurses and techs would fold back Mom's gown, only exposing the smallest necessary areas to my avoidant eyes, this nurse unsnapped the gown from Mom's shoulder and threw it back. It all happened so fast I couldn't turn my head; I couldn't even avert my eyes. There they were, like three-dimensional arches in front of McDonald's, my mother's breasts. I put on my best clinical self and looked elsewhere. I told myself at least it wasn't her other parts.

Mom's leads got adjusted and the nurse left the room. Tom, my partner, came in and asked, "What's so funny? You two are laughing in the middle of the Emergency Room like you're in a comedy club."

We filled him in. Through his own laughter he looked at my mom and said, "Gloria, that's why I love you and why I love him. At the darkest hour you two can be as inappropriate as a pair of adolescent boys in biology class."

Tom ran home to attend to some things. Mom and I turned on the *Today* show to see what was happening in the rest of the world. When the second repetition of the news came on, I glanced at my watch and recognized it was time to call my boss and let him know I wouldn't be in to work today.

I stepped outside, flipped open my Nokia and dialed my boss, Sam. "Hi, it's Mike, you're not going to believe this. I am at the hospital; they think my mother had a heart attack."

"Well, good thing he was in the hospital at the time, they could get to him fast," he replied.

"No, no, not my father, my mother! I am in the ER with my mother, who has most likely had a heart attack," I explained as calmly as I could. His confusion was understandable. Just twenty-four hours before I had collapsed into a chair in his office and recounted the events of my father's hospitalization that weekend for a possible stroke.

"You've got to be kidding. How are you coping?"

"Oh, if only I was." Since humor was my typical response to stress, tragedy, tension, even death, I would love to be making a joke like this; that I was such an unlucky schmo I had two parents get sick on me in less than four days. My voice faltered.

He must have heard it because he came back, "Seriously, are you okay?"

I didn't know how to answer. Somehow, seeing my mom's breasts had disarmed me. I wasn't sure why and I needed Sam's usual humor to ground me. I was thankful to have Sam, my new boss, with whom I could release some anxiety through laughter. Why would he get serious on me now?

~

This medical drama had begun as soon as I had arrived home from work the previous Friday. My parents were in Jersey on a house-hunting trip. Their dream of a retirement in North Carolina near my oldest brother, Phil, and their grand-children had succeeded only in giving my mother fodder for her kvetching. She had managed to find an anti-Semite on every corner in North Carolina, although she was always searching for it, like the hidden toys in a *Highlights* puzzle. She had been miserable from day one, except when with the grandkids. She worked hard to convince my dad he was miserable too. They had decided to move back to New Jersey, near where Tom and I lived. They had come north to house-hunt. The visit wasn't convenient for me because I had recently made a huge career change, from being a clinical psychologist to being a financial consultant. I was working hard to get clients and was attempting to limit distractions. I made it clear I wouldn't be available to help them house-hunt, but they could stay at the house.

When I walked in the door after work that Friday, I was a bit surprised to see them already home. I was less surprised that Mom was sitting in the living room in the dark. She could be the Jewish mother in the old joke, "How many Jewish mothers does it take to screw in a light bulb? ... None, I'll just sit here in the dark."

"What are you doing home? I thought you'd still be checking out places."

"I think your father's having a stroke," she said. "He was driving funny, crossing lines and raised dividers. In the mall parking lot, he couldn't figure out how to get to where we needed to be."

"You let him keep driving?" Mom had stopped driving several years before, after her diabetes became so brittle she would have episodes of blacking out. It probably never dawned on them that they could call a cab.

"I made him drive right home. I wanted to call an ambulance but he refused to go to the hospital, so he's upstairs napping."

"What do you mean refused? Why did you give him an option?" My mind went into overdrive. I wished Tom were home from work so I could lean on his calm demeanor and was relieved he wasn't spending this Friday night on Long Island taking care of his mom.

I knew that with a stroke time could be of the essence, that there was a window of opportunity for intervention. I made a guess that the window had passed for Dad and the best course around his resistance was with food. As soon as Tom got home, we'd grab a quick bite and then go to the urgent care center. Dad was okay with that, although he kept insisting Mom was overreacting, "I'm just tired." Looking back, I probably should have called an ambulance in case we were still in the window of time, but I knew he would put up a stink, that Mom would be reaching a point where she would need to eat, and being Friday I knew Tom and I would not want to deal with any resistance.

We went to Primavera, their favorite pasta place. When the check arrived, Dad insisted on paying but could not figure out how to sign the credit card slip. Frustrated, even with my direction, he handed me the pen and had me sign it for him. Now Tom and I were seeing what my mom had seen earlier in the day, and we gave each other concerned glances.

I liked the doctor at the urgent care. He listened to my dad's and my mom's accounts of the day. He completed a chest X-ray and some neurological testing. The chest X-ray revealed Dad had pneumonia and so was probably not oxygenating well enough. We left with a prescription for antibiotics and a strong recommendation that he get a CT scan the next day.

On Saturday morning he seemed to be more like his "regular self." He did not seem confused or at all disoriented. He didn't want the CT scan.

"It's a waste of time. What's it going to show? That I have an old brain?" At seventy-eight, he did have an old brain, but it had remained sharp. He still read a paper every day and loved his paperback thrillers.

"Dad, the test takes like ten minutes, and it's not like an MRI where you get all claustrophobic." I was wishing he were easier. This had to be scary for him, and I wanted to be supportive, but he could make it so hard.

"I know what a CT scan is so don't lie to me. When they see the brain tumor, then they'll want to operate. If they operate, I'll die. Or worse, I'll be a vegetable."

"Well, if that's so, you better hope you are kale. Since no one really likes it, you'll have a better chance of not being eaten."

"You're just sick. We should get your brain checked," he snapped.

"It has been," I said. "They discovered I've been doomed by genetics and they can't help me." I had a big grin on my face, but my mother's grin was even wider. He was going to get mad because he would feel we were ganging up on him. I defused it the best way I knew how. "Mom, they haven't decided which of your DNA caused the problem."

Mom finally ended the argument by announcing, "Artie, get in the fucking car. We're going to the hospital for the test. If not, I'm not getting in the car with you, ever again, even if I have to walk back to North Carolina." I loved my mom, but I sure didn't get an empathy gene from her.

The test was quick. They asked us to wait while the doctor read the results. When they sent us home, we concluded everything was normal.

~

The phone was ringing as I opened the house door. "What do you mean he has to go back to the hospital and be admitted? Why the hell didn't they tell us that while we were there? It was hard enough to get him to go for the test. Now I have to convince him to go back to the hospital!" So many choice words were going through my mind, but I knew this was just a nurse from the doctor's office, not at all connected to the hospital. She had as little power over her job as I had often had over mine in my days in healthcare.

"Mr. Keren, I agree with you. Certainly, their procedures were not designed to consider the patient or the caregivers."

Her acknowledgment was just the right thing. My rage calmed and I felt rational again. "I'm sorry if I snapped at you," I said. "He's giving us a hard time and now this is going to be a task, convincing him to go back to the hospital."

"Good luck," she said, and added, "Don't forget to take care of you."

Despite his grumblings and deliberate foot-dragging, we got Dad in the car and to the hospital. Never a good patient, Dad complained bitterly about the inconvenience of being in the hospital, about the view, about sharing a room, about the plastic-coated mattress, about the dried mystery meat that came for his lunch, about just about everything. He dismissed our concerns; he dismissed the doctor's concerns. It was a repeat of the excuses he gave the doctor the night before. We ignored his litany, made a list of what he would need, and left him to the care of the nurses and doctors.

~

I stopped by the hospital on my way to work on Monday to help Dad get shaved and eat his breakfast. I didn't know it then but this would be my first stop every morning for the next six weeks. In spite of the fact that he would do very little for himself, he would fight me on almost everything I tried to do for him. He got annoyed if I asked if he wanted his bed adjusted; got irritated when I tried to set up his shaving kit; snapped when I straightened out his nightstand and lap tray. The only time he allowed any of us to help without protest was when it involved bringing food from the snack bar instead of making him eat the regular hospital food.

My new job was very understanding, encouraging me to take whatever time I needed.

After work I stopped and picked up some pastrami sandwiches, a family favorite.

Dad was in good spirits when I arrived. He seemed to thrive on the attention of the doctors poking and prodding, technicians pushing his gurney through sterile halls, and the small talk with aides and cleaning staff. Mom looked tired. She was ready to leave when I arrived. She had been there since lunchtime. We ate our sandwiches; I helped Dad change his PJs and get cleaned up a bit, said my "good nights," and helped Mom to the garage.

We drove home and talked on the way. Mom started. "Thank God a podiatrist is coming to cut his toenails tomorrow. Hallelujah! And one of the other doctors said he had a mass on his kidneys. I can't tell you how long I've been trying to get him to go see a podiatrist."

"What do you mean he has a mass on his kidney? Does he have cancer?" I was panicking; she seemed oblivious.

"Oh, I didn't hear him say that." With one eye on the road, I glanced at her, with my other eye, in disbelief.

Tom was home when we got there. That was a rare treat as usually he wouldn't have finished with patients for at least another hour. Unlike me, who was never in love with my career in clinical psychology, Tom loved the field and had a thriving private practice. Late hours were the norm for him. We all got in our PJs and watched a little TV before heading to bed.

At two o'clock there was a timid knock on my door. Despite my deepening sleep, I heard it and woke up. "Mom?"

"I'm sorry, boys, but I think I need to go to the hospital … I'm having a heart attack."

I bounded out of bed and called for an ambulance. I was too tired to register anything but doing what needed to be done. Feelings, I could have those later.

The EMTs arrived quickly and wasted no time examining her. Mom's EKG was confirming her suspicion. They wanted to take Mom to the closest hospital, which was in the opposite direction from the one where Dad was. It was probably a difference of five miles, but having them in different hospitals, in opposite directions, would make my complicated life even more so. As they began to explain that it was policy to go to the closest hospital, I dropped to my knees and clasped my hands together. "Please, please take her to the hospital, where my dad is."

The lead EMT replied, "Well when you put it like that, I can at least try to get clearance from my boss." The boss didn't seem to see any problem with it, so off we went.

At that time of morning the roads were eerily empty. Tom and I arrived while my mother was being moved from the ambulance to an examining room. I handed the nurses a sheet of her current medication, her two-page medical history, and her insurance information and began my bedside vigil. Mom seemed scared, despite her feigned indifference. She often had wished out loud for her life to be over, but she responded to medical emergencies with the speed of someone who wanted to be helped.

~

After my call to my boss, I walked the halls of the hospital for a bit to clear my head. I stopped by the gift shop to buy some tissues for Mom. I knew she would need them.

I stopped at the snack bar and got myself a blueberry muffin. It wasn't very good, but it did bring my mind back to my very early childhood when my mother would take me to the neighborhood bakery. I loved their blueberry muffins. They had a crispy sugar coating on top that just added to their spectacularness. So many of the loving memories of my mom revolved around food. Those bakery trips not only let her love me with special treats but also marked the start of our special relationship. I took a few bites of this blueberry disappointment and tossed the rest in a garbage can as I headed back to Mom's room in the ER.

Tom was sitting with Mom when I returned. He looked refreshed and alert. I envied him his break. He handed me a bagel. We all sat in silence for a time and pretended to watch the TV. A short time later the cardiologist came in and informed us that, indeed, Mom had had a heart attack and she was to be admitted. They wanted to run more tests and then decide on a course of treatment. He seemed nice enough, concerned and attentive to Mom, respectful of the place Tom and I held in Mom's care. We couldn't take that for granted. There were so many stories of gay loved ones being excluded in the hospital. Tom had no legal or family standing in their official eyes despite our twenty-two years together.

"One last thing," Mom said. "When I'm admitted, do not even think of having me share a room with my husband. Unless, of course, you want a suicidal patient on your hands."

The doctor looked at me with the most uncomfortable expression. I just shrugged. Her statement was not unexpected, but it was embarrassing to have her put this so bluntly to a total stranger. I was saddened to hear her say it out loud. Her disdain and contempt for her husband of forty-eight years was evident to most. Deep down, I will always believe she felt some love for him, but it was so hard for her to express it. Her life had left her cold and disappointed. She was born at the start of the Depression, her parents separated when she was three, and her loving but angrily disappointed mother raised her. My father was the convenient target for all her bile. I had lived with it forever, but as I grew older, I became less tolerant of her kvetching about him. While, as a child and teen, I was her confidant, as I aged I had often felt myself to be the mediator. It wasn't a role I chose. I had always longed for sitcom parents; the ones you knew loved each other.

The doctor left. Mom rang for the nurse to get her a bedpan. Mom sat and stared at it. The look on her face, the frustration of being dependent was taking its toll on her. Like Dad, Mom was not a great patient; she just had a lot more experience with it than he did.

~

The day dragged on, with blood tests, doctors visiting, and mundane conversation between the three of us. It was getting towards lunchtime, and I realized

Dad was probably getting anxious about not having heard from Mom yet. If Mom looked at Dad with contempt, Dad saw Mom as his everything. He had grown so dependent on her that he couldn't separate his dependence from his love for her. I asked Mom how she wanted me to handle it. "Just tell him. He's got his own issues to be handling. Now, I need the bedpan again."

Tom and I took the elevator up the two floors from the ER to the Neurology unit. When Dad saw us walk in together, he immediately asked, "What's wrong?"

"Mom is downstairs in the ER. She's had a heart attack," I said.

"This is my fault. I put too much stress on her. I shouldn't have come to the hospital!" he said with tears in his eyes.

"Dad, if it's anyone fault it's probably mine. I shouldn't have given her the pastrami yesterday, all that salt and fat. But there is no time for blame. Neither of us caused this and there is too much to do to sit around taking credit."

"When can I talk to her or see her?"

"Let's get her settled in a room and we'll see what kind of arrangements I can make."

"Do you think they'd let us share a room?"

"I doubt it, Dad. She'll be on a cardiac monitoring wing and you don't need that."

It was hard enough, his being here. He didn't like that I was taking so much control, but he had the courtesy not to fight me that day.

I helped Dad place a call to his brother. When he finished, I asked him if I could get him anything else.

"Maybe some pretzels and a Coke."

Tom jumped at the chance to get away and headed off to the cafeteria. I again asked if I could do anything else.

"Could you look at this?"

He threw off the sheet and lifted his gown in one swift movement. I was shocked; I had had no time to react. His roommate, too, was shocked and rolled over in his bed as I reached for the curtain to hide the scene from the roommate and the hallway beyond his room. Assured he was now visible to only himself and me, I tried to stare at a place on the wall beyond his head to avoid seeing what I really did not want to see.

"It's all irritated up here, on top of my penis where the tube is," he whined.

"Dad, they said that might happen with the catheter and left some cream for you to put on it. Remember?" I attempted to control my voice so as not to betray my irritation and disgust.

"So where's the cream?" he barked. "Could you put some on me?" he said, calmer upon recognizing his vulnerability in my face.

I tried to locate the cream without making direct eye contact with his penis. The cream wasn't on the nightstand, and I couldn't find it on the windowsill either. It must be on the lap table. I was going to have to look, to see. I took a deep breath. Yup, the cream was right there, on the lap table, and his penis was right there in my line of vision. Not since I was seven and he was teaching me how to shower had I seen it. I could remember having showered with him, I must have seen it, but I had no memories of it back then. The mind is such a wonderful thing sometimes. This time I did not believe I would be so lucky. This image of his penis would be seared onto the IMAX screen of my memory for the remainder of my life; an image not of virility, but of a gravity-lengthened tube and its wrinkled pals down below.

"So, can you put the cream on? It's really irritating," he pleaded.

"Dad, I know you don't feel well. I can do many things for you, but I think you can do this for yourself."

"I only ask you for one thing …"

I bit my tongue. Tom and I had been very attentive of him the last few days and now were taking care of his wife as well. "Dad, I'm not comfortable with it and you can do it yourself." I would not submit to his total dependence. I would find my limits along the way, but I had a memory, a very vivid one. It was my senior year of high school. I know it was mid-spring because each day was marked by the anxiety-provoking peek into the mailbox to see if I had gotten any college acceptances. My grandmother, his mother, had had a heart attack and was in a hospital slowly dying. I would accompany my father on the twenty-mile drive each night because he didn't want to drive alone. My grandmother looked so small in her hospital bed. She was sick. I didn't recognize then, though, that she was dying, and they didn't tell me. One night, she began to complain bitterly about her rectum being dry and itchy. Seventeen-year-old me had no desire to hear about this, no less see it. She turned to my father and asked, "Could you rub some Vaseline on it for me?"

I'll never forget the shade of white he turned. "Mom, I'll get the nurse, I'm not going to do that for you."

"Why not, I used to do it for you when you were a baby." Of course, that was fifty-one years prior.

As much as I didn't want to do it or see it, I was siding with my grandmother in my head. Was that really such a big deal? Wouldn't I do it for my mother when the time came? Now I was seeing the reality that I wouldn't. I could not know how often this scene might play itself out as I assumed caregiving responsibilities, as he had then. Like me, he had a capable sibling who was very happy to let him do the work.

Dad grabbed the tube and his penis and began to apply a portion of cream. I think he could have waited till I had left the room, but things were getting tense and I didn't want to upset him anymore, or myself. Having to get the last word in as he closed the tube of ointment, he said, "I bet Tom would do this if he had been here." I doubted it but let him hold on to his belief, at least for now.

As if by magic a voice outside the curtain said, "What would I do?" Tom poked his head in but withdrew it as soon as he saw my dad was exposed. I threw the sheet over Dad and called for Tom to come in.

Dad popped open his can of Coke, grabbed the pretzels, tore them open, and began to eat. Amazing, those were all tasks probably more difficult than putting ointment on his penis. With a mouth full of pretzels, he asked Tom, "Wanna see the irritation on my penis?" It might have been the stroke, but when Dad was sick he usually would get regressed, demanding, and forget his sense of decorum. I forced myself to remember that he was sick and uncomfortable, that I could find empathy for strangers in my life, that I had to keep it flowing for him throughout this ordeal.

Tom and I left the room. I began to bang my head on the wall. Tom came over, put his arm around me, kissed me on top of my head, and led me down the hall.

"Why me?" I cried, wondering how Tom had managed not to be in the room for both of today's genital sightings. This day was getting very long, shaping up to be a drama in need of a Greek chorus and it was only one in the afternoon. Not only was I being thrust back into the healthcare world I had recently fled, but also into the family drama, of which I had worked so hard to control my contact.

"Let's grab some lunch," Tom said.

"I want to check in with Mom first. God knows what they are doing to her down there." I felt guilty leaving her alone in the ER.

We turned into the room and Mom was looking frustrated. "I have to go again and no one is answering the ringer."

So much of this day, our interactions with each other and the staff revolved around bedpans and staff attentiveness.

"Well, I can help you get on and we'll wait in the hall, but I'm getting a nurse to get you off." This was getting to be a lot. We got Mom situated without any "wardrobe malfunctions," pulled the curtain, and went and stood just outside the door.

The nurse came by. "Your mom is ringing."

"Yup. She needed the bedpan. Couldn't she at least use the commode? This is making her truly miserable."

"No!' she snarled and headed off down the hall.

"Nazi," I muttered under my breath. "Mom, how you doing?"

We left Mom on the bedpan and went to get some lunch.

After lunch we returned to find Mom sitting in a wet bed. She had been calling for a bedpan but had given up the wait. We both knew she was humiliated, but she was also used to hospitals so she didn't even sound angry.

I found a different nurse this time, and she was willing to come in and help Mom. She told us she would be there in a minute. As I was walking away, I heard her pick up the phone to call Mom's doctor. She came in a few minutes later and in her most annoying, kindergarten teacher voice called out, "And what has happened here?" Was it her intent to humiliate Mom even further? She didn't know whom she was dealing with this time.

I answered, "She rang and rang, but no one came to help her. She's sick, you know, and can only hold it so long. Perhaps you didn't realize she's in a hospital bed?"

Mom gave me a look that said, "I'm stuck here, don't provoke them."

"The doctor has ordered a catheter for you. Let's get it in and then we can change the sheets," the nurse sang. The tech accompanying the nurse yanked up Mom's sheet. And there it was, her most private of places. I hadn't seen it since the moment of my birth; and then it was from a totally different angle. I had scored the perfect trifecta today. I am a great tourist, but in one day I had seen the three places on Earth I never wanted to encounter.

"Uhmm … I think we'll wait outside," I said to the pair. "She deserves a little privacy." Mom blew us a kiss.

Tom went to hug me. I squirmed away. I needed some space, some air. I needed something with which to poke my eyes out. I hadn't killed my dad and I hadn't "lain" with my mom, but in these three sightings some sacred boundary had been crossed. I felt as though my eyes should have at least melted. I felt a deep understanding, a kinship perhaps, with Oedipus, and his decision to stab out his eyes after realizing what he had seen and done. More than that, like Oedipus with the oracle, these events were foreshadowing a major change in my life, a shift in relationships and perspective.

I had always had a fascination with death. When the other boys around me would talk about wanting to be a fireman or a policeman I would think to myself, *I want to be an undertaker*. My fascination was always about death, but now I was confronting the reality of dying, and it was very different.

Emergency Rooms can be lonely places. So much activity going on around you, but if the staff isn't working on you it's like you're invisible.

The sun was starting to set when they told Mom she had a room. I kissed her goodnight and got in the elevator to go to Dad's room. Dad had a million questions, but eventually he realized I could barely keep my head up or eyes open. "Can I call her room?" he asked.

"She is sleeping now. I'll set it up for tomorrow. Her phone isn't even turned on yet." I tucked him in, gave him a kiss, and dragged myself to the garage.

~

On the drive home I started to laugh out loud as I was reflecting on the situation. I was forty-four years old and in the throes of a midlife crisis that had driven me to a major career change. Nine months before I had made the decision to leave behind my career as a clinical psychologist, to abandon the ever-changing and devolving healthcare environment to pursue riches as a financial consultant for an investment company. All the talk about healthcare reform may have been leading to change, but it all focused on how care gets paid for and not on how it was delivered. As the power of insurance companies to dictate treatment grew, it became harder to deliver quality care. Now, I was being dragged back into that environment and experiencing the impacts from a new, more frightening perspective. Staffing patterns and overburdened caseloads, caused by the dash for inadequate payments by the insurance companies, were now having an impact on my loved ones.

2

The Time Before

Eight years earlier.

The phone woke me from a sound sleep. The clock seemed to say three-thirty but without my glasses it had been getting harder and harder to actually read the clock from bed. I looked over at Tom, who was either still asleep or pretending to be to ignore the phone. I had moved the phone to his side of the bed several months prior because his parents, spokesmodels for expressed emotions, especially anxiety, seemed to have no decorum when it came to appropriate times to make a call to share a thought. In my family, if you made a call after nine at night it better be an emergency, after ten someone better be dead (and even then, they'd still be dead in the morning so why wake us?). But life with Tom included many late calls about anxious thoughts.

I gave him a shot to the ribs. "Get the phone! You know it's your family."

"What ... oh, yeah." He picked up the receiver. "Slow down, Mom. What happened?"

I thought to myself, Jim, Tom's dad, must be on another bender, but as the half of the conversation I could hear continued I realized it was more than just drunken ranting and fighting, that Jim had had some kind of emergency. "Mom, just take a cab. Don't worry about the expense ... Call me back when you know more ... Wait, what kind of surgery? ... Mom, get to the hospital and get the whole story ... Sure, call as soon as you know."

When he hung up, I asked, "What's going on? What's the matter?"

"It seems Dad is in the ER at Nassau County General. He was found lying in the street opposite one of his bar hangouts, passed out with his head bleeding."

"Oh shit. Do they know anything?"

"Well, Mom is a bit frantic so she didn't have much information. She could tell me he had bleeding on the brain. They're still running tests. He's conscious and still drunk."

"Oh shit!" I'm ashamed to admit my private thoughts were more along the lines of, *Dumb shit. He deserves it for putting us through this. All his drinking and no one ever confronted him, pushed him, or challenged him. I doubt his own doctors have any idea what an alcoholic he is. Joan, I bet, never told them.*

I held Tom tighter and said, "I'm sorry. What are you going to do?"

"Right now I'm going back to sleep, at least until she calls again. I'll probably have to drive out to Long Island later."

I knew he'd be snoring in a matter of minutes and I would spend the next several hours tossing and turning. Going back to sleep was never a skill of mine.

~

Tom and I had met in December 1986. It was a blind date; a blind date he didn't even know he was on. A friend of mine was dating a friend of his. The two of them thought we might hit it off and devised a plan where they would co-host a party, invite us both but not tell Tom I was his date for the evening, since he had a moratorium on blind dates.

Since I lived in the Bronx, where I was a full-time graduate student working on my doctorate in clinical psychology, and they all lived in Highland Park, New Jersey, an adjacent town to Rutgers populated by graduate students and psycho-therapists, I would have to travel to this party and stay sober. The party was held on my dad's birthday. Since my parents were living near to the party, I combined events. I drove out to have dinner with my parents and then went to the party.

Judy, my friend, lived in a typical New Jersey garden apartment, not overly spacious, but laid out well for casual grad-student entertaining. When I walked in, the first thing I noticed was that there was only one other man visible to me. The man I saw in the middle of the floor playing a drinking game with some of his colleagues was not a beefcake beauty but, to use an Irish saying Tom's family would gift me, "he was better than a poke in the face." Shawn and Judy introduced me around. It wasn't until we rounded the corner and entered the small, overcrowded kitchen that I saw there was indeed another man at this soiree.

The man was introduced as "Tom." Shawn or Judy had probably told me I was supposed to be meeting "Tom" prior to the party, but I didn't store his name because I assumed any introduction they made at the party would include an aside of "This is the guy we wanted you to meet." Tom was pretty skinny and I immediately grew concerned my large size would turn him off. What really stood out for me was his hair. It was reddish in tone, surrounded a bald top, and curled under in a Prince Valiant kind of way. *Incredibly unstylish, and really not attractive,* I thought to myself. Because the kitchen was so tight it was hard to move around, and because Tom was a good conversationalist and an even better listener, I spent the rest of the evening "trapped" in the kitchen.

Eventually, it grew late and I had a long ride back to the Bronx. As I was walking to the door, Judy said, "So what did you think?"

"Tom was okay. I'd see him again. Give him my phone number and have him call me if he's interested."

I heard from Judy the next day. Once he had gotten over his annoyance at being set up, he had told them to give me his number. So, basically, we both were interested enough to encourage the other to call, but neither of us wanted to risk the first move.

We spent about six days playing phone tag to each other's answering machines, deliberately timing the calls for when we assumed the other wouldn't be home. Finally, we did connect on the phone and arranged to meet.

We had a nice time on that date. We discovered we both loved to read, to eat, and to watch Disney movies. We ended the evening at Tower Records, his favorite destination in the whole city of New York. He could spend hours just touching the albums (vinyl was still the predominant mode), browsing the covers, and listening to the samples. He was shocked to learn as we approached the store that I had never been there. On the busy corner of Broadway, he stopped dead in his tracks, looked me in the face, and announced to all of New York City, "What? You're a virgin?" I'm sure the staring crowd assumed he meant sexually.

I quickly pushed through the revolving door and looked at him in disbelief. "Big deal, it's just a record store. I go to Sam Goody." I didn't realize that to a music lover I had just revealed a crucifiable heresy. But I'm not a music lover. I don't hate it; I just don't have enough of an interest to pursue the ever-changing list of popular artists. Late the morning of the second date my phone rang. "I've been putting off making this call. I really didn't want to disappoint you, but I'm really sick. I think I have food poisoning."

My mind filled with doubt. "How sick are you?"

"What do you mean, how sick am I? I'm too sick to come up to the city to meet you."

"Are you too sick for company?"

There was dead air on the line and he finally said, "Why?"

"'Cause I'll come out and visit. If it's food poisoning, I'm not gonna catch it. I'll just come out and keep you company."

"You'd do that?"

"Sure. I already had the evening committed for you, so I really don't have an alternative plan."

"Okay," he replied, somewhat uncomfortably. "I can't believe someone would want to come out and hang with a sick person he barely knows. You're so sweet."

He was right and he was wrong. I was sweet, sometimes. What he didn't know was that the last man I had dated, a twenty-year-old Cuban who still lived at home, had vanished from my life by claiming illness to cancel the last three dates we had set up. It had been a whirlwind. The night we met we had spent making out on a pool table in a Greenwich Village gay bar. Somewhere in the second hour of the make-out session he had pledged his undying love to me. Two dates, one sleepover, and he grew tired of me but being twenty didn't know how to end it. So I ended it. Now, if Tom wasn't really sick, I wasn't going to waste weeks. If Tom was giving me a story because he couldn't say it directly, I was going to find out.

I showed up at his door with cans of Campbell's soup, some Special Tea Cookies, and a coloring book with crayons. When Tom tells this story it's here that he adds, "That was the point when I fell in love." For me, I was slower to fall, but I was at least reassured that he was really interested. The evening ended with us engaged in an outing to the bedroom marked by AIDS-anxiety-ridden sex. We would not have our first fight until we started apartment hunting six months later. That was when we really began to identify the differences that make a relationship.

~

I lay in the bed, the first signs of the sun poking through the shades in our bedroom, wondering when Joan would call us back. The phone rang, disturbing my reverie and Tom's sleep. He picked it up on the second ring. I heard a lot of "uh-huhs" and "oh no's." The words brain surgery, swelling, and coma were repeated a number of times.

Tom got off the phone and said to me, "This isn't good," and started to hold back tears. I tried to hug him, but he brushed past me to the bathroom. When he finished peeing, he turned on the water in the shower. I reached in behind him, shut it off, and said, "Tell me what's going on before you get in the shower."

"Okay, but I don't want to hear your opinion of this," he said. "From the best the police can piece together, my father had been quite drunk and even though the bartender had tried to cut him off, he had stayed around and closed the bar. Anyway, seems he was trying to get to his car, tripped on the curb, and hit his head."

I kept it to myself but I did think, *At least he didn't get in the car and take someone out with him.*

He continued. "Doctor says that because his brain had shrunken from age, it bounced a bit when he hit the pavement so he not only has a brain bleed on the left side where he fell, but there is an equivalent bleed on the opposite side. They want to try surgery to stop the bleeding and reduce the swelling, but he would be at quite a great risk for a good while even with the surgery."

I asked a bunch of questions about functioning, but they had no answers, wouldn't for days. As psychologists we both had knowledge of brain functioning, and it wasn't comforting.

I knew enough to know his mother wouldn't even entertain the question of whether Jim would want this surgery. Tom probably wouldn't have entertained it either. I also believed Jim would have wanted it.

I may be frantically anxious, but I'm good at making plans and moving to action in a crisis. "So why don't you take the first shower," I said. "I'll walk the dog. Please eat some breakfast. Who knows when you'll get to eat anything today. Leave me a list of any errands or calls you need me to make."

There's never a good time for a crisis, but our lives were really not in a place where we could afford an emergency expense. We had both left our jobs in community mental health a few years prior and were both trying to build private practices in a competitive, but seriously changing, healthcare environment. Time out of the office was time without pay. We barely took vacations and were working through all but the worst of colds, aches, and pains. Now we were going to suffer. I couldn't say it out loud, or maybe I did, but because of Jim's alcoholism we were going to pay, again. I was furious. It made it very hard for me to be compassionate.

I channeled my anger into functionality. I called Tom's patients for the next two days. I called his shrink and cancelled his personal appointment. I loved Tom and assisting in this crisis was my duty. It carried me forward.

On the treadmill that day, I turned the tunes way up and played out furious battles in my head where I got out my rage at what his "asshole" father, Jim, had done to us. I probably did two or three more miles than usual that day.

~

My relationship with Jim, Tom's dad, wasn't horrible, but I never felt close to him. He was too foreign to my experience. I was the son of Jewish non-drinkers. My parents lived the sacrifices parents were expected to live for their children at the time, doing what was expected. Not Jim. Jim came first. Tom couldn't go to Princeton as his guidance counselor suggested because Jim was too paranoid to fill out the financial aid application. When he was upset with Tom, Jim would start the car and threaten to take him to an orphanage. He had a hard time being proud of Tom because Tom had surpassed him in many areas.

There were so many ways children came first in my home when I was growing up. Entering Tom's family clarified the extent of them. My dad worked to support us, not because being a margin clerk was a satisfying career, but because it was what fathers did. Moms too. I also knew my mom stayed in the relationship for the children.

When we first decided to move in together, Tom's parents were less than thrilled. They knew Tom's first lover but believed he was only Tom's roommate. He had come out to his parents in the years between and they had settled into an uneasy peace, ignoring that Tom had refused to promise them he would never have sex.

When Tom and I got involved, they made it clear I was not welcome to their house, especially not during the day. In Jim's paranoid mind he believed if the neighbors saw me come to the house, they would know he had a homosexual son. We tried to put him at ease, promising I would wear a dress and even cover my face with a kerchief. The humor was lost on him. They both worried I would give their son AIDS.

During one tense phone call, Tom tried to calm their fears, offering to tell them about "safer sex" if they wanted to hear. Jim had slammed the phone down, disgusted. Joan, his mom, settled in, an eager student at the ensuing lecture. As Tom recounts the story it ended with his mother asking, "Do you like that oral stuff? Your father always wants it, but I think it's gross." Way more than either of us really wanted to know.

Jim and I could talk history and politics. He and Joan both loved my cooking and looked forward to when we would have them over. Religious differences were smoothed over. They participated in our home rituals around Passover and Chanukah with a mixture of curiosity and fear. Tom would reassure them that he loved our rituals but had no interest in converting.

As we neared our ten-year anniversary, we began to discuss a desire neither of us had allowed to come out before because we doubted its possibilities. We wanted to have a baby. We knew that wasn't possible but were willing to settle for adopting one. Many of our friends, straight and lesbian, were beginning to have children. We didn't know other gay men who had adopted, but we knew they were out there. I knew my parents could be wonderful grandparents; we had watched them with my niece and nephew. We also believed, if they could get past the non-traditional nature of our family, Tom's parents would make wonderful grandparents, Jim especially. He had interests in sports and woodworking that Tom had never been able to share with him. Joan would relish dressing up a baby, reading to a toddler, and encouraging the studies of an adolescent. On reflection, I don't remember his parents ever sharing any thoughts about our dream, but as with most things concerning us, they would eventually come around.

We decided we would proceed with our plan and our first step was to get married. There was a synagogue in our community where the rabbi was very progressive, and he had been marrying lesbians under the chuppah for several years. We joined the temple, settled in, and picked a date. My parents were very excited. There would finally be a Jewish wedding in the family. Interfaith marriages abounded among my extended cousins, but most had had secular ceremonies. My own brother and his wife had finally agreed to having dual ceremonies, but only after months of screaming fights.

Tom's parents rebelled against the idea. It wasn't because we were getting married in a synagogue; we could have shut that argument down by agreeing to get married in any church where the priest would agree to marry an interfaith couple, on the altar, and offer the sacrament of marriage. No, for them, it was the question of visibility. Actually, for Jim it was the question of visibility. I believed Joan, Tom's mom, was secretly thrilled at the idea of a wedding but didn't dare disagree with Jim. After a lot of ear-piercing phone calls, late-night tears, and a few threats, later withdrawn, they agreed to come to the wedding. Jim refused to participate other than to attend, but Joan agreed to walk Tom down the aisle and even do a reading on the pulpit at our Aufruf the night before.

Our friends, my family, and our extended families all prepared for the day with joy. From weaving a chuppah and crocheting yarmulkes, to baking our three-tiered, gold leaf–encrusted wedding cake, everyone was getting involved. We had a big wedding party—six attendants, four chuppah holders, flower girl, ring bearer, and readers and musicians who were all playing a part. Despite the struggles, this was to be a ceremony bathed in the love and light of family and friends. Even if it would not be recognized by the state of New Jersey or the United States of America, could that really matter given all the love that was being returned to us?

The night before the ceremony was interesting. An Aufruf is a ceremony that takes place in the congregation on the Sabbath before the wedding. Prayers are said, blessings are offered to the parents of the groom and groom (in Judaism, our parents were entering into a relationship that has a name: machetenim). Since there was to be a bar mitzvah in the synagogue in the morning, we knew it would be crowded. We didn't know the bar mitzvah boy or his parents, but we had asked the rabbi to please let his parents know the Aufruf would be happening. Not only did we not want any gasps of surprise from his guests in the congregation, but also the bar mitzvah family provided the oneg—post-service reception—and we wanted to offer to share the expense. The rabbi never did. So, although it would end as a joyous evening where Tom's Irish Catholic relatives would join the congregation in a special music program, replete with folk dancing and singing, there was a moment when the bar mitzvah boy's grandfather stood up while we were being blessed, announced, "In a shul you do this? I never …" and walked out of the congregation. We didn't let his outburst mar our joy or disrupt the ceremony, but the congregation saw how when you're gay, even in the most accepting places, you must always prepare for that moment of rejection, or worse.

Afterwards, I apologized to the boy's parents for the rabbi's neglect. His mother wished us loads of nachas (joy), dismissed her father-in-law as a rigid old bigot, and stated, "My son will never forget this evening. None of my family will."

The next evening, as we were lining up to proceed down the aisle, Tom informed me his father had had a change of heart. He had agreed to walk Tom down the aisle with Joan. Through the tears of joy filling my eyes, I went to hug my father-in-law and to thank him. He stiffly accepted my hug and then added, "I realized I was the only fly in the ointment. So here I am."

"Jim," I replied, "the why is not important right now. You've made Tom happy, which makes me happy."

The reception was a blast. It is still referred to as "the best gay wedding our families ever had."

~

The wedding was eighteen months prior. We were slowly making our way through the paperwork and interviews in preparation for the adoption. But now Jim was in a hospital bed, fighting for his life. Or rather, Joan and Tom were fighting for his life. I can't say what Jim was thinking in his coma; and I was finding myself once again resentful of the way his selfishness was messing up our existence.

Jim would survive the multiple surgeries he had during those first few, crucial days. I calmed down enough to take my place at his bedside through the vigils. As he emerged from his coma and the extent of his deficits became clearer and clearer, I even managed to find compassion. I'd help with his feeding, cleaning him up, and pushing him into the sun at the hospital solarium.

It began in mid-May. As the months wore on, there was a great deal of physical and occupational therapy, hospitalizations for pneumonia and urinary tract infections, and more therapies. Tom would make the trip out to Long Island every Friday. I would frequently join him; but there were times I would stay home and resent the intrusion into our lives. While Jim grew more dependent, and weaker, I watched as Joan began to emerge as an independent, strong woman who was finding a circle of friends and a myriad of interests. It was my growing admiration and eventual love for her that blossomed most through it all.

Jim ended up in the hospital just before Thanksgiving with another urinary tract infection. The months of physical illness and incapacitation had worn Jim down to a mere shell of the fit man he had been. Thanksgiving morning Jim's nurse dropped the bomb that his kidneys were shutting down and we'd have to make a decision about dialysis, very soon. Over dinner, I pushed my point. "He's still alive, alert, and reasonably aware. Ask him what he wants to do."

The next day we gathered at Jim's bedside and discussed the options with the doctor. The doctor started, "So Jim, after all the infections your body has fought off, and all the surgeries and treatments, your body is shutting down."

"What exactly does that mean?" Tom asked, knowing his father would want to know.

"Well, your kidneys are failing. We would like to start you on dialysis."

Jim grunted and shook his head no.

"Dad, not so fast," Tom said. "Doctor, are we talking about dialysis as a temporary way to get the kidneys working again, or will it be permanent?"

"Good question. At this point I would say your father will need dialysis several times a week forever. He's not a candidate for a transplant so I don't see him getting off it."

Jim's headshaking grew more aggressive. The doctor continued, "Mrs. Johnson, I don't think your husband will be able to return home. He'll need more care than could probably be provided at home."

Jim managed, in a dry hoarse voice, to say, "*No!*"

Tom looked at him. "Dad, are you saying you don't want the dialysis?"

Yes! Jim's emphatic nodding said. "No more," he managed to say.

Jim passed in his sleep, as the thirtieth of November was becoming the first of December. Tom and I had gone home the evening before so we could get back to our practices and make some money. When the phone rang a little after three in the morning, I didn't get upset. I just held Tom as he talked calmly to his mother and they both spoke of how Jim's pain was over. He invited her to call back if she needed to, that the time didn't matter. It didn't. Tom assured her he would be out there by eleven and they would do whatever they had to do.

As I spooned up behind Tom after the phone call, I said, "It's not just the pain of the last six months he's now free of. It's the pain of his horrible childhood in the orphanage, the loss of his mother and stepbrother he knew for such a short time, yet loved so dearly. All that pain is gone."

"You know he loved you," Tom said.

"I know he tried, but like every other relationship he tried to have he got in the way of himself and made it hard to love him back … I'm glad I got to know him, and I'm glad he made you so strong. As much as some of those lessons hurt you, I benefit from them every day." I could feel Tom start to cry so I shut up and just held him.

When, at last his shoulders stopped quaking, I joked, "There is a bright side to this, you know. He died on December first so your mother will get his December benefits check and get to keep it." He kicked me.

Tom stayed with his mom for a few days after the funeral. One night on the phone I said to him, "You know, I hate you for one thing right now."

"Yeah, what's it today?" He kind of laughed at me.

"You not only taught me how to take care of a sick and dying parent, one who wasn't always easy to love, you set a standard of care I'm going to have to meet when my own parents are dying. You were so attentive to them both. You were loving, kind, patient … all those traits I have no idea where I'll find when it's my time to provide. So, yeah, I hate you for that right now."

3

CHANNELING AURORA

Those first few days of having Mom and Dad in the same hospital quickly settled into a routine. I would either go to the hospital early, before work, to try to see their doctors, or I would run over during lunch to bring them some outside food or just to check on their comfort. This usually included getting orders for food, toiletries, or reading materials to be delivered on my after-work visits.

I was tired but I continued to be very focused at work. This routine was giving me structure and was honestly benefitting me. I was scheduled to go to Boston for a business trip. I was going to represent my firm at a LGBT business expo. I was very excited. Despite how new I was to the firm, I had been chosen to represent them, and I was feeling a bit panicked that my hospital responsibilities would force me to cancel. Boston was my old home and I was looking forward to a chance to visit old friends. Mom and Dad were insistent that I go. Tom had offered to cover everything on the medical front, but he had parental agita of his own: His mother had been struggling with chemotherapy for uterine cancer for a while and he was needed out on Long Island most weekends. I asked my brother, Stuart, to come out from his home in Ohio for the weekend to spend some time with Mom and Dad. Tom could help him if there was a crisis, but at least Stu could cover the visits.

Thursday at lunch I went to the hospital. Mom was still feeling weak, but not so weak that she couldn't complain about the nurses. Actually, her complaints were a sign she was feeling more herself. I could tell by looking at her (and smelling her) that her basic needs were being met. She was clean, her meds were in place, and in spite of her complaints the nurses checked on her regularly. She asked questions about Tom and me, about work, about the dogs. She was excited she would see Stuart over the weekend.

It was mostly unsaid, but I could tell from her complaints that she missed her regular doctors in North Carolina ("He's no Dr. Smith"), her usual hospital ("The food here can't compare to Duke"), and mostly the motivating visits of her grandchildren. As I kissed her good-bye, I told her that either I would come by right after work or I'd sneak in with Stuart later in the evening after I picked him up from the airport. She blew me another kiss as I walked out the door.

I got in the elevator and headed for Dad's room. As I turned into his room to shout a greeting, I realized he had a new roommate and so my typical wise ass comments, even a loud "Good morning, what the hell are you still doing in bed?" might disturb this new patient.

I approached his bed and was greeted with the repugnant stench of human waste. Dad looked up from his paper and said, "You're late!"

Happy to see you, too, I thought. "I went to see Mom first," I said with a smile, trying hard not to breathe too deeply. "Dad, did you mess yourself?"

"Yeah, but it's not that bad."

"What do you mean? Not that bad? Did you call for a nurse?"

"I did. I've been waiting. They must be busy."

"How long ago was that?"

Looking at the TV, I asked him if the show had been on when he first rang, and recognized it had been an hour he was waiting. *No one is going to ignore my father!* I thought to myself.

I excused myself to go to the nurses' station. "Don't make any trouble," my father pleaded. "Remember, I'm stuck here." I knew he meant stuck in the hospital, but I stifled a giggle as I interpreted it as glued to the bed by his shit.

"Have they been mean to you or mistreated you?" I asked, my suspicions fueled by his comment.

"No, but if you get them in trouble, they'll ignore me all the time."

"They're already ignoring you. How much worse can it get than letting you sit in your own shit for an hour?"

I turned and left the room. How could he tolerate sitting in it like that? Reading his paper as if his dirty sheets were just some new kind of comfy cushion. I approached the nurses' station. Several doctors were writing notes in charts.

There were four women in decorative hospital scrubs chatting about that week's *American Idol.*

"They better not send Bucky home," one announced. "He's my dream."

"Bucky, you dream about Bucky when Ace is up there on the stage? You're nuts," another said.

The third added, "But they both suck."

I cleared my throat. They ignored me. I called, "Can I get some help?" A nurse came over to where I was standing. "My father has defecated on himself. He rang for help about fifty minutes ago but no one has responded."

"Oh, I'm sorry. Who is your dad?" she asked.

I gave his name and pointed to his room. "Oh, he's one of Marcia's patients and she's out to lunch right now," she continued.

I took a deep breath and adjusted my volume upwards. "Are you saying that he needs to sit in his shit until she comes back from lunch?"

"No. No. Let me find someone to help clean him up." She smiled.

I turned to the other two and said, "By the way, you're both wrong, Eliot is the hottest on this season and would make the best husband." They both looked at me, mouths agape, as I turned and walked away, feeling somewhat satisfied with myself.

When I got to his room, I saw the lunch cart sitting in the hall. I walked in and there was the food guy propping my dad up and pulling his tray in front of him.

My blood began to boil. I don't suffer fools easily. "Excuse me, what are you doing?" I asked, contempt leaking from my speech.

"I'm giving him his food. He's hungry," he answered, seemingly oblivious to my sharp tone.

"Can't you tell he's sitting in shit?"

"So?"

"So, would you want to eat your lunch sitting in shit?" I asked him.

"I'm doing my job, *shit* ain't my job." All over the hospital signs were posted reminding staff that patient comfort was everybody's business.

"Leave him alone, Mike, he's just doing his job," my father said to me, adding a soft "Thanks" to the food guy. The guy retreated from the room, quickly.

I pulled the tray away from my dad. "Where the hell *are* they?" I went back to the nurses' station. Sure enough, there was that nurse back in the *Idol* conversation.

"Excuse me…. *EXCUSE ME!*"

She turned around while shooting me a look that said, *What now?* "Yes," she said.

"He's still sitting in his shit. No one has come by ... well, except for the lunch guy who informed me in no uncertain terms, 'Shit ain't my job!'"

"Sorry, I told the tech to go in there. I'm on break now, let me get Marcia for you."

She turned her back on me while I silently fumed. A linebacker of a redhead approached the desk. "What can I do for you, sweetie?"

"First off, you can not call me sweetie!" I responded. "You can get someone in there to clean up my father. He has been sitting in his own shit since you left for lunch and your colleagues have ignored him and given me a runaround." At this point I know my volume was high. My voice had been deepening and I hoped I was making sense. I slammed my hand on the counter for emphasis.

I sensed a long-awaited moment was about to occur. When I first saw the movie *Terms of Endearment*, I was so impressed by the scene where Shirley MacLaine, playing Aurora Greenway, is standing and storming at a nurses' station, outside of her daughter's hospital room. Her daughter, played by Debra Winger, is dying of cancer. She can get her pain medication every four hours. At four hours and one minute, Aurora sets out to get the meds for her daughter. She is the ultimate mother bear protecting her cub, and you are not sure if the nurses will survive the encounter. I tucked the scene away as a model for the future, and I thought it might have arrived. Shirley won an Oscar for that moment, and I was preparing to win mine in the halls of the hospital.

A tech walked by the desk and Marcia called out to him, "Mr. Keren needs his bed changed and to be cleaned up. Could you go in there and assist him?"

"As soon as I finish with this other room," he replied.

I looked at Marcia. "I guess you're going to have to do it yourself, huh? Because, you know, he is not waiting another minute in that bed."

"Of course, sir, I'll get right on it," she replied as she came around from behind the station and headed for my father's room.

With all the drama, I realized I had been needing the bathroom for a while and now my bladder was pressing. As I was washing my hands and rinsing off my face, I looked up in the mirror. I half expected to see Shirley MacLaine staring back at me. It wasn't; it was just me. A bit red-faced, but still put together. I returned to Dad's room.

The curtain was drawn around his bed. Behind it I heard Marcia, the tech, and my father chatting. Marcia was leading the cleanup. "Oh, this really is a mess," she said, "perhaps we should have you in a diaper." She was gentle and tender with my dad but also used the voice a kindergarten teacher would use with her kids, but, Marcia was a "good one." My upset was upsetting my dad. Not only that, but I had worked in medical settings long enough to know nurses could be vindictive. I also knew they probably worked short-staffed and covered more patients and more paperwork than was reasonably expectable.

"How would Aurora deal with that?" I wondered to myself. Certainly, she wouldn't ignore it; but then again, her daughter was too sick at that point to shut Aurora down. My dad still had enough spunk to be angry with me. I chose to say nothing more at that time.

Marcia and the tech emerged from the curtain. I heard Dad before I saw him, but his voice was more chipper. He looked better. Surely he felt more comfortable. I noticed his lunch sitting on his bed tray. "One more thing, do you think you could call down and get my father a fresh tray that's hot, now that he can eat it?"

Marcia turned, glared at me, but said, "Of course."

After she walked away, I lifted up the cover and saw it was a cold fruit plate. I turned scarlet. Dad said, "Can you push that over so I can eat now?"

I ran out after Marcia. "Thank you for taking care of my father," I said. "You don't have to call the cafeteria; he was served a cold lunch so he can still eat it."

"Don't mention it," she replied.

I went back to Dad's room. He was watching the news and eating his fruit. "Feeling better?" I asked.

"Yes, but did you have to make such a scene?"

"I guess you don't mind sitting in shit. I guess it wasn't ruining your appetite for lunch," I replied angrily.

He started to cry. "What do you want from me? I don't feel well. I can't do anything. I'm stuck here. I don't want any trouble."

"Dad, I know you don't feel well. We're all very worried about the both of you But I'm only trying to protect you, to make sure you get the best care, and to make sure your needs are being met by the staff. I mean you couldn't help that you messed yourself. Your meds are probably wreaking havoc on your stomach and you can't exactly get out of bed to walk to the bathroom. They have to answer the buzzer."

"But you got so angry. You were yelling at them," he said.

"Gee Dad, I wonder where I got that trait from?"

He smiled at me sheepishly. "I'm sorry. I know you are trying to help me, help Mom, and still have your own job to do."

"It's okay, Dad. We'll work it out."

I gave him a peck on the cheek and turned to walk out into the hall. Just before the elevator there was a door marked Unit Nurse Manager and it was open. I knocked on it.

"Hi. Come in. How can I help you?" asked a pleasant, middle-aged woman in business attire. "My name is Louise. I am the nurse manager for the unit. Has there been a problem?"

"Hi. My name is Mike and my father is Art Keren. And yes, there has been a problem." I went on to recount the events that just unfolded. She listened very intently and promised she would speak to all the parties involved.

"One thing. I've worked in hospitals and I know human nature and I'm worried about retaliation. My dad really is pretty dependent right now."

"Of course," she said. "I'd be worried about the same thing. I will address that, too." I was feeling very reassured when she added, "Dr. Keren, why don't you take my card and leave me your contact information? That way we can keep each other well informed."

There is a God, I thought to myself as I walked to my car.

~

Later that evening I picked Stuart up at the airport. As we were driving to the hospital, he had a few questions about Mom's and Dad's medical conditions and what he should do in certain circumstances, if things turned bad or they wanted to perform certain procedures. I reassured him that mostly he was there to keep them company and hold their hands. I wanted to say wipe their butts, but I was afraid he'd get on the next plane home. If a medical crisis arose, he could call Tom or me for help.

At the hospital, Mom brightened up as soon as he walked in the room. Stuart had brought her pictures of his girls to keep her company and of course she gushed. Sometimes, it felt like all that mattered to her was being a grandmother. I could spend my life caregiving, but without the little ones I could be tossed aside. I always felt small and petty when I got jealous of my nieces and nephew. They had gotten a wonderful grandmother in my mom. She could be with them in ways she could never be with us. Sometimes, I would watch her with them and wish I could trade places with them. She was unambivalent about being a grandmother, something I don't think she could honestly say about being a parent.

Tom and I had lost our desire to adopt after Jim died. The burden of that caregiving, the loss and despair, the curtailment of all that brought us pleasure had convinced us we did not want to give it all up to raise children. We would focus on being uncles. We could spoil our nieces and nephew and send them back to their parents when we were done. But, sadly, I would never know the joy of watching my mom grandparent my children. In retrospect, we both deeply regret that decision.

Once, right after college, I asked her if she ever wished she hadn't had children. She told me she never regretted it but she envied women today who could do it by themselves, without a husband.

Stuart and I visited a bit with Mom and then headed up to Dad's room. He, too, brightened when Stu and I walked in. The one who's there, the one who does it all, has his lights dim when the novelty walks in. I was so happy to have Stuart there, but I'd be lying if I were to say a part of me didn't wish Dad got that bright when I walked in.

I don't think Dad ever questioned being a parent. Dad had no problem telling us when he was proud of our accomplishments. He attended my concerts, plays, and back-to-school nights, but his attendance was more out of obligation. He could be a verbal critic of the event, but he always followed it up by taking us all to our favorite local ice cream parlor. He loved when Stuart had played lacrosse and would get to every game and scrimmage he could. When Phil was the water boy/equipment manager for the football team, our father became president of the Dad's club and went to every game.

The problem with Dad's fathering was in his anger. He couldn't control his rages. He wasn't violent (occasionally he would try to spank us, which would mostly make us laugh) but he was loud. On weekends we lived in fear of waking him up. He was up at five a.m. daily and on the train by six, so he would try to "catch up on sleep" on the weekends. We kids wanted him up. We would play right outside his door, not loudly, but hopefully with just enough enthusiasm to rouse him from his slumber and suggest we do something. It never really worked.

Between his rages and my mom's shaping of my perceptions, it was hard for me to find the love, or to feel it. I saw him as silently fulfilling his duty.

We visited a bit and Dad told us about his doctor visits that day. One doctor was concerned about a shadow he saw on my father's kidney during an X-ray or sonogram. Dad wasn't sure which, but he didn't have any doubts when he said, "I'm sure it's nothing."

"Have him call me." I pointed to the stack of my business cards I had left for him to give to his doctors. Then I thought, *Or he can talk to Stuart, who can relay it all to me*. I wanted Stuart to be involved, to feel responsible in this caretaking project.

Stu gave him his copies of the recent kid photos and we took our leave. On the way to the car, Stu said to me, "So what should I do when I'm visiting him?"

I couldn't process this question. It seemed like he was asking the obvious. "Talk with him," I said.

"About what?"

"Well, you could reminisce. Talk about things you have done with him. Talk about your work. Talk about the kids, marriage, the neighborhood, the news, anything. You know, this might be a good time to work through whatever it was that happened between the two of you that has made you so angry with him. He's captive; he has to talk about it. If he's approaching the end you don't want it lingering." Stuart gave me a look. "Or you could bring a deck of cards and just play."

We were quiet the rest of the way home. In the morning I would take him to rent a car and I'd be off to Boston. I probably would not get home before his flight left to take him home. I had to trust he'd do all right by them, that he was no longer just my beloved little brother, but an adult who could handle things. I was appreciative that he at least came in to relieve me; I could count on him.

4

A Very Sick Woman

The ride to Boston was a pleasant four hours all to myself in the car. I played the radio, sang to no one at the top of my lungs, and thought about how my next car should really have a built-in recording studio so I could get these sessions onto a CD and let the world know how talented I was. Two pit stops and a snack later, I was there. I started calling around town to make plans for that evening with my local friends. I was chatting with one when another call came through. Checking the caller ID I saw it was Tom. I excused myself and took his call.

"What's up?" I asked.

"It's your mom." My mood sunk. "It's not an emergency but we have to make some decisions," he said.

"Thanks. It was a great ride. I'm doing just fine," I replied.

"Sorry, between patients, but I wanted to make sure I got you," he said. "Your mom needs a cardiac catheterization and they want to move her to Memorial. They feel she is a high risk and they can accommodate her more safely over there."

"I knew I shouldn't have come. Now I have to turn around and come home," I said, assuming my worst worries were coming true. This lifelong gift of power over life and death could be a burden at times. I had convinced myself that leaving was a mistake; no one but me could take care of them or make decisions the way I could. "I'll grab a meal and come back home."

"You don't have to come home. Stu and I have everything under control, I just wanted to bring you into the loop."

I calmed easily. "When are they going to do the Cath?"

"They're trying to set it up for Monday morning, but they'll transfer her on Sunday. She's mad she has to wait that long; she wanted it this afternoon."

"She'll be my mom till the end … So she doesn't mind the transfer?"

"No. Of course, your dad is a bit crazed about it, but …" He didn't have to finish the sentence.

Dad was absolutely panicked that my mom wouldn't live to take care of him. He couldn't imagine a life without her. Once, Tom had given her a ride to the store and she turned to him and said, "I really hope I get a few good years to myself after Artie dies." How does a son-in-law respond to that?

~

The rest of the weekend passed easily. I got home in time for dinner on Sunday evening. My older brother, Phil, had driven up from D.C. to be there as well. Over dinner we settled on a plan for the next day. I would be at the procedure in Morristown while Phil would spend the time with my father. Stu had to get back to Ohio, to work and his family.

We went to see the two of them. Dad was in good spirits since the nurses had wheeled him down to see Mom, who told him to stop worrying. Actually, what she said was, "Knock it off or I'll purposefully code during the procedure." She was irritated because she had spent the day waiting to be moved and only at supper did she learn the move was put off till right before the procedure. She had to spend another night before her transfer.

"Mom, calm down," I said. "It takes time to prepare for the arrival of the Queen."

Mom stuck her tongue out, thinking I had made the crack about her, but I was really referring to myself.

We tucked Mom in, wheeled Dad back to his room and went home. In the car, Tom turned to me and said, "You know, she isn't dead yet, you're still the princess." In that one statement, he was letting me know I was doing okay, but not to overreact.

I slept listlessly that evening. I had not "been through a dozen of these procedures," the phrase Mom had adopted to dismiss our concerns. I had been pretty much excluded from Mom's health concerns while they were in North Carolina. It was always some variation of they didn't want to worry or inconvenience me. They succeeded in making me worry more, which I sometimes thought was Mom's goal. It felt like it was a punishment for not calling them every day.

~

The doctor called my name in the waiting room. I waved and he came over and introduced himself. He was loaded down with a number of medical charts and a laptop. He gestured for me to sit and he took the seat next to me. He took out some photos that looked like they were straight out of *Science* magazine.

"This is your mom's heart. As you can see there is a great deal of damage there. I've never seen a heart with so many stents," he said.

"Actually, I'm not a cardiologist and really don't know what you are showing me. Could you please explain what I'm looking at?"

He looked at me and I knew he was feeling put out. I wasn't sure if it was due to my question or his discovery that I was not a "real doctor." I held my tongue. But I was there for my mom, and arguing with him was not going to help her.

He began to point out the stents in the pictures and the areas of heart muscle that he called "dead." He said, "Your mom really is a sick woman. How long has she had her heart problems?"

I explained that she had had her bypass in 1991, fifteen years prior. That she had done well for four or five years but had stopped going to cardiac rehab when she had to change facilities and the new one had treadmills instead of a track for her to walk. Her health had deteriorated over the last ten years, with numerous catheterizations and stents and a worsening of her diabetes.

He explained that the stenting had gone relatively easily considering all the hardware already in place that he had to make his way around. "She should do okay with this one, but her next one may be her last!"

Boy, was that a subtle punch in the wake-up clock. "That's not good."

"No. She's a very sick woman."

I kept it in my head, but what I was thinking was, *I know, but what about her heart?* What I said was, "Can I see her?"

"She'll be upstairs in her room in about an hour."

I called over to my father's room to let him know all was well. He picked up the phone on the sixth or seventh ring. "Hullo?" he said tentatively.

"Hi, Dad, it's me. I wanted to let you know the procedure is over and Mom is doing okay. I expect to see her in about an hour."

"So what time are you going to be over here?" he asked.

"Dad, I'm going to stay here until I see Mom all settled and comfortable. Tom and Phil are there with you, so I may not make it over there."

"Oh." His voice faltered with disappointment. "When she's up for it, make sure Mom calls me."

Somehow, in the last eight days his dependence had transferred to me. He was totally fine for the three days of my trip, but now that I was back in the area, he couldn't stand that I might not come by for one day.

"Okay, Dad, but don't get freaked out if it's not today. Mom will probably sleep all day. Can you put Tom or Phil on?"

"Here's Phil. Take care of Mom."

"I will, Dad, I will," I said. As if I wouldn't.

"So, how's Mom doing?" Phil asked.

"According to the doctor, she came through okay. How are things over there?"

"He was himself. I'm glad Tom is here. He can really calm him down." I could hear the *I can't wait to get out of here* in Phil's voice. "Tom's leaving for the office, wanna talk to him?"

"Nah, tell him I'll call him later unless he has something pressing." I really hate the phone and I wanted to get off before my dad asked to get back on with me.

"You doing okay?" Phil asked. He was capable of concern, but I'm not sure what he would have said if I said no.

"Yeah. My conversation with the doctor was interesting, upsetting actually, but I'll tell you about it when I get home."

"Oh. I'm actually going home myself this afternoon, to D.C., now that everything is okay. I actually want to come see Mom as soon as she's in her room and then hit the road. How 'bout I come have lunch with you at that hospital?"

I couldn't say no, what excuse would I give? My ambivalence really sucked. He was reaching out with one hand, but then with the other he was actually jumping ship, again. I agreed to meet him in the hospital cafeteria.

I was gagging down a cardboard hamburger and some lukewarm fries that had clearly been under the heat lamp too long when he sat down with his tray. "How was Dad?" I mumbled.

"Okay. Anxious to hear from Mom."

"Any doctors come by while you were there?"

"A few."

"Which ones, what did they have to say?"

"I think the guy for his lungs. They gave him that thing you blow in. And another one who was talking about some tests, but I left the room to give them some privacy."

"Did you ask Dad after? What did they say?" Was that a reasonable question? I was feeling frustrated. I didn't want to get nasty here in the cafeteria but did he not feel some investment in being part of this care team?

"No. Dad and I were mostly talking hockey and watching the news."

One … Two … Three … I counted slowly to myself and focused on the french fries. He had at least kept Dad occupied, and maybe Tom had picked something up while he was there.

"So, Mom should be upstairs in a few minutes. It was really shocking to get the doctor's account of what he found in there."

"What do you mean?" he asked between bites of his potatoes.

"Well, how much damage she has and how many stents are placed. I didn't realize she had had so many procedures."

"Oh, that was a lot?"

"She has seven stents in there. Did the doctor ever tell you just how sick a woman Mom is? There are major areas of her heart muscle that don't function anymore."

"I never really spoke with her doctors back home. Dad was always there so I never felt the need."

"Did Dad ever talk to you about it? Did Mom?"

"Nah and I figured if I needed to know, they'd've told me."

I needed some dessert, chocolate could keep my rage down, chocolate or Tom, and he was at work. I couldn't believe what I was hearing. Was I unique among men, caring about my parents and wanting to know what was happening? Was I unique in being involved? How could he have been so uninvolved when he was right there?

~

My mind flashed back to 1991. Mom and Dad were still living near us in New Jersey. Mom had her first heart attack on Presidents' Day. Tom and I had rushed to the hospital and had been by her bedside or helping Dad for a week. It was easier then because we both had full-time jobs and could use our time off without worry about meeting the bills.

It was two days post-op from her triple bypass. She was still in the ICU. Her recovery was slow and they were keeping her in a coma to facilitate it. We could see her for fifteen minutes every three hours. Dad and I had made every one of those visitations. Triple bypass was still a big deal back then, not the routine procedure it has become.

Phil walked in following his drive up from North Carolina. He said his hellos and then blurted out, "Okay, you can rest easy and take a break, I'm here now!" While my father looked relieved at this, I did my best not to choke him. At least he could entertain Dad for the evening, maybe take him out to dinner and make sure he ate.

The three of us headed out to the hall. I said to Phil, "It's not as bad as it looks. They have her in a coma to aid in recovery."

"Oh, I wasn't worried. I thought she looked pretty good." Was he really in the same room with us? The woman had tubes coming out of her in every which way, she had no color, and she was unconscious.

"I'm going to run up to New York City and see my friend Paul for dinner. I figured as long as I was here, might as well kill two birds with one stone. Dad, I'll probably get in late tonight so don't wait up for me," he said as he disappeared down the corridor.

I turned to my father. "Come on, Dad, let's go get some dinner. What do you want to eat?"

As we walked to the car, I was questioning my anger at Phil. Was I unreasonable? Was it unfair for me to think he might actually come up and be helpful? Shouldn't the oldest be shouldering more responsibility? Given the duration of his visit, it felt like he was showing up just to confirm we were telling the truth about her being sick. I wished I could chalk up my irritation to anxiety and being overwhelmed, but it was an old family story for me.

~

The November preceding this crisis, before there had been any thought of their moving back to New Jersey, we visited them in North Carolina for Chanukah/Thanksgiving. I was struck by how sickly they both looked.

At one point, in the car, on the way home, I turned to Tom and said, "I think this will be our last holiday with them."

"Why, it wasn't that bad this time. There were no major fights and your dad barely snapped at your mom."

"Oh, I'm not saying that; I just think they both looked at death's door." Tom took my hand and we drove in silence for the next hundred miles listening to the show tunes we had blasting from the stereo.

5

AURORA RETURNS

After lunch, Phil and I went to visit Mom, who had been moved to her room. I was surprised to see her sitting in a chair, as usually patients were kept immobile after stenting with sandbags pressing on the entry points in their legs. I asked her nurse about this.

"Oh, those were the old days, no one does it that way anymore. Your mom has pressure bandages on her legs. She can walk when she's ready."

"Wow," I said, "things sure do change." I kept my eyes fixated on the spot, as I was sure her hospital gown would fill with blood flowing from the spot at any minute.

"It was great of you to come up for today," Mom said to Phil.

"No problem, but I really have to be getting back. I want to let the kids know you're doing all right and I have a conference call first thing in the morning," he said.

Sure glad we didn't inconvenience you! I thought to myself. There goes any relief I was hoping for. I wondered how he was going to report back since he hadn't asked my mom how she was doing or anything else.

"This is my roommate, Norma," my mother said, pointing to a shockingly obese woman in the next bed, "and those are two of her daughters."

I waved, introduced myself, and turned back to Mom. "How're you feeling? Any pain?"

"Nah, they gave me something. I'm just waiting to get something to eat. I'm starved."

"I'll go check and see if you're getting a tray, but then I really have to take off," Phil said.

While he was gone, she said to me, "I'm glad you two are getting along." I just smiled and left her to her fantasy.

He came back and said her tray was expected any minute. He gave her a kiss and took off. I turned to Mom. "So, is it okay if I call Dad and you say hello, so he can stop worrying?"

"Whatever."

I had him on speed dial in my cell and he answered on the fifth ring. "Hullo!"

"Hey, were you sleeping? I have someone who wants to say hello, but the doctor says, 'Don't tire her out.'"

Mom took the phone and in her best fresh from anesthesia, God I don't really want to be communicating with anyone voice, said, "Hi, hon! Just wanted to let you know I came through okay and you can rest easy."

She was silent while she listened to his chatter. She did roll her eyes a few times, then I heard, "Well my phone is not hooked up yet. I'll let you know when it is." And she handed the phone back to me.

"Okay. Okay. One of us will be over for a bit tonight. No, Phil has gone home already."

"So what is she in for?" I said, nodding toward Mom's roommate after I hung up with Dad.

"She had a quadruple bypass three days ago; she just got moved here from the step-down unit." She looked good for three days post.

Mom's tray arrived and along with it six more visitors for Norma. Of course, Mom's Jell-O was not sugar-free and the broth wasn't low salt; Mom didn't care, she ate it anyway. Her sin couldn't compare with what was going on at the party in the next bed. One of her visitors had baked a tray of macaroni and cheese, and Norma was sitting with a spoon eating it right out of the baking tray. How I didn't scream, "Really, three days after bypass and your goal is to see if you can refill your arteries before you even leave the hospital?" Still puzzles me. They were all laughing and joking, taking up far more than their share of half the room. Most significantly, since Norma had the bed next to both the window and the bathroom, her crowd was blocking both. I was visibly annoyed by this but Mom just dismissed it. That is until she got a stomach cramp.

"Come on, I'll help you to the bathroom," I said.

"No, I'll just get a bedpan. I don't want to disturb them."

"That is ridiculous, Mom. I can help you or I can get the nurse to walk you."

"Just give me the bedpan and close the curtain!"

Of course there was no bedpan by my mom's bed. I rang for the nurse and rang for the nurse. When she didn't come, I went to flag someone down and ask for a bedpan. When I got back, Mom said, "Too late! And I got the runs to make matters worse."

I was annoyed. What took them so long to get here? Now they'd have to come clean her up. I pulled the curtain and heard a "Phew!" from the other side. If I was a fighting man, I would have thrown a punch at that point, but Mom was cool as a cucumber.

They came in to clean Mom up; I waited in the hall. When they came out, I followed the nurse back to her desk.

"Hi, I'm Mike," I said, "Mrs. Keren's son. I don't know if you know but her husband is in a nearby hospital right now so I am the contact person if there is a problem. I was concerned because my mom is a diabetic and should be on a diabetic and low-salt diet and her tray was clearly not either of those."

She checked my mom's chart and said, "Thanks, it's clear from the chart but for some reason the doctor didn't order special diets. I'll make sure he does."

"Thanks. If you don't mind, could I see the medications he ordered? Mom has so many sensitivities I have to be careful." I was really not trusting the hospital. The diet is a simple oversight but could have really bad consequences. I had made sure to provide these doctors with a printed copy of my mother's medical history, with all her meds and drug reactions, but there was no guarantee they'd use it.

"Well, that's not very typical," she said.

"Well, I'm not very typical. Besides, it's just part of my job as a good and caring son. I can't have been the first caregiver to ask for this."

"Well, let me ask my supervisor."

While she was off getting her supervisor, I grabbed Mom's chart, which the nurse had left on the desk, and turned to her medication orders. They were all there, but there was one I didn't recognize. I wasn't sure if it was a generic name I was unfamiliar with or a new med all together. The nurse and the supervisor returned together.

"Excuse me, what are you doing?"

"I'm looking at my mother's chart. Your nurse left it right out here for anyone to look at, so I figured it would be okay for me to look at her chart." She didn't dare go any further in chastising me, but the nurse would probably get reprimanded later.

"I'm sorry, Mr. Keren. She should know better than to leave the chart like that. I'll make sure it doesn't happen again. Now, how can I help you?"

"First off, while I introduced myself to your nurse by my first name, I also made it clear that if we're going to be formal, my title is Dr. Keren. I've already been made aware of one mistake in the doctor's orders, so I wanted to just look at them to make sure there were no others."

"Of course, Dr. Keren. What kind of physician are you?"

"I didn't say I was a physician, I said I was a doctor." I was revving up; Aurora was yearning to break free.

"I just have one question, what is this med for?" I said, pointing to the one name I didn't recognize.

"Oh, that's for her high cholesterol."

"Is it a statin medication?"

"Yes, it's the newest one. It has been very successful."

I swallowed hard. I flipped the chart closed and pointed to the big red sticker that said ALLERGIC TO STATINS.

The nurse turned pink, then red, and then flushed white.

I turned to the medication charting section; each page had a red sticker that said, ALLERGIC TO STATINS. Aurora wanted to ask, "Can your nurses read?"

"Well, it looks like the doctor had his resident do the orders."

Aurora could restrain herself no more. I was starting to yell. "And unlike in other hospitals, are your nurses not the front line and are they not supposed to check such things when they take the doctors' orders and transcribe them on the med sheets?"

"Yes Dr. Keren." She backed a few steps away. I must have looked scary.

Finally, Aurora yelled, "THEN WHY WAS MY MOTHER GIVEN A STATIN?! NO WONDER SHE SHIT HERSELF. NO WONDER SHE COULDN'T HOLD IT WHILE YOUR NURSES TOOK THEIR SWEET TIME!" Aurora and I took a deep breath. "Please let her doctor, not the resident, know I'd like to speak to him. And have the Director of Nursing come up as well."

I was aware I was standing in the hallway, at the nurses' station. All kinds of folks were walking by. I wondered how I looked to these others. Did they see me as nasty? Entitled? Contemptuous and privileged? Perhaps. But maybe they saw I was in a fight for my mother's life and sweetness and diplomacy were beyond me at that point. Maybe, just maybe they recognized Aurora and thought to themselves they hoped their family would fight as hard for them.

I turned on my heels and returned to Mom's room, where the party was still in full progress. Mom was in her bed. I could tell the incident had wiped her out.

"Well, figured out why you had the runs. The doctor's resident prescribed you a statin and the nurses gave it to you. I'm a bit concerned we may have to travel far to find someone competent to take care of you. For now, please ask about every pill they offer you."

"Calm down. I shit myself, I'm not dead. Mistakes happen."

"You're welcome!"

The director of Nursing was the first to arrive. I barely let her introduce herself when I began recounting the past hour. Aurora and I attempted to be conciliatory, but I was not sure how successful we were being. "So then, I went to find a bed pan and it took minutes to even locate one. By the time I did, it was too late. Then, when I went to talk to Mom's nurse, she was kind of rude, seemed put out that I asked about the medications and then she left the chart unattended on the desk when she went to get her supervisor. I guess I got kind of snide in my anger."

"Well, you didn't make friends with the nurses," she said, laughing, "but you were angry and probably overwhelmed. I hear you have your plate full with caretaking." *Finally, a mensch*, I thought.

"I do. And I guess I apologize, although I do feel justified in my anger. These runs are what happen every time. This was avoidable."

"Certainly was, and I will make sure it doesn't happen again. I am truly sorry. Is there anything else I could help you with?"

"Is it possible my mom could get a quieter room? We didn't realize the cardiac wing had party suites." I just couldn't control my sarcasm, "A private room or maybe just a roommate with a smaller family." I followed her out into the hall.

"I really am sorry," I said, "but it's hard to be in two places at once and I want to know my mom is safe. She's worried that if you throw Norma's visitors out Norma will blame her."

"I got you. We'll move your mother and take care of the party and please, don't worry more than you have to."

What a smart thing to say; she knew she couldn't tell me not to worry at all. She got it. She also responded to me without worrying that I would use her words in a lawsuit. I was calming down nicely. Now if I could just keep Aurora in check when the doctor showed up.

The nurses had Mom packed and were wheeling her in her bed before I got back to the room, a nice private one across from the nurses' station. When I went back in the room Mom was sound asleep. I turned on her TV and caught up on some CNN.

Mom was quickly snoring again, and I was settled in to wait for her doctor. I must have dozed in the chair because the next thing I knew they were bringing Mom a dinner tray. I glanced at my watch and realized I must have been asleep for an hour and a half. The plate was both sugar-free and low sodium. Mom wasn't thrilled, but she picked at the baked, skinless, flavorless chicken and mushy vegetables. "I'm not really that hungry, but tomorrow could you bring me some Mrs. Dash?"

"Anything for you, Mom. Do you want original flavor or one of the varietals?"

"Original is just fine, anything for some taste in the food." She picked up her sugar-free ice cream and ate it heartily, even though it was mostly soup. "How'd you get me this room? It's not going to cost me, is it?"

"Better not. I just asked them to move you out of the party suite to a quieter room, preferably one where your roommate has a smaller family."

Mom giggled a bit.

I realized I still had not heard from her doctor. I went to ask at the desk. Perhaps he had come when I was sleeping and chose not to wake me. They said they had not seen him and offered to send another page. I thanked them and went back to Mom.

I was tired, hungry, and knew I still had to see Dad. I said my goodbyes to Mom and told her I'd come by at lunchtime the next day. When I got to my car, I called the doctor's office and left a message with the doctor's service, "This is Dr. Keren. I have been requesting to speak with you for six hours. I do not want to hear from your associates, nor do I want to hear from your resident. Someone made a medication error this morning that could have killed my mother; it will certainly complicate her recovery. I expect to hear from you before ten o'clock this evening. Thank you." I was still angry and anticipating dismissal and condescension.

My visit with Dad was very short. Since I could barely keep my eyes open, conversation was difficult as well. I assured him all was well with Mom and headed out. It was actually after visiting hours and I used that as an excuse to keep it short.

I was halfway home when the phone rang. I checked the screen, did not recognize the number, but assumed it was the doctor, so I pulled the car over and took the call.

"Mr. Keren, it's Dr. X, what can I do for you?"

"Mr. X, it's Dr. Keren!" I said. What he didn't know was that Dr. Aurora Greenway was listening in as well. "Don't know if you are aware, but someone wrote for my mother to be on a statin. She received a dose when she got back to the room and soon after had a reaction. It's pasted all over her chart that she is allergic to statins, how could this have happened?" I did my best to keep my rage from overflowing.

"Well, I don't have her chart here so I don't know for sure. But your mom is not allergic to statins, they just give her diarrhea."

"Doc, call it an allergy or call it a reaction, but they don't just give her diarrhea, they give her diarrhea so excessive that she has three times ended up in the hospital needing IV fluids due to dehydration. Were she not already receiving IV fluids, I'm sure they would have needed to be started this afternoon."

"So now you're a physician?" he replied.

"No, but I know my mother." I could feel Aurora smiling at me.

"I'm sorry, Dr. Keren. You're right. It's late and we're both tired. I will follow up with my resident and your mother in the morning. Your mother's lucky she has you on her team."

"Thanks, Doc." I said, just before I disconnected.

I walked in the door and fell into Tom's arms. He wanted to comfort me with words but I put my fingers to his lips and just relished being in his arms of strength. I was lucky. Aurora didn't have Tom, but I had both of them. Together, we'd get through.

6

BLUE EYE SHADOW

What was happening in New Jersey was only half of what was going on for us. Tom's mom, Joan, had received a diagnosis of uterine cancer the previous autumn. Joan was a lifelong participant in the physician's loyalty program. Her Family Practice doctor still called himself a General Practitioner. He treated her diabetes and did her annual physical and had since she first moved to Long Island in the late 1950s after Tom's birth. He was slowly ceding much of his practice to his young son (by young, he meant fiftyish). Specialists were not in her vocabulary and she had not seen a gynecologist since her post-pregnancy follow-up when Tom was born.

When Tom got a call from her in which she embarrassingly told him she was "bleeding down there," he immediately told her to go to the gynecologist and learned she didn't have one.

"Mom, you have to see one."

"Why can't I just go see Dr. J.?"

"Well, maybe he could refer you to a gynecologist, but since he doesn't regularly examine you or do Pap smears, I'm not sure we should trust him on this."

"I trust him on everything."

Tom didn't answer that. It would hurt her feelings to insult her doctor and wouldn't help the discussion to progress. "Mom, why don't you ask your friend Amy? I'm sure she has a gynecologist and maybe she would go with you to the exam."

Since Jim's death seven years before, Joan had experienced an awakening. She was a bright and curious woman who discovered the world when she was freed from stifling relationships. Her mother, who while loving, was a strong and dominant matriarch and left little oxygen for Joan. Not pushed to excel, Joan never recognized her smarts and talents. She left her mother's home for her marital bed.

Jim was another force: A vortex of control needs whose anger and alcoholism kept Joan in an ever-shrinking universe. She did love him, and they depended on each other. When Jim died, Joan had a crowd back to the house after the funeral. There were maybe twenty-five folks enjoying coffee and cake, allowing Joan to share her memories. A frequent comment that day, however, was how Jim must be turning in his casket with all the people in his house. Jim did not allow company; he would say it was too taxing for the cesspool (sewers had replaced the cesspool some ten years before but it didn't change his cautionary warnings). Jim and Joan knew the neighbors but had no relationships. They went out only with Tom and me, or occasionally with distant relatives who still lived in the New York area.

Joan, when widowed, made a group of female friends that was a testament to the power of women's relationships. They helped her to discover the strong, bright, and well-spoken woman who had been living inside of her. They went to the movies, they went to the theater, they went out to eat, and mostly, they listened and supported each other through the ups and downs of their personal plights. They were a diverse group—religions, political leanings, educational backgrounds, and experience of the world—and somehow, Joan ended up the center of them all. She had tolerance for them all even when they didn't all tolerate each other. She babysat for kids and grandkids in the neighborhood. Dog-sat for Tom and me when we would travel. And she discovered a new passion: ballroom dancing.

Joan became a Salsa Queen. Her theme song was "Dancing Queen" by Abba. Two or three nights a week, she could be found at the local Arthur Murray studio. Now, it's true these places could wipe out a widow's fortune, but within reason, the studio and its dance parties gave Joan a sense of freedom and ability she had never experienced. We loved watching her grow, develop her own tastes and sense of style. She updated her wardrobe and bought every blouse she could find that was bedazzled. "Foxy Lady!" read our favorite one.

Despite the updates to her look, however, no one could convince her to change her makeup. Some women won't leave the house without lipstick, for Joan it was her blue eye shadow. Not even a trip to the MAC store with her "two gay sons" and a consultation with an expert could convince her to try a new shade.

Amy was her next-door neighbor and had been for most of the fifty years they had lived there. But after Jim died, she became one of Joan's best friends and a great resource for Tom and me when we couldn't be there. She took Joan to the gynecologist and for the handful of blood tests, CT scans, and MRIs that led to Tom and Joan sitting in a surgeon's office.

"Joan, I believe the best course of treatment for you would be a full hysterectomy," the doctor said.

"Oh, okay," Joan said sheepishly, still the old-fashioned patient who wouldn't dare question a doctor's recommendation.

"Well, are there other options?" Tom questioned.

"We could just remove the uterus and leave the ovaries, but I recommend the full hysterectomy. It greatly reduces the chances of later metastases."

They accepted the doctor's recommendation and scheduled the surgery for two weeks hence. All of this had gone down four weeks after I had begun my new job. On the morning of the surgery, I went to work. My work at that point involved studying for my upcoming exams to be licensed as a stockbroker. Attempting to concentrate was futile. About one o'clock I went to my boss and said, "It's useless, I can't focus. I belong on Long Island."

"Of course, get out of here. Be where you should be."

I texted Tom, "Thinking of you. Hope it's going well." I didn't let him know I was on my way. Partially, I wanted to surprise him and partially, I didn't want him to be worrying about me on the road.

He texted back, "They started late, but she's in there now. They said she should be out in about another hour or so."

It was the days before smart phones. I was typing on a flip phone keypad, three letters to a key, so I just threw out some capital Xs and Os.

When I got to the hospital and found Tom in the surgical waiting room, he was deeply involved in reading an academic paper. I startled him when I stood in front of him and stepped on his toes.

His startled annoyance quickly turned to a grin of pleasure as he jumped up to hug me. It was strong and long. Finally, I asked, "Any news?"

"She's out of surgery and I'm waiting to get to see her in recovery. You'll be able to come with me." Before I could say anything, he added, "What are you doing here, how did you get away from work?"

"I just told Sam this was where I belonged and he told me to go."

"I'm glad you're here."

When the nurse brought us into the recovery room, we went to opposite sides of Joan's bed and grabbed her hands. She opened her eyes and smiled at us. We both broke out laughing, simultaneously. As she stared at us with her relieved and satisfied look, we both saw it at the same time. There, on her upper eyelids, was her blue eye shadow. They may have scrubbed the rest of her clean for the operating room, but they recognized the eye shadow's importance to her and let her wear it. She may no longer have her uterus or ovaries but she was still Joan, as long as she had her blue eye shadow.

They didn't let us stay long in recovery with her. I kissed her goodbye and told her I'd see her Friday night or Saturday. She asked me if I'd bring the dogs out to visit her. I'd told her we would see how she was doing.

Before I left, Tom and I met with her surgeon.

"The operation went fine, not at all complicated. Your mom should make a full recovery," he said.

Tom let out a sigh of relief, but the doctor's body language suggested there was more.

"Now we have to wait for the final biopsy results, and I'm sure we got all of the tumor, but initial cell typing suggests that even though it was in the uterus it was an ovarian cancer cell type. If that is the case, an oncologist would probably want to have your mom do a course of chemotherapy."

We both felt deflated by this news. We knew ovarian cancer was far more aggressive and much more frequently terminal than uterine cancers.

"So when will we know?" Tom asked.

"We should have the results back within two weeks."

I had worked during grad school in a pathology lab preparing specimens for slides and had my doubts that it would really take this long, but I held my tongue. I felt like a visitor in this family drama despite all my years of being part of the family. I wasn't sure of my right to ask questions or have opinions.

A course of chemotherapy treatments was decided upon. The oncologist assured Joan and Tom that they would be able to control the side effects—primarily the nausea, but Joan would likely lose her hair. Joan had thin hair as it was, and someone told her it would probably grow back thicker and curly, which actually held promise for her.

Tom would take Fridays off to spend with her; she would go to the cancer center every third Friday for her chemo. Joan was a patient during the time the center moved into a new, bright and shiny facility with separate cubicles and personal flat-screen TVs for each of the patients. The patients, Joan included, hated the setup. It turned what had been a social and supportive experience into a very isolative and lonely one. But Joan had Tom at her side, and the doctor was right about her nausea being controlled. Joan was indomitable. She would rise from her treatment chair, free from the IVs and monitoring hardware, and announce, "I need a drink and dinner. Let's go to Mateo's," her favorite Italian restaurant, where she would eat a plate of spaghetti and meatballs and sip her scotch.

She did well with her chemotherapy. She did lose her hair but rejected uncomfortable wigs and sported flashy, sparkly turbans. Her energy was good. She felt well. Tom went out for her follow-up appointment after the third round of chemo.

"Joan, you did so well. You are looking good and your numbers are great. We had worried about your ability to tolerate the chemo at your age, but you came through just fine," the doctor said, adding, "I'd like to recommend we do two more treatments."

Joan looked confused, and Tom asked, "Why?"

"Well, in a younger person we would always recommend a minimum of five. We recommended three because it is considered a good compromise for a compromised patient, enough to raise the odds of survival while minimizing the intrusion of side effects. But since your mom has responded like a young woman, I think we should do the whole course."

Tom asked about the research and was provided with more numbers and stats than either of us had dealt with since graduate school. They supported the doctor's position but didn't contain answers to questions about accumulated side effects as treatment progressed. Both Joan and Tom were leaning towards consenting to the additional treatment when I arrived on Long Island and joined them for dinner.

I listened as Tom made the case for the additional chemo.

"What is the risk of side effects with the additional chemicals? Is it cumulative? Does it grow with each treatment? Or, would we have seen them already if they were going to happen?" I asked.

Tom couldn't fully answer my questions. "Joan, how do you feel about more treatment?" I asked.

"Well, the doctor thinks it would be good for me."

I didn't feel good about the idea. It was tempting fate in my mind. But, I was just a son-in-law. The hospital wouldn't even acknowledge my relationship to Joan because of the laws. I kept my concerns to myself until I was alone with Tom.

"Tom, I don't know about the extra treatments. What if they do make her sick? If there's no signs of metastases or spread at this point, why tempt fate?"

"You know my mom. She'll listen to the doctor. Besides I think she should do it."

"Well, could you at least ask the doctor about cumulative risks and such?"

"Okay."

The extra sessions began and Joan's nausea remained under control. But within days of the fourth session, she was complaining about numbness and tingling in her legs and feet.

"Neuropathy," her doctor informed them. "Probably from all your years of being a diabetic."

Well, it certainly was possible, but one interesting side effect of the chemo was that Joan's sugars were better controlled than they'd been in years.

"Could it be from the chemo?" Tom asked.

Her General Practitioner conceded it could be an interactive effect. The oncologist was reluctant to acknowledge the possibility, but by the time of the fifth session Joan was using a quad cane at home and a walker outside. There was no more dancing and going out with the girls was a whole lot more difficult. The neuropathy would persist long after the chemo ended. There were hours of physical therapy and myelograms to check the nerve damage. She was frustrated.

I was sad for her. Our alive and vibrant Joan was somehow diminished. Oh, she still kept her spirit, that never really wavered. But, her life was shrinking back into the little Cape Cod house in Bellmore, Long Island, that had been so constrictive for her before. We began to spend even more time on Long Island with Joan.

7

DAD GETS A FAN

It was a long spring. Mom sprang back from her heart attack with few complaints or complications. When she was released from the hospital, I convinced the doctors to refer her to a rehab until she had the strength to climb the steps in my house. As big as my house is, there is no bathroom on the main floor. If she couldn't do the steps, she would have to stay on the second floor, in the bedroom, all day. I knew that would be intolerable. I located a facility near home and after a week of physical therapy she took up residence in our guest room.

It was fun to have Mom around. She would join Tom and me at the movies or out to dinner. She kept Max and Chelsea, the dogs, company, and they her. I'd take Mom to the hospital to see Dad most days after work. She never wanted to stay too long and Dad, feeling guilty, didn't complain when we left rather quickly.

Dad's recovery was going much slower. His initial hospitalization lasted more than a month. When he finally was stabilized on medications for his breathing, blood pressure, and esophageal issues, he was severely weakened from lying in the hospital bed for as long as he had. He was going to need rehabilitation. This was going to be a tricky proposition to broach with him. He believed rehabs and nursing facilities to be firetraps.

As expected, Dad initially said no. He argued he was working with the physical therapist at the hospital and was now able to get out of bed and go to the bathroom. He neglected to acknowledge that he did need assistance. I was firm. Neither Tom nor I were prepared to give him that level of attention. If he was going to come to our home, he would need to be able to not only get to the bathroom by himself but also get down the stairs. He could not stay in the hospital long enough to achieve that, and rehab was the only way.

Neither Tom nor I had been particularly impressed with the quality of care Mom had received at her rehab, so we started checking out ones close to our home. Tom had previously worked in a mental health program for the elderly and their caregivers and therefore had a good deal of experience with nursing and rehab centers. He volunteered to check out two of them in our town. The afternoon of his visits I got an excited voicemail from him. "Oh my God, this place is incredible. I would bring my parents here in a heartbeat. The staff is pleasant, competent, and seems very caring. Best of all, there was no smell of urine. You have to come see this place."

He was right. The first thing you noticed at Norwood Terrace was the absence of the smell of urine. That's very unusual for a nursing home. The second thing you noticed was that there were not rows of overmedicated old people sitting in the hall, staring into space and drooling. Security seemed a bit lax, although there were days I wouldn't have minded if someone did steal my father. The staff was as Tom described them. They had a bed available on their sub-acute rehab unit. The hospital social worker spoke to their social worker and after forty-seven days Dad was out of the hospital.

Dad seemed to like the place. The nurses were very attentive to him and tolerated his often off-putting humor. He had a very nice relationship with his physical therapist, a young man named Jimmy. Dad would talk about him constantly. Since I would get to visit only in the evenings and on weekends, I didn't get to meet Jimmy till way into Dad's stay, but Dad wasn't complaining and that was a good thing.

Norwood Terrace connected Dad with a gerontologist who would be able to follow him while he was there and beyond. This doctor was more concerned with the growth they had discovered on my father's kidney than any of the doctors had been during Dad's hospital stay. He ordered a few tests and remained concerned. He sent Dad to see a surgeon, and both doctors concurred that it should be removed. A surgery was scheduled.

The surgeon was based out of a huge teaching hospital in New Jersey, the site of my mother's first heart surgery. Dad was not thrilled at the prospect of more hospitals, but the doctor convinced him it was essential the tumor be removed.

He was placed in a room in the new cancer treatment center and he *was* thrilled with its amenities: big-screen TV, stereo system, his own refrigerator, and privacy.

The surgery went well and Dad had no complications. They wanted to keep him in the hospital for five days to recuperate. The plan was for him then to return to Norwood Terrace to further his recovery. By the second day after the surgery Dad was back to his old self and was asserting demands.

"You know you could offer to bring me some food once in a while."

"Dad, you've only just started back on solid foods. If you want something special, why don't you just ask? Don't have to be nasty."

"Sorry. Okay. I'd really like some clams on the half shell."

"Dad, come on. How about something that will be a little easier to get as takeout. I'm not going to start opening clams for you here in the hospital." He began to pout a little. "I could bring a shrimp cocktail or a shrimp salad sandwich," I offered.

He settled for a shrimp cocktail.

"All right, we'll bring it back with us after we go eat." Mom and I were both feeling hungry and she needed to eat regularly.

"Oh, I have to wait?"

I leaned over to give him a kiss. "See you later." I wasn't going to respond to his demands and impatience.

We picked up a shrimp cocktail after dinner and braced ourselves for his complaints when we returned to the hospital. He munched happily on a few of the shrimp. He alternated sucking the end of the shells to get out each last drop of meat and dozing off while his head snapped on his neck. Recognizing his tiredness, I suggested he save the rest of the shrimp for the next day and put them in the refrigerator next to his bed. We kissed him good night and left him to the nurses.

~

The first words out of his mouth the next day when Mom and I got to his room were, "I think they want me to die."

I wanted to make a joke; the words "So they've gotten to know you?" were on the tip of my tongue, but I could see the fear, sadness, misery, and concern in his eyes, so I switched modes. "Dad, what's up? What makes you say that?"

"They left me lying on the floor, forever. Nobody came. Thank God for the visitors next door."

"Whoa, back up! Who left you on the floor? How did you get on the floor? I'm not following."

What followed was a timid confession that he had gotten out of bed on his own, against doctor's orders, to retrieve his shrimp. When he was bending down to open the fridge, he fell and couldn't get up. He was yelling and no one came until a visitor from next door walked by, saw him, and went and got the nurses.

I hadn't liked the layout of this unit from the time Dad got admitted. His room was far from the nurses' station and invisible to all unless you were walking the hall. I really had to question the architect. On the other hand, I know my Dad, and he doesn't listen when he doesn't want to. He might love the attention of the sickbed but when the attention is gone, he is impatient. Add to that those tempting shrimp and one might understand why he would take such death-defying risks as to get up and open the refrigerator.

Dad's next-door neighbor's son came by and confirmed Dad's story, but no one could really say how long my dad laid on the floor. I checked in with the nurses and they assured me the doctor had been made aware of his fall, had him checked over, and did not determine any injuries or complications. They could not tell me how long he had been there, nor could they tell me how long might have gone between their checking on him. At least they were honest. I was upset it had happened, but I think there was only my father to blame.

The nurses offered to move him to a room a bit closer to the nurses' station if it would make him feel more comfortable. "No, I just want to get out of here before they kill me."

"But Dad, you're the one who tried to kill himself for shrimp. At least if you were closer, they could hear you easier, maybe you wouldn't be getting out of bed on your own."

"Look. Even if I shouldn't have gotten out of bed, they still left me lying there forever."

"*Forever?*"

"I was on the floor calling for an hour."

"An hour, were you watching the clock?"

"No, but …"

After quizzing him on what was on the TV while he lay, helpless, on the floor, we ascertained it was likely less than half an hour. That's still a long time, but it didn't suggest neglect.

Dad was deflated and pissed. "Now my son is fucking Sherlock Holmes? Does it matter if I was only there for ten minutes? Nobody came, nobody cared."

Mom finally piped in, "Serves you right. Stop being a pain in the ass."

"Mom, that's not helpful right now. I'm sure Dad was scared and embarrassed."

"You just pamper him," she muttered.

"Probably, Mom, and I pampered you, too, when you were laid up. In fact, I still pamper you and I don't mind doing it. Now, please apologize."

"Hmmph!"

Great, besides dealing with Dad's care, I was refereeing the War of the Roses. They were two people perfectly matched to drive each other over the brink for a lifetime.

I tried to play peacemaker and stated that I would talk to the doctor and the folks back at Norwood to see if we could speed up his return.

"Did you ever get your shrimp?"

"No."

"Do you want them?"

"Yes."

We raised the back of his bed, pulled his tray table over, and put the shrimp in front of him. He was grinning from ear to ear. Probably felt he had a victory. He was losing control and now he felt he had some back. Dad seemed to let the conflict with Mom roll off his back, but she was sitting in a chair, watching the news and ignoring her husband. I would ask why she even came, but I knew why: It was what she was supposed to do. She would get a ride, take a cab, or wait for Tom or me to bring her, but she would not let a day happen where he could say to himself, or even worse to another, that she didn't come visit.

* .

They released Dad back to the nursing home the next day. He was in his element there. He thoroughly enjoyed the attention of the nurses, rehab therapists, and mostly his physical therapist. Jimmy was becoming God. "Jimmy this," "Jimmy that." It was a constant monologue. Maybe Jimmy was the son he always wanted.

Thin-skinned and programmed for jealousy, I pondered his magic over my dad. I had to see him in action for myself.

One day, I went to visit early hoping to observe my dad in physical therapy. I was a little surprised by what I saw, never having been in a physical therapy area before. It was a long, narrow room filled with gym equipment, balls, poles, loops, and ropes. It was like a compressed version of my most vivid gym class nightmares. In a semicircle, among the clutter, was a line of about ten residents of varying ages from fifty to death. Most were sitting in wheelchairs. Some were engaging their hands or legs with different apparatus or pieces of equipment.

Jimmy and two therapy assistants were making their way around the circle assisting residents. Dad was in the center of the line attempting to pull his legs apart while they were wrapped in a large rubber band–like contraption. Jimmy approached Dad, removed the band from his ankles, and rolled him over to the parallel bars to do some walking. Dad never stopped talking. I didn't need to hear him to know the jokes he was telling. I had heard them over and over again my whole life. The best of them I may repeat occasionally. My favorite was the one he would say to every toll taker on the highway, "Hey. Where's my cookie?"

But here was my answer to the magic. Jimmy was laughing and laughing hard. Dad had found a soul who enjoyed his humor, who seemed to genuinely like him. This was the source of "Jimmy, Jimmy, Jimmy."

8

THE GUEST ROOMS

"Artie, Mike and I found an apartment. It's perfect. It's a ground floor with a bedroom, den, living/dining area, kitchen, laundry room, and two baths. The development seems quiet. Mike says we can afford it."

"Oh, Mike says!"

I excused myself and left them to chat. Dad had been on the rehab unit for several weeks and was making good progress. The doctor was talking about releasing him the following week if he continued to improve. It was mid-May and the apartment would not be ready till July 1, so I would have him in my home for at least a month. A challenge for sure, but we had no other choice. Their condo in North Carolina was on the market and the realtor claimed there had been a good deal of interest. She didn't want my folks to settle for too low an amount.

I poked my head back in the door. "Is it safe?"

My father was wearing a big smile and Mom didn't look upset or aggravated. "Of course, we were just talking about what to have sent from North Carolina and what to leave behind." Had my father's crack been my imagination? My family was skillful in their avoidance of emotional content.

It had been settled; they wanted to sign the lease. Mom let her realtor know they wanted to have the unit sold and closed by July 1. That happened pretty easily. They got a good price and began planning for their move, starting with Mom's decision that they would heretofore be sleeping in twin beds. No surprise, my parents would now be living like a 1950s sitcom couple. My own Lucy and Ricky, probably more like Fred and Ethel.

Dad was to get out during the last week of May, until he developed a fever during that last weekend. Blood work suggested an infection and he was started on an antibiotic. Monday rolled around and he was still feverish. Further testing revealed he had developed a MRSA infection. Methicillin-resistant Staphylococcus Aureus (MRSA) is a virulent bacterium that breeds in care facilities and has grown resistant to most antibiotic treatment. Left untreated it could be fatal. It would require intravenous administration of very strong medications. The first step in the treatment was for Dad to have a port installed in his chest, where the medications could be administered.

The next day started out to be a good one. I made some sales, despite the distractions. With a few minor bumps, having Dad in the nursing home was good for getting into routines. I was tempted to go out to lunch to celebrate my good sales but decided to eat at my desk again. I was mid-chew on my sandwich when the phone rang. I swallowed quickly and picked up the phone.

"Hello, RBC, Michael Keren …"

I barely got my greeting out. "Mike, it's Mom. There's a problem and Dad is in the Emergency Room. He's at the same hospital where he went to get the port installed."

"What? Why? Why there?"

"He was getting his infusion and had some kind of reaction to the medication. He couldn't breathe. The ambulance just took him and didn't ask where to, but his doctor is there, so it probably makes sense."

"All right. Are you still at the nursing home? Should I pick you up on the way to the hospital?"

"Yeah, I'm here. I'll wait for you."

"Be there within the hour."

~

In mid-June the hospital decided he could be released. Because I insisted he have physical therapy during his hospital stay, he had not deconditioned much. The doctor suggested he go back to Norwood Terrace but I envisioned that as not ending well. The last few months had come to feel like an endless in and out, back and forth. If Dad could get in-home physical therapy and a visiting nurse, I thought we could handle him at home and his physician agreed. After some brief lessons from the nurses on the care of his surgical wounds, medication regimens, and a few other orders, I drove Dad to our house and settled him into the guest room.

The transition went easily. He was getting an aide for two hours a day to help him wash and dress. A visiting nurse came regularly to check his wounds and track his vitals. And the physical therapist came daily, for an hour. Mom handled his meals. I installed four hundred channels of cable on the TV in the guest room and there were plenty of books for him to read. When I got home from work, I would check in with him and take Mom out shopping or for a bite to eat. As he felt stronger, we would take him out to eat as well.

The weather was getting warm so he could sit in the backyard with the dogs for a bit, and the physical therapist could walk him on the block or even around the corner. If it was still light when I got home, I could take him walking as well. He was still fairly unsteady on his feet, though, so I asked him not to go walking in the neighborhood alone. If it took fifteen minutes for someone to respond to him on the ground in the hospital, it could take ten times that to be found in the neighborhood.

Dad still had one surgical wound that was not totally healed. It required cleaning and dressing each evening. It was not in an inaccessible place, but he insisted he could not do it for himself. Mom refused, so it became our bedtime ritual. I would don latex gloves, remove the old bandage, visually inspect the wound, wash it with saline, and cover it with antibiotic cream before rebandaging it. The multiple steps quickly became a boring routine. It was easy and at times a bonding moment, but it also wasn't necessary. He could do it himself. Once or twice, I would pretend to skip a step, and he always caught it and reminded me.

The second full weekend he was with us both of my brothers, Phil and Stu, came to visit and to help out. I had the brilliant idea that Stuart should take a bandage-changing turn. He wanted to help, I wanted him to feel included, and I wanted him to try to bond a bit more.

We took Dad out for dinner that Saturday evening. Getting him back and forth was a bit of a production. He was still a bit wobbly and was growing frail, but it was a pleasant dinner. Phil spoke excitedly about the company he was working for in D.C. It was an educational start-up that was selling preschool programs around the country. My liberal bones were assaulted by the idea of this business and their overly profit-driven model of education, but I seemed to be the only one to recognize that money spent on such programs was money not spent on public education. Stuart waxed on about his kids. They were growing quickly and were finishing another year of school.

We got home and all gathered around the TV. After an hour Dad said he was tired and wanted to go to bed. "Would you come up and do my bandages?"

"Oh, Dad, Stu's going to help you out tonight, give me a night off."

"But he doesn't know how to do it."

"You do, and you can tell him what to do."

"But I want you to do it." He was getting annoyed. We all could see it in his face.

"Dad, please, let me do something. Michael does so much, I want to do this and give him a break."

"A break. Am I a burden?" He started to cry and stomped up the stairs. He must have been in better shape than we realized because he managed a good stomp.

Stu looked at me, I looked at him, and Phil didn't make eye contact at all, he was busy on his Blackberry. He was always busy on his Blackberry. "Should I go up?" Stu asked.

"Nah. At this point it's just easier if I do it."

"You sure?" Stu offered.

"Yeah, I appreciate your willingness to do it. And for your sake, I wish he wouldn't carry on so. It's strange, for sure, but it's making memories."

"I'll cherish them forever," Stu said.

I climbed the stairs and tarried over washing my hands for a lot longer than I needed to.

"Okay, Dad. Let's get this changed."

"What happened to Stuart? I thought he was going to do it."

"Really … I wouldn't subject him to you after that show downstairs." Dad didn't respond, he just exposed his stomach and let me do what I had to. "That's it. No lullaby for you tonight." He got it. He had pushed the envelope too far and he had to watch his behavior. We weren't employees of the hospital or nursing home he could push around.

Sunday morning dawned bright and sunny. Stu had pitched in this morning, walking the dogs and running out to get the *New York Times*. Tom was being a slow poke getting up and dressed. Mom had eaten her corn muffin and drank her tea. Phil was in his guest room texting away on his Blackberry. I heard Dad call.

"What is it, Dad?" I called, walking up the stairs to see what he needed; of course, making the mental note that Phil was only eight steps away in his room.

"I want breakfast."

"Okay, why don't you get washed up and come downstairs to eat."

"What's everybody eating?"

"Well, Mom just had her muffin and tea. There's bagels and cream cheese. I could scramble you an egg if you wanted. Cheerios." He grimaced. "What's the matter? You wanted Rice Krispies?"

"What are you boys eating?"

"Well, Tom, Phil, Stu, and I are going out for brunch."

"So why can't I come along?"

"Because it's our time. We have stuff to discuss."

"It's not fair."

"Wasn't it you who taught me that life is not fair?"

Major pouty face.

"Sorry, Dad, but I'm not budging. Now if you want me to help you downstairs and get your breakfast, you better get washed up." I helped him to get out of bed and put on his slippers and robe and walked him to the bathroom. There was still no movement from Phil's room with an offer to help, so I stood nearby in case he needed some assistance. When he was done, I helped him negotiate the stairs and got him seated at the table.

"Cheerios, bagel, or an egg?"

"I'll take a bagel, what kind do you have?"

"There's poppy, sesame, and plain left."

"No salt?"

"You ate the last one yesterday, which I'm sure was a joy for your system." Somehow this bright, sunny day was producing clouds in the house. I'm sure I was contributing to it, but my patience was feeling tested.

Tom came bounding down the stairs. "Good morning. Everyone sleep well?"

"Of course," my dad said. "Like a rock, as always." Tom was probably the only one Dad would put the bright face on for when everyone else was feeling his jabs.

"So what's the plan? You running a marathon today?"

"No, you're going out to breakfast with my sons while I'm stuck here in the house."

Tom ignored him and turned to me. "What's up with Phil? Heard him on the phone, seems pretty irritated."

"Got me? Does he need a reason?" Tom laughed. "I assumed he was talking to home."

"I didn't want to listen in, but what I heard didn't sound like it," Tom said.

Just then we heard the sound of Phil coming down the stairs. He emerged carrying his backpack and duffel bag. "I got to go. No time for breakfast," he said, barreling past us all and pushing open the storm door.

"What the hell is with him?" Mom asked. We all shrugged.

He came back in and headed up the stairs again. When he came down he was carrying his laptop and some paperwork.

"What's the rush?" Dad asked.

"You're not going to come to breakfast with us?" Tom asked.

"I said I got to go, and I have to go," he snapped.

"But you just got here," Mom said. "What's the matter?"

"I just have to go!" His voice was getting more pressured and agitated. "Just leave me alone."

"I don't know what crawled up your butt this morning, but it's not us. Either tell us what's going on or knock it off. We're your family, not your punching bag." Just as I finished Stu walked in with the dogs. He looked at me, then around the room, and just kept walking with the dogs into the kitchen.

"Bye, I'm leaving." And with that Phil walked out the door.

I followed him to his car. "What the hell is going on?"

"I can't tell you."

"Are you okay to drive?"

"It doesn't matter, I just have to go."

"Why? Are you okay to drive?"

"Just leave me alone!" He got in his car, slammed the door, and drove off.

I was worried about him driving, maybe more about someone he might hit than anything else. I knew Mom and Dad were going to be upset. They loved having all their boys around. I was probably glad. His being here made Mom and Dad happy, but he wasn't or couldn't be helpful. I tended to think it was the former. He was always excused from all hard labor when we were growing up. It was as if the orthopedic issues he had as a toddler were a lifelong handicap; my parents still held on to their anxiety about him despite the issues having been treated and cleared when he was a toddler. Maybe it was the firstborn syndrome. I don't remember him ever shoveling, cutting grass, painting, or even fixing things. Certainly, when it came to taking care of Stuart as a baby, there was no expectation on him. Prince Philip.

I went back in. Everyone was at the table watching Dad eat. "Did he tell you anything?" Mom asked.

"No. He just sped off."

"Probably had a fight with Karen," Mom said. "Wouldn't be the first." Phil was living in D.C. during the week and commuting back to Raleigh on weekends because he couldn't find work near home. His marriage to Karen had seemed tense for a very long time, and Tom and I privately speculated whether Phil was trying to get out of it by working so far from home.

Dad asked, "Where the hell did he get that temper?" We all looked at him in astonishment; we all had inherited our tempers from him. Phil's was probably the worst. Tom and I had once considered going on a cruise with him and the kids until we observed him rage at his son, Daniel, in the lobby of a movie theater. He had no control over his temper at all, and we decided we would not be stuck on a boat with him under any circumstances.

~

It would take some time, but the source of Phil's agitation that morning would eventually emerge. We had, in fact, witnessed the end of his marriage, and it had not come as passively as we imagined. It was a drama involving the internet, a one-night stand, and blackmail. Phil being Phil, he didn't ask for help or advice. He got angry and did nothing.

True to her word, his blackmailer told his wife the whole story. She told Phil to not come home. A messy divorce proceeded from there.

If there is a hero in this part of my story it is his ex-wife, Karen. While the drama was proceeding in New Jersey, Karen was in North Carolina packing up my parents' condominium with her friends. She was packing when she got the call from the blackmailer. Had that been me I would have told my brother to get his ass down there and "Pack up your own parents' place," but she didn't. She packed it up, attended to the closing, and took care of moving on that end. I admire what she did, her inherent goodness in seeing it through, and feel much closer to her now than when she and Phil were married.

~

The rest of the weekend went quietly. We even managed a nice, quiet dinner together at one of Dad's favorite local places. I drove Stu to the airport Monday morning and headed to work. By Wednesday the routine was beginning to feel normal and mindless. I was lying in bed that night reading myself to sleep only vaguely aware of the conversation that was going on between Dad and Tom in the next room. It sounded friendly enough. All of a sudden I could hear Tom yelling. This was significant because in all of our years of marriage I am the only one I had ever heard Tom yell at and that was rarely. I started to pay attention.

"How dare you say that! Mike is doing everything to make you comfortable, to see to your health. You know he could have just said for you to go to the nursing home until your apartment was ready."

"Control, control, control. That's all he's doing. It's like I'm a prisoner here in this house. He's forbade me from going out."

"Grow up, Artie. He just doesn't want you walking the block alone. It's an old street; the sidewalks are uneven and choppy. None of us want to deal with you breaking a hip." Tom was really yelling.

"Yeah, yeah. That's my problem, isn't it?"

Tom's voice was calming a bit. "Well, that's one selfish way of looking at it. If we were to just dump you in a hospital somewhere afterwards and not turn our life upside down for you, it would be just your problem. But you know we wouldn't do that."

"Oh, so now I'm a burden? You feel that way too?"

"Don't go there, Artie."

"Well, I am. You do think of me that way, right?"

"Look, Artie, I'm done. You owe Mike an apology. You are damn lucky to have him. Your other sons certainly count themselves lucky that we've taken up your care. Frees them up a ton, doesn't it? Why don't you take your frustrations out on them?"

Before he had a chance to answer, I could hear Tom walking out of their room and over to ours. He came over to the bed and sat down next to me. "I'm sorry. His griping was just getting to me. When he started to make it about you, I just flipped. How dare he?"

"What are you apologizing for? You were defending me and I'm appreciative. It might be a bit uncomfortable for a few hours but it will pass over. And don't you dare apologize to him before he apologizes to us. I mean that. I will be mad then."

"Of course I'll apologize to him."

"Tom, let him stew in it or he'll keep it up. His moods and demands are more of a burden than his care. A few hours of discomfort and he'll be on his best behavior for a few days."

"But …"

"No buts. I'm sure by tomorrow night it will have passed over. Now say good night to my mom and come to bed."

He went downstairs to say good night and Mom followed him back up. She knocked on my door and came and sat on my bed.

"You know you and Tom do too much. Don't listen to anything he says."

"Mom, I don't feel like it's too much, I just do what seems to need doing. If not wanting him to go out by himself is holding him hostage, then let him go, but I swear if he falls, I'm done!"

"I'm done, too, and he knows it. Just be thankful you don't have to sleep with him."

"You know you can sleep on one of the pull-out beds in the other room if you don't want to sleep with him."

"Now that would be the proverbial fart in church. We would never hear the end of it. No, I'll stay in that room."

Mom leaned over and kissed me on my cheek. "You know I really do appreciate all you guys are doing. And so does he. I love you."

"I love you too."

9

A GOOD DEATH

There was a period of time, mid-to-late adolescence, when I considered becoming an undertaker. Death fascinated me. I had first seen death as a preteen when my mother's uncle, Buddy, had died suddenly. His wife, a much younger woman and not Jewish, had him laid out in an open casket prior to his funeral. The corpse fascinated me. I found the makeup disturbing; even at the age of twelve, I could tell he had on way too much. But what really got my attention was that the undertaker had failed to trim his nose hairs and his stood stiffly and prominently beyond the end of his nostrils. I couldn't stop staring.

I had also been fascinated with the images I had picked up of the way he died. He was travelling a very busy road, three to four lanes of fifty-miles-per-hour traffic in both directions, when he had a "massive heart attack." The others on the road were lucky because Buddy's wife was able to get control of the car from the passenger seat and bring the car safely across three lanes of traffic to rest on the road's shoulder. Some called her a hero. I couldn't help wondering how I would've felt if I was in the car. For years afterward I wondered how I would die and who would be with me. I also became obsessed with letting people know I wanted to be buried in my most broken-in jeans, a T-shirt, and bare feet. I didn't want to look as uncomfortable as Uncle Buddy did in his blue suit; and please God, trim my nose hairs.

~

When spring became summer, I think we let out a collective sigh of relief as it felt that we had gotten my parents through the worst of it and they were on the mend. We moved my parents into their apartment just after the Fourth of July and were now free to leave them to their own devices if their kvetching or griping at each other became too much to bear.

There were a few fun times as we still spent a considerable amount of our "free time" with them, or Joan, or all three. My parents enjoyed going out to Joan's as it could be melded with a visit to old neighbors or their favorite old ice-cream haunt.

One Sunday evening in early August we had taken Mom and Dad out to dinner near their new apartment. When we returned to our home, though, we were not greeted by the sound of both dogs' nails clicking on our hardwood floors on the other side of the door. In fact, there hadn't even been a bark from either one of them. *Very strange*, I thought, anxiously turning the key and pushing open the door. As I looked inside it was obvious neither one of them had come to the door. Pushing the door open farther I saw Chelsea awkwardly lying at the bottom of the stairs with a pained look in her eyes. Max was not to be seen.

"Come here, girl," I called to her. There was no movement. I called for Max but heard no response, not even the familiar jingle of his tags. I moved over to Chelsea and reached down to pet her. She just looked at me and whimpered. Tom came in from taking the garbage cans to the curb and joined me on the floor by Chelsea's side. We again tried to coax her up, and she began to unwind herself from her curled-up position, but her whine grew more persistent.

I left Tom to see if he could get Chelsea standing and went to look for Max. Max was a scaredy cat (dog?); a Norwegian Elk Hound, his breed lived in caves but was known to take on elk and other large mammals. He had maintained his preference for cave-dwelling, and as is often the case I found him under the bed, but this time I could not coax him out. He was trembling. I surmised he was probably upset about his sister downstairs and wondered if he bore some responsibility for whatever had caused her pain.

Eventually, with the use of his leash and a cookie, Max came out of hiding and agreed to go out. When we got downstairs Tom had still not gotten Chelsea on all fours.

"Let me take Max out to go potty, and then we can carry Chelsea out and see if she'll go on the lawn. We did eventually get her standing outside long enough to pee, but then she instantly laid down in the puddle she had created. This was serious and Tom and I agreed we needed to take her to the emergency vet. We bundled her in the car, gave Max a bowl of food, and headed back to the veterinary ER.

The clinic was hideous. Cheap, chipped linoleum lined the floors and the lower walls. Hospital blue paint and bright fluorescent lights rounded out the non-homey feel. Chelsea was shaking, and we were the only ones in the waiting room. I kept Chelsea, all seventy overweight pounds of her (like fathers like daughter) on my lap and hugged her close. Tom filled out the paperwork and a tech came to take her away.

"Can't we be in there with her?"

"Sorry, it's against policy."

After a few minutes of arguing he eventually let us carry her back to the examining area but quickly shooed us out. Meeting the doctor, it was apparent the policy was meant to protect the doctor from the necessity of human interaction and not for the safety of the dogs.

Listening to our report he gave a cursory feel of her legs and hips and suggested we get an X-ray to see if the hip was dislocated or broken. We were banished to the waiting room and struggled to find something to divert us from the stacks of four-year-old magazines. We reminisced about the Saturday fifteen years prior when we had gotten Chelsea from a big shelter by Tom's parents' home. She had always been a bundle of love and kisses.

When the ER vet came to the waiting room, we noticed by the clock it had been over two hours. There were no formalities; he just looked at us, not really making eye contact, and said, "The hip is broken, please sign here so we can put her to sleep," while pushing a legal document in our direction.

We looked at each other and both shook our heads. I began, "Thanks for the diagnosis. I'd really like to have her vet take a look at the X-rays before we give up on her. Could you give her something for the pain and let us take her films?"

Seemingly annoyed or put out, he responded, "Sure, but you'll have to sign a release of responsibility for us."

Extremely agitated and aggravated now, we both said, "No problem!"

The car ride home was fairly quiet. Chelsea was snoring lightly in the back seat as the pain meds must have made her drowsy.

The morning after dawned brighter, not just the sun, but Chelsea seemed a bit more chipper and tolerated standing to pee on the lawn. Our vet, Kurt, had some good news for us as well. When we got to his office we were led right in. Kurt joined us on the floor with Chelsea to do his examination. He stared hard at the X-ray and asked a colleague to have a look as well.

"I don't think we are looking at a break here," he said.

Tom and I both sighed loudly in relief but when Kurt suggested we try physical therapy, we both heard the ka-chink and saw dollar signs. It was a relief to hear it was something we would do ourselves, at home, with a towel to support most of her weight while we gently walked her. It was, however, much more difficult than it sounded.

Chelsea hated that towel and walking her like that was exhausting. We kept at it for two days. By the third day she was no better. She was definitely in pain, only trying to get up when we offered to take her out. She looked sad and resigned.

On Thursday I came home to find her lying in her own wastes; she had not touched her food and water. I wrapped her in a towel, carried her to the lawn, and tried to clean her up. She hated it and wanted none of it. We called the vet and arranged to put her to sleep the next morning. I knew I wished someone would be there to do that for me when I reached that point.

When Tom came home from work we all laid on the floor, even Max, who came out from his hiding space. We could have taken our Christmas card photo that evening.

In the morning when we walked into Kurt's vet office, we were greeted with sympathetic hugs and seen right to one of the consulting rooms. They had already laid down several comfy-looking blankets, lit the room by floor lamps rather than the fluorescent overheads, and even had cushions for us to sit on if we chose.

Chelsea was shaking and we tried hard to comfort her. I had a thought but hesitated for a moment. She had a favorite activity that was often hypnotic for her. I tossed off my flip-flop and put my toes by her face. Her head turned and the tongue emerged. Soon she was in an orgy of licking and snorting as she went. She calmed down, the shaking stopped. Kurt readied the needles and explained to us what Chelsea would experience.

Time seemed to go quickly. She slowed and stopped her licking, put her head on her paws, closed her eyes and left us. Kurt listened through the stethoscope and confirmed she was gone from our corporeal lives. Tom was crying. I held his hand tightly. My tears wouldn't come. I wasn't less sad, just not able to access my tears. Kurt excused himself and told us to take as much time as we needed.

We hugged and kissed her now lifeless body. We hugged each other, again and again. At no time did we stop petting or hugging her.

We knew we had to move on. We called for the tech, who covered her up, and we went to check out. All the staff gave us hugs; the patrons in the waiting room expressed condolences and hugged their dogs tighter. Chelsea was to be cremated. I wanted her interred at the crematorium and memorialized on their memory wall; Tom wanted the ashes back. Chelsea still sits in a box in our dining room.

10

A Bad Death

Five weeks later, Labor Day weekend, we would be back in another Emergency Room. It began Sunday morning. Tom and I lay cuddling in bed deciding where and when to go to brunch. The phone rang. We let the answering machine pick it up.

It was Mom. "Boys, are you there? I need some help."

I snatched up the phone, "What's the matter, Mom?"

"It's your dad. He hasn't been able to swallow all weekend and now he's too weak to get out of bed. He's refusing to go to the ER."

"Put him on." When he got on the phone I continued, "Dad, if you can't get up, you can't fight this. Mom is going to call an ambulance. We will meet you at the hospital. Now put her on." I didn't even give him time to respond to my order.

Mom got on. "Mom, call the ambulance. We'll come pick you up and follow it to the hospital."

Seven hours later we still didn't know much about Dad's condition. They could not tell if he had a stroke or if this was due to his esophageal issues. The ER was overcrowded and the staff overwhelmed. We knew he was to be admitted, but no one could tell us how long it would be till he got a room.

We decided to address our hunger and go to dinner. After eating I insisted that we all go back to the hospital to say good night. No matter how I was feeling, I could not just abandon him in the hospital. I needed to reassure him and to leave my contact numbers for the doctors and nurses.

He was sleeping when we got to his bed. We woke him and he reported no news. I checked in with the nurse. He'd probably be moved upstairs about ten-thirty. It was eight o'clock. "I have to go home," Mom insisted.

"Go!" he said. "Nobody really cares anyway!"

I looked pleadingly at Tom. "Could you take Mom home and get her settled?"

"Of course."

They walked away. Dad began to cry. I held his hand. "I don't want to kill her, the stress can't be good."

"Then make it your business to get better."

"This really fucks things up. I'll never get my car back now." That had been the focus for the last four weeks. He had begged to drive again. Mom was petrified by the prospect. We had insisted he undergo a senior driving assessment. Dad had an appointment for Thursday of that week. He was in reluctant agreement to this plan. He didn't like the teasing that it would be like the bumper cars he used to take us on when we were kids. On reflection, I think Dad knew they would recommend he surrender his license. This was the beginning of his loss of will to survive. Dad without a car was Dad without a role in life, pretty amazing for a man who didn't learn to drive till he was almost forty, going from public transport rider to suburban family chauffeur.

"Dad, if that's the case, we'll deal with it then. Right now, we have to find out what is going on with you. Let's try to take this one step at a time."

He grabbed my hand harder. Why couldn't he say the words his hands were conveying? Why did I need him to?

Tom returned about nine o'clock and Dad was moved to a room about an hour later. By coincidence, Dad's first roommate was a neighbor in their development, and his wife became a great help as she drove Mom back and forth to the hospital each day.

Those days after Labor Day lacked the excitement that made me love fall. I didn't have the feeling of rebirth: the excitement of the potential of a new year, new TV season, the rebirth of autumn. I felt dread.

Dad was scheduled to have an endoscopy that Wednesday afternoon. I knew he would have liked me to be there, but I didn't offer. Mom complained that he wanted her there. "What the fuck for?" she complained, wanting to be anywhere but there.

"I guess he needs his hand held."

"He's such a baby." She had such contempt for his neediness.

"Mom, do what you think is right, but you know that if you don't go, you'll hear about it. You can take a cab if it's not convenient for your friend."

My phone rang at one p.m. I was between cold-calls. "Something went wrong … you have to get over here."

"Mom, what's the matter? What happened?"

"He's in Intensive Care on a respirator. Just get here."

I let Sam, my boss, know and got to the hospital in forty-five minutes. That meant I had probably gone ninety miles per hour for much of the trip. I found his room and entered to see wires and tubes everywhere. He was conscious and trying to talk.

When his nurse stepped in, she began to talk about him and I asked her if we could step out in the hall. It was annoying and rude how they would talk about the patient, over the patient. Shelby's famous line in *Steel Magnolias* mumbled as she came out of an insulin reaction rang in my ears! "Don't talk about me as if I'm not here."

So, I learned Dad had a heart attack in the prep area before the endoscopy. They wanted to intubate and informed him it was the only way to save him. I'm guessing he was panicked as his yes answer contradicted his living will. When the doctor came in, we heard that Dad had suffered a great deal of damage. His lungs weren't working well. He needed the respirator to support his breathing while they attempted to strengthen his heart.

I went to the hospital twice a day. I'd go before work to see if I could catch either his heart or lung doctor doing rounds. Dr. Rosen, my gastroenterologist, who was coordinating his care, kept me informed, but I liked to get my reports directly from Dad's doctors who were calling the shots. Basically, the cardiologist was reporting that his heart wouldn't strengthen until his lungs improved; the pulmonologist that his lungs wouldn't improve until his heart strengthened. Clearly, they were talking through Dr. Rosen and never to each other.

I brought Dad a wipe-off board to communicate with us. One day, the cardiologist saw him trying to write a message to us and he got angry. "He shouldn't be wasting his energy talking to you, he should save it for his recovery!" The next thing I knew the nurse came in and hung a new bag of medicine on his IV. He had ordered an induced coma. Was this punishment? Could he not have talked to us first?

One morning about a week into this nightmare, I caught up with Dr. Rosen. The story was still the same and neither the cardiologist nor pulmonologist talked to me or to each other.

"He didn't want to end up this way. I don't know why he said yes to the respirator, but he was always clear that he didn't want to be on life support for an extended period of time. The specialists are useless. Is it time to talk about taking him off the machines?"

Dr. Rosen did not seem surprised by the question. "I think it is still early. Let's give it till the end of the week."

"I'm okay with that, Doc, but promise me this. You will set up a meeting with the other two doctors, my mother, and myself so we can hear it from them and make a decision."

Dr. Rosen agreed. I went to work that day cheered, thinking the team might finally work together.

Friday came. I had not heard from Rosen and sat waiting for him in Dad's room, slowly fuming. When he arrived he was somewhat surprised I was so angry; he had not followed through on his promise and was very apologetic. He was sympathetic and very empathic and so I calmed easily. He did tell me that the doctors had not changed their reports. I asked, "If he were your dad what would you do? Would you keep him waiting in the induced coma? Would you terminate treatment?"

"I think that is a fair and reasonable question, as long as you recognize we are not the same and neither are my father and yours," he started. "I think I would remove him from the life support."

He went on, "My father and I have had many conversations about the topic. We're both doctors, have watched the slow decline of life for such patients, and observed its impact on the family. I know neither of us wants to live a subsistence life, attached to machines without being able to enjoy the things we love. I also know you have been a better caretaker than I would probably be. Your bedside vigil waiting for doctors and information each day before going off to work, the way you clean your dad up when you get here (yes, the nurses tell me about it). They've seen you shaving him, moistening his lips, telling him about your day." He stopped talking and reached to clean his glasses.

I was amazed at his honesty. Of course, I thought, he would be a good, no excellent, caretaker in a different way. I imagined as a "real" MD he would get the respect of his colleagues demonstrated in giving time and reasonable, clinical explanations. Maybe the doctors and nurses would give his dad extra attention and treat him with dignity. But, I'm sure he would be there to hold his father's hand as I had been doing for mine. We agreed to reconvene in early afternoon to have my mom sign the consents to remove life support.

When he left the room I glanced at my watch. He had spent nearly an hour with me. I turned to Dad and told him I'd be right back and went to the cafeteria to get a Diet Coke, my "drug of choice," and a piece of cake (carbs are a must in any emergency recovery pack) and took a seat by the window. Gulping my soda, I dialed Stu.

I filled him in and asked if he wanted to be there when we pulled the plug. "I think I have said what I need to say, I'm not as close to him as you are. I'll stay here, but keep me in the loop." I wished he would come; I just enjoyed his company, but I knew he would pick up the phone if I called.

I knew Phil was passing through on his way to his college reunion this weekend. I called him to see what time he would be here and if we should wait for him.

"I was going to stop for lunch, but I'll drive right through. I should be there when you and Mom meet with the doctor at one p.m."

"You can grab a sandwich on your way upstairs."

"Okay, see you then."

I closed my phone, shoveled chunks of cake in my mouth, and washed them down with the Diet Coke. I had a nagging what-if. My fear wasn't that I was making the wrong decision but that I might be plagued with doubt about it, forever. Could I make it go away with another piece of cake?

I went and got Mom at their apartment. "But I haven't eaten. Why do you need me for this?"

Despite my rage, I lovingly responded, "Mom, he's your husband, has been for forty-nine years. He may be dependent, or maybe it's something else, but he has adored you for all that time. You owe him this." There was no response, so I continued, "We can get you a burger at the cafeteria." They knew how to make them just the way she liked them.

When we got to his room neither Rosen nor Phil had arrived. Tom walked in. "I cancelled my appointments. I thought I should be here."

Phil arrived. Mumbled a greeting and pulled out his Blackberry to check a text. Dr. Rosen followed right behind. He repeated what he had said previously, adding that Dad would, if he ever got off the respirator, need nursing care and a feeding tube for the rest of his life. When I asked him what the end would be like my mother threw me an impatient look. I loved her. Couldn't she at least put on an appearance of a grieving wife? As if she could read my mind, she said, "So what are we waiting for?"

"Well, I assume there are releases and forms that need filling out."

"Yes, there will be a quick review by the administrators. I will start things rolling," Dr. Rosen said and left.

I turned to Phil. "How was the drive?"

"It was okay. Do you think I have time to run down and get a sandwich?"

"Sure, can you bring me back a Diet Coke?" I said to the back of his head as he walked out the door.

Turning to Tom, I said, "Thanks so much for coming. I know you were hoping to see your mom today."

"Of course I'm here. I'm part of this family and I belong here."

Phil returned with his sandwich and without my Diet Coke. Once again he had his face in his Blackberry. "What's so interesting on the phone?"

"It's just my girlfriend."

I didn't really need to ask. Now that his split from his wife was official, he was involved with another woman pretty fast.

When the doctor returned, Mom signed the papers and I witnessed them. Dr. Rosen went to see the administrator while the nurse stayed to talk to us. I made a few jokes in honor of the occasion. I was still me, after all. Mom sat staring blankly into space and Phil continued to stare at his Blackberry.

The nurse was terrific, warm, friendly, and empathic. When it's my time I hope I have a nurse like her. I know I had and have high standards for the nurses and doctors who treat me, my family, and loved ones. I feel entitled having worked in healthcare settings my whole adult life. But, it's not an easy job. Medical care-givers are overworked, criticized, and suffer the minimal staffing and budgetary restraints imposed by insurance companies who remain focused on cost controls (and making more money).

I started to talk to Dad. I couldn't tell you what I said, I just remember holding his hand. I felt sad, sad for him, and sad for me. This was his end, surrounded by family who he desperately wanted to be closer to but who couldn't bring them-selves closer to him. Well, I would. My feelings were real. I was determined that he would feel I loved him as he left this world, even if I didn't really know him or couldn't let go of some past resentments.

When Dr. Rosen returned, the respirator was shut off and the tubes were pulled out. IVs, except for his sedatives and painkillers, were withdrawn. His monitor stayed on but the nurse turned off the alarm. I took a seat by his right hand, Mom by his left. Phil was on his "Crackberry" at Dad's feet, where he would text unabated and undisturbed. I hated that device and whoever was on the other end. Tom moved between the three of us, giving supportive hugs, back rubs, and shoulder squeezes. I hugged him back.

I had expected it to go quickly, but for the first hour there wasn't even a drop in his heartbeat or respirations. As a family we weren't great conversationalists in the best of circumstances, and the silence around me was deafening. I switched back and forth from watching and talking to Dad to staring at his monitor.

At some point, Tom got up and kissed Mom goodbye so he could head out to his mother's. I walked him to the elevator just to get a moment's reprieve. He gave me a very tight hug and told me to call if I needed him. On the way back to the room, I grabbed a soda and a bag of cookies. One of the best things about this hospital was that they carried these amazing cookies in their snack machine. If anything could make death easier it was these cookies. They were an addictive and guilty pleasure for me. *Carbs are always better than feelings.*

I reclaimed my seat by his side. At one point the nurse caught me looking at Dad's monitor and began to chastise me for not paying him more attention. "But he doesn't feel like talking to me," I begged, "there's not much else to do." Did he hear that exchange in his coma fog?

"If I catch you looking one more time, I'm turning the monitor off." She gave me a wink and a pat on the back as she left the room. I wished she had given Phil a lecture.

An hour and a half into our vigil, the monitor started to waver. Every few minutes there was an unusual blip on the heart line of his monitor. His heart rate was becoming irregular, but his pulse and respiration were still strong.

Tired of sitting, I grabbed a washcloth and began to wash Dad's face and hands. I put some ChapStick on his lips and wiped away the flaking skin where the tubes had irritated his chin. "I can't have Bebe (my grandmother, his mother) see you looking so disheveled when you see her again," I said to him and to nobody. I got some lotion and rubbed it on his hands, which had grown cold. I combed his hair, which had grown long for him, although it still did not touch his ears. I wondered if he knew I was doing all this for him. Did he know we had removed his life support? How did he feel about that? Did he appreciate that we were there with him, or would he have rather been alone?

From then on, it went pretty quickly. I continued to hold his hand and alternated between watching him finish the work of dying and watching the monitor. I told him, "It's okay to let go, Dad. We'll miss you, not forget you."

The only sound in the room was the clicking of Phil's Crackberry. There was no dramatic moment. I felt he was gone, but there were still a few sporadic blips as something electric was happening in his chest.

The nurse appeared at the door.

"It's over, right?" I asked.

"I have to give a listen and the doctor will too, but yes. He's gone."

She listened and looked up at me. "Nothing."

"Not even some old Sinatra tunes, maybe a little verse of 'My Way'?"

The nurse choked back a little giggle as I held my tongue. I so wanted to blurt out one of my favorite literary lines, "Marley was dead! Dead as a doornail, dead." I guess I am a drama queen.

The nurse told us to take all the time we needed. I called Stuart. Phil announced, "I have to hit the road."

"Where are you going?"

"You know I'm going up to Rhode Island for my reunion."

I imagined I looked astonished. He was still going? *Is it me, or is that fucked up*, I thought. I could only picture him at the reunion, his former classmates asking what was new and he replying, "Not much, my father died this afternoon." It felt cold.

Maybe my mother would have liked him to stay around that weekend. Maybe I could use some help with the arrangements, or he'd stay to sit Shiva with me. Or maybe I just didn't understand because I hadn't enjoyed my college experience the way he did his. I never wanted to return for a reunion. Or maybe, I had just grown up and had my priorities straight. Would he spend his reunion glued to the Crackberry?

I called Tom to let him know it was over.

"What, so soon? I thought we'd have days … I would have stayed if I had realized it would be over that quick."

I wondered to myself if he had heard the same reports from the doctor that I had.

He was still in the car. "Do you want me to turn around?"

"No. We have a bunch of stuff to do. You go spend some time with your mom and I'll see you at home after."

"You're sure? My mom will understand."

"No, go. Don't worry about us." I clicked off my phone. I glanced at Mom. She looked a bit pale. "Mom, are you okay?"

"I'm not sure. I think my blood sugar is off. I feel kind of funny."

Switching back to caretaker mode, I ran and got a nurse. "Could you come and take my mom's blood sugar? She doesn't have her meter and she's feeling funny."

"Oh, I'm sorry, but I can't. The machine only works if it reads a patient's bar code first. Since your dad is already listed as deceased, we couldn't bill it to him." She was trying in her voice to be caring, but I only heard officious.

"All right. Hopefully she doesn't die on your watch." Her name tag read Ruth, but I felt it should read Ruthless. "Can I get her a glass of orange juice, maybe a graham cracker, or would you have to bill the corpse for that as well?"

Mom drank her juice and felt better. As we left Mom thanked the staff for their attention to my dad and us. I apologized to Ruth.

PART
TWO

11

The Memorial

Leaving the hospital after Dad died, I wondered to myself what Mom was thinking. If I asked, I doubted I'd get a response, or it would be a response I wouldn't want to hear. I imagine she would deny any sadness and probably just announce she was glad to be done with the process. He went first as she had hoped; would her final years be what she hoped them to be? I didn't envision her having a widowhood like Tom's mom, Joan: a widowhood marked by good friends, new hobbies, and personal discovery. I expected Mom'd find new things to complain about, maybe play a little mahjong, and hopefully spend more time with her grandchildren.

Mom and I went back to her apartment. We had things to do. First up was calling the North Carolina Cremation Society. Despite its official and formal-sounding name, it was a business that did prearranged cremations for their customers. Mom and Dad had arranged theirs several years back; a serious task in the long wait to die that was their retirement.

I first learned of the society during a Thanksgiving-weekend visit to my parents in North Carolina. The family was going to celebrate Chanukah over the weekend.

Leaving Tom's parents behind with their extended family, Tom and I settled into the four hour drive to North Carolina and braced ourselves for the weekend. These visits, as in many families, could be trying. While I loved my parents, they were chronically unhappy with their adopted home outside of Raleigh. Inevitably, we would be besieged with stories to justify and fuel their unhappiness.

Like me, Mom could put a humorous spin on most tales of woe, but her anger and sadness always came through.

We looked forward to seeing the kids and having Chanukah. We loved spoiling all of them. The Chanukah celebration was a great chance to do that, and Tom and I would often get their lists and buy everything. We loved seeing Stuart and his wife, Karen. The four of us had created some shared history and enjoyed being with one another. My brother Phil, however, was always a big question mark. His temper and his interactions with his wife, also a Karen, always were a threatening cloud over any event. She'd been a Keren more than fifteen years and it was still hard to know her, as my brother seemed to keep her on edge.

The afternoon of our arrival seemed fairly uneventful until my father asked me to join him and my mother in their bedroom for a few minutes. As I entered there was an aura of excitement in the air, Christmas-morning excitement. I couldn't imagine why, but I hoped they were going to tell me they had come into some money and were paying off my student loans. To me, it was the only thing that could justify such glee.

My father withdrew a long, manila envelope from his dresser drawer. "Your mother and I want you to have this."

I took the envelope; it wasn't thick with cash nor was it thin with a letter or check. It held a credit-card-sized plastic card. "What is it?"

"Your mother and I have arranged for our cremations. When the time comes, you and your brothers won't have to worry about a thing. This is a card you should carry with you in case we are with you when we die. So you know what to do."

"Thank you," I said, barely containing the confusion and revulsion I felt. Why were they so excited to give this to me? I put it in my wallet and tried to forget about it.

Several years later we were back for another visit. It was the year my father was to turn seventy-five. My mother wanted to throw my father a surprise party but she had been told by several of her extended family that they would not travel to North Carolina to attend. She was clueless that it was, in part, that she had painted such a negative picture of the place to everyone that nobody wanted to spend time there. Her disappointment was pervading the entire weekend and fueling her vitriol about the South. Eventually, I could take no more.

I walked out of the living room during one of Mom's extended litanies and tried to hide in the guest room. She followed me in. Feeling cornered, I turned to her and asked, "Mom, you know that cremation society?"

"Yeah, what about it?" I had disarmed her by seemingly changing the topic.

"I was wondering, do they have doctors on staff who come out to make sure the dead are really dead before they cremate you?"

"I guess." She looked puzzled. "Why?"

"Well, I was thinking that when you went to sleep tonight, I'd call them and just have them come pick you up and cremate you. End your misery."

She turned and walked out of the room. "And my misery!" I added under my breath. I could feel my father laughing out in the living room.

~

Now, we needed them for real. Prearrangements really did make it easier. Mom and I met with a funeral director that afternoon who was to take care of the cremation. He seemed surprised we did not want a funeral. Dad had never left instructions and Mom had no use for one. She looked at me surprised, however, when I asked him if we could rent a space for a memorial service later on. There were to be no obituaries, and Mom had no interest in urns: A cardboard box would do her just fine.

Driving back to her apartment, I turned to Mom and said, "I'll be sitting Shiva on Monday afternoon and evening. I hope you'll join me."

"Why, no one will come."

"Stuart's coming. Tom and I will be there. I'm sure at least our friends will come by."

"If you insist."

"I do!" I said, adding, "Oh, and I spoke to Stu and Phil. We are going to have a memorial service in a few weeks. We'd like it, and the grandkids need a chance to say their goodbyes."

"I think it's a waste of time and money, but it's yours ..." She trailed off, and I let it end there.

We stopped for a quick dinner and ate in silence. I helped Mom make a few phone calls to family and realized I needed to get home to walk the dog. Mom saw no need to stay at my house that evening, nor did she want me to come back and stay with her. She was determined to make this day seem no different from any other.

The next day, Saturday, Stu came into town. He wanted to be useful and planned on staying to sit Shiva with us on Monday. It was a relief to have him there to absorb some Mom. She continued in her stoicism and only expressed an urgency to get on with her life.

Monday, Tom and I were running errands, getting ready for Shiva. Stu was taking Mom to do things she needed to do. Just before lunch the phone rang.

"Mike, it's Stu. Mom and I were at her clubhouse signing her up for mahjong and she fainted. The ambulance is on the way. She wants you to meet us at the hospital."

"Never a dull moment, is there?" I muttered. "Okay, make sure they know she's diabetic and that she's had the recent stressor of Dad's death. She's probably dehydrated."

I got to the hospital at the same time as the ambulance. Stu's face softened as he was relieved by my arrival. Her blood sugar was a bit low, and I was right: She was dehydrated. They started her on an IV drip and left her to marinate in a curtained stall in the ER. She was actually in good spirits being attended by her two favorite sons while we waited for the test results to confirm my dehydration diagnosis.

The worst part about curtained ER stalls is that curtains don't make good boundaries. You can't lean against them like a wall. You can see the shadowy form of anyone passing by and you can hear the conversations of the sick next to you.

While we were crammed into Mom's curtained stall, her neighbor's heart monitor alarm went off. Staff came running. We couldn't see the drama, but we could hear it. The curtain that separated us was constantly flapping as nurses, doctors, and techs bumped it in their frenzied activity. When they went to defibrillate, you could hear "Clear!" and then the electrical pop.

Someone said, "Nothing." More frenzy and another "Clear!" She died alone in an ER She was probably scared before she died. Dying alone in an Emergency Room, frightened with no one to hold your hand, has to be one of the worst ways to die. Mom's ER neighbor lay there on a gurney for a good deal of time. Death was only a curtain away. I'll say this for her: She was quiet. I think we all would have preferred a noisier family; we'd had enough death for the weekend.

Suddenly, it was two o'clock. The time we had set for Shiva. My phone rang.

"Where the hell are you? The house is full of people." It was Tom.

"Sorry, Mom hasn't been released yet."

"Well, leave Stuart there and get home. These people are here to see you."

Tom was right. Stu could handle this. I got in the car and headed home. The house was packed with friends and colleagues I didn't expect to see. It was overwhelming; my mind was back in the ER.

Mom and Stu showed up about three o'clock. Mom was gracious, if a bit surprised by the crowd. Stu pitched right in. The crowd thinned at five o'clock and we had two hours till the next group was expected.

My work colleagues had sent a tray of sandwiches from a local kosher deli and we settled in to enjoy them. It tasted so good, and I hadn't eaten since my morning bowl of Cheerios.

The evening visits brought my current work colleagues. I was touched they came. It was a first for all of them. They were young guys, right out of college, and Shiva was foreign to them all. Tom, trying to put them at ease, offered them all a beer and they accepted. I had never seen beer served at a Shiva; perhaps, if the deceased was an immigrant, a bit of schnapps, some slivovitz, but beer, unheard of.

At some point Joan called. "Mike, I really want to be there with you and for you. I was going to take a car, but it's just too much for me by myself. I promise I will come to the memorial."

"Oh, please don't feel bad. I know you want to be here, and I feel your presence, especially in the gifted son you share with me." She started to cry. "Stop that, Mom, we're not there with your oil can." I had only recently felt close enough to call her Mom and it pleased her so. When she initially pushed for me to do so, even before Jim had passed, I had always responded that "One mother was enough."

She started to laugh, getting the *Wizard of Oz* reference immediately. "Well, just know that I love you."

"And I love you too."

The next day Stu and I helped Mom to sort through papers. Midmorning I got a call from the funeral home. "We have your dad's death certificate, finally. Before we send him to be cremated, we need you to identify the body."

I was a bit shocked, as I had been assuming he was already burned up. It seems the doctors had been passing the buck around and no one had actually signed it till Monday night, three full days after he died. Good thing we weren't doing a traditional Jewish funeral; it would have really messed up his plans.

I went back to work on Wednesday. In a month Tom and I were going to Paris for my forty-fifth birthday: dinner at my favorite Paris restaurant. I needed to save my time off for the trip.

My brothers and I planned the memorial. I pushed for a date before I went to Paris so it would not be hanging over my head as a big "to do" upon my return. They agreed, and I sent out an invite and arranged for some catering.

The plan was for each of my brothers and me to say a few words. I asked Dad's brother, Gerry, to speak about my dad as a kid. He agreed, reluctantly.

The day of the memorial we had a full house. There were three generations of cousins from both my dad's side and my mom's. There were friends of ours, friends of our parents, and friends of my brothers. My mom, seeing that folks had really come out to say goodbye, asked if she could speak despite initially refusing.

There was a podium but Mom chose to stand at her chair. "I want to thank everyone for coming, for their support. I especially want to thank my boys. They have taken such good care of us." In one sentence, all that Tom and I had done had been equated with my brothers' contributions. Maybe I'm petty, but her comment cut me to the core.

Uncle Gerry got up and told two stories. The first was about my father as a little boy. It was kind of funny and set a tone of compassion. His second was a tale of my father getting mugged on his way to class at City College. "He found me in my class. He looked so lost when he walked in. You could tell he had been crying. As he told me the story, my classmates in my graduate seminar looked on. I remember feeling embarrassed by this happening in front of my classmates. But I was his big brother. There were six years between us and he had always looked up to me. I excused myself to my teacher and took him home, to the Bronx. By the time we got home, he had calmed down. I don't know if my mother ever knew what had happened that day."

I had not heard the story before but it reinforced my image of my father as a frail and vulnerable man. It was a poignant start to the day.

Tom was up next. He was his charming self, and he was able to get laughs from the crowd over some of his recollections. He closed by recounting the way he would see my father beam when he talked about "his boys" or looked on at his grandchildren's play. "Artie loved them so, even if he didn't say it enough."

My brothers and I did not coordinate our eulogies, but we each spent at least some time focused on his work. Phil reflected on how he and my dad would often commute together when he got his first post-college job at the firm where my dad worked. Those commutes were filled with chatter about whatever game had been on the night before. Phil shared a love of watching sports with him.

"My dad loved his job," Stuart began. Most of his sense of Dad was of the long hours he put in and the intense work ethic my father had. He also shared memories of our dad watching him play lacrosse.

When my turn came, I began with "my father hated his job." I focused on his work ethic and sense of duty. His work structured his life and when he was unemployed for a year he was totally lost. "I was only eight, but I remember seeing pain in his face almost every day."

I also was pleased to reflect on the Dad I got to know when I worked summers in his office. This was a version of my dad who was well liked and respected for his ability. His job kept him from home and family, but he stayed at it to give his family a home. "Working with Dad, I was impressed by how much he was liked and respected by his colleagues. They saw him as smart and fair. They asked him questions and came to him for advice. This was not the same angry guy who we tiptoed around through my childhood."

I shared a few more thoughts about how he had instilled in each of us a solid work ethic. I reflected on some humorous moments, mostly about times he would get angry with us for really dumb things. I closed by talking about the stories I heard him tell about "his beloved City College." I surprised myself at how teary I became as I ended, "Dad, you didn't always know how to tell us you loved us, but you showed us. I don't know if I said it until you were sick. But I thank you for all you did and hope you are at peace and feel safe."

Memorializing my dad was a great experience. I got to highlight the good parts of my father—his pleasure in his grandchildren and in his sons' accomplishments. He loved to show us off, to beam with pride. My father didn't feel very successful in life, but he did feel he had raised great children. Somehow, he had.

My parents had emphasized education to their children. I had taken that push too seriously, but he supported, however he could, my path to my doctorate. He referenced his time at City College of New York frequently, even had a CCNY sweater tucked away in a drawer. I knew it had been an important time for him, so I was shocked when I sat down and Mom leaned over to whisper in my ear.

"Your father never graduated from City College. He went there for two semesters. He was a dropout."

I couldn't respond to my mom at that point. Why would she tell me that right then? Both my brothers confirmed this fact, however, expressing amazement I had never known. I was shocked. How could I, the one who listened and gathered all the family tales, be the only one who didn't know this? I thought back to my freshman year of college when I was so unhappy and thinking about dropping out. My father was in a panic. Now it made even more sense. He felt stuck and limited by not having that degree and he was scared I would be in the same place.

Leaving the funeral home, the director handed Mom a box with Dad's "cremains." "Put it in the trunk till later," she said to me, as if he were a bag from a shopping trip.

My house was filled with people and they were spilling out onto both the front and back lawns. I heard some wonderful stories of my father that day; his older cousins telling of his tag-a-long ways and his younger cousin speaking of him admirably. Mom's family acknowledged his having taken care of my mom. They knew she had never been that happy. They didn't dislike him, but they saw him through her eyes. All of our friends who had known him were able to share nice memories of time with him. My father had always loved meeting and spending time with our friends. They remembered his graciousness.

When everyone had left, Mom said to me, "Thanks for putting that together. He would have liked it."

He would have. He also would have enjoyed watching his sons work together on it. He would have loved to see those cousins who he had not seen in years who came out to say "goodbye."

Paris was beckoning. I had three days to get through and piles of laundry. The day was perfect except for Mom's need to dispel my belief that Dad was a college grad. I was angry but decided to put off dealing with it.

12

"And then she said ..."

"And then she said, 'Joan, now that you're cancer free for six months, it's time to start caring for the rest of you. When was your last mammogram?' Mom's face turned white." Tom had called me from his mom's when he decided to stay there for dinner.

"'What's the matter, Joan? You look like I scared you there,'" Tom reported on the doctor continuing.

"'I've never had one,' Mom admitted."

"'Joan Marie, you're killing me! You never had one? You need one now.' They talked about Mom's discomfort about the procedure. 'If you're very worried about it I could give you something to relax you beforehand.'"

As Tom told me that last bit, I was having a growing sense of foreboding. Tom said he asked, "Doc, can we schedule it through your office? So I can arrange it for a day that it will be easy for me to get here?"

"I bet I can get your mom in this afternoon, so you won't have to make too many trips," she told Tom.

Tom recounted how they went from the doctor's office to get some lunch and kill a few hours until the scheduled mammogram. He described how his mom was unusually quiet over lunch and he had to push her to talk about what she was thinking and feeling. She finally let it out, referencing my mother.

"Why do I have to get a mammogram? Gloria never gets them anymore."

He continued, "Mom, Gloria doesn't get mammograms because she is angry and depressed. She claims she wouldn't get treatment, so why bother getting the tests. She is not you. You want to live; you're just tired from all you've been through. You miss your dancing, you hate your cane, but you're still loving life."

It was true. My mom had been refusing all mammograms and colonoscopies; basically, any intrusive procedure that might diagnose a more serious illness. Her plan was that if she got cancer and couldn't stand it, she would just overdose on her insulin and end her life. Of course, that contrasted with the speed in which she would call for me and an ambulance at the slightest tightness in her chest.

"So, what was the day like for you?" I asked Tom. I did not share my sense of foreboding. Why be pessimistic?

"I was focused on comforting Mom, I kind of ignored my own feelings. I mean, I was worried, but …"

"And now?"

"I am just trying to focus on the positive. I can't believe she has never had a mammogram. Her doctor …" He didn't finish the statement.

"Malpractice."

"Old-fashioned. She should've switched to his doctor-son years ago."

"So, when will she have the results?"

"I'm going with her next Friday."

"Ugh … I can't believe you have to make that trip again, so soon. Do you want me to meet you out there after work?"

"Why should both of us make that trudge?"

"All right, just know that I will, if you want. Maybe you can bring her back here. Have her spend the weekend."

~

Neither of us was surprised when the mammogram showed a suspicious growth. I could hear the concern in his voice over the phone. "So, she has to see a surgeon for a biopsy before we can do any more. That's next week. Amy is going to take her."

Amy, her next-door neighbor, had become an important source of support for Joan. She would often take Joan to doctor appointments, even though she was dealing with illnesses in both her own mother and her husband.

"How long until the biopsy comes back?"

"About a week. We already have an appointment for the following Friday."

"I don't know what to say. I wish I was there to hold you, tell you it's going to be all right."

"I know," he said. "How was your mom's appointment?"

I had taken Mom to meet a new endocrinologist. Mom's sugars were all over the place lately. Mom didn't care, but I worried. Her cardiac and pulmonary issues were constantly demanding our attention.

"He was a nice guy. Seemed to know his stuff."

"Did she like him?"

"Yeah, she did. Surprising."

~

"It was positive, early, but positive all the same. She's scheduled for a mastectomy in two weeks." I could hear the resignation in Tom's voice through the phone. I didn't know what to say.

"How's she handling it?"

"You know Mom. She wanted dinner at Mateo's: her usual scotch, soup, salad, chicken parmigiana, plus all the bread. She just plunges on. She's dealt with everything else, she'll handle this."

Joan really was resilient. All she had been through and there were so few complaints; never let depression take hold.

"I'll take off the day of the surgery. Come be with you."

"Thanks. I'll probably come out the night before, but we can talk about it."

~

The surgery went without a hitch. The oncologist believed the surgery was all she needed—no chemo, no radiation. She got fitted for prosthesis and resumed her life. Shortly after, we drove with my mom to Long Island to celebrate Mother's Day with Joan.

Over dinner Joan thoroughly surprised us. "I think I should sell the house."

"Where's this coming from, Mom?" Tom asked.

"It's just not fair to you boys to have to keep coming out here all the time. After my breast surgery I realized how much work you boys missed, how much time you spent driving out here to take care of me. I should probably just move out to New Jersey to be near you."

"Mom, that's thoughtful," I said. "I won't lie and say it's nothing. But it's also a relief to us that you have such a strong group of friends. Have you thought what it will be like to leave them behind?" I also thought to myself that I hoped my mom didn't say anything like "It's about time." While she did enjoy Joan, she found her to be somewhat selfish when it came to our time and her expectations.

"Mom, thank you for thinking of us like that. I agree with Mike, though. There's a lot to think about, but we will definitely help you with whatever you decide."

"So where in New Jersey would you want to live?" my mom asked.

"I'd really love to live where you live, Gloria. I love your apartment. And all the people I've met through you are so sweet."

"That would make our lives so easy, but that should not be your primary concern," I said.

"I think it would be fun. Joan and I could hang out. Weekends we could all do things together. Maybe travel," my mom added.

I looked at her in awe. After all this time she could still surprise me. I would not have thought Mom would have ever seen such a move as a positive for herself.

"Then it's settled. I'm going to move."

Our moms spent the rest of the meal making plans for their future. Mostly, there seemed to be this developing plan for us all to go to Las Vegas. I certainly thought a trip together could be fun, but Las Vegas was not on my list of the top one thousand places to see before I died. The only thing that interested me in Las Vegas was the Liberace Museum.

By the following Wednesday, Joan had appointments set with three realtors. She also had a possible buyer for her house, as well. This was really happening.

Joan signed a lease for an apartment in a building across the parking lot and the other side of the pool from Mom. Tom and I committed the next three weekends to cleaning out the Bellmore house.

~

"Oh my God, I haven't seen this in forever!" Tom was standing over a small wooden toy box. I walked over to see what he had found. Inside were some old children's books, a few photos, and a good deal of dust. Clearly, it was the toy box itself that was bringing the memories.

"I guess we're going to move that to our attic."

"Do you mind?"

I'd have just been a totally insensitive asshole if I said I minded. "Of course not. We have plenty of room." The year before Tom and I had rented a forty-foot Dumpster and emptied out much of the junk we had accumulated over the previous fifteen years in the house. As Joan sorted through what she wanted to take to her new apartment and what she would get rid of, I realized there might be more things heading to our attic.

As moving day approached, Joan's buyer began to get cold feet and itchy palms. It was mid-2007 and the housing market was beginning to deteriorate. The buyer wanted to renegotiate the deal. Joan felt insulted by the last-minute attempt to get her to reduce the price. The deal died.

The house was listed with a realtor. We cancelled the lease on the apartment. And we waited and lived our lives.

13

MARY POPPINS

Not long after Dad passed, Mom and I went for her checkup at the cardiologist. He was not pleased with her EKG.

"Gloria, are you having any chest pain?" he asked.

"A bit."

"I'm going to send you to the hospital. I think you need a cardiac catheterization. We can't handle it here, so I'm going to set you up with a colleague."

That time we ended up in the big teaching hospital where Dad had his kidney removed and ended up on the floor of his room. They were ready for us when we arrived, although I was made anxious by my struggle to understand her doctor through his heavy accent.

Eventually, we decided to trust Mom's doctor and allow this doctor to do his job. Everything went well. Mom needed another stent placed but there had been no complications. Mom was brought to a room and I was informed she would probably sleep for most of the evening. So I went home.

When I arrived in the morning Mom was livid. She was so upset I thought she would dislodge the stent if she didn't calm down. Eventually, she was able to tell me what happened.

"I woke up. I'm not sure what time it was. But my legs felt wet. I looked down and my sheet was soaked with blood. So I rang for the nurse, and then I yelled."

Looking at Mom's sheet, this had clearly passed as it was clean and no blood was visible. "This nurse wandered in. I mean taking her sweet time. She takes a look at me and says, 'That's not good' and turns around and walks out of the room. I started to yell some more."

I was getting really concerned at the story, but I let her continue. "I don't know how much time passed, but it wasn't a short time, and a new nurse comes in. She introduced herself and immediately saw there was a problem. She lifted my sheet and started to take off the bloody bandage that was on my leg, where the catheter had gone in."

"Did they have to do anything else? Was it still bleeding?" I asked.

"It had stopped. They put a new pressure bandage on it and let the doctor know. I still don't get why they don't use the sandbags anymore. This never happened then."

What I came to understand was that the first nurse was getting off her shift and so had not taken the time to respond to what was a crisis for Mom. The day shift nurse was my hero. She actually told me she had reported the previous nurse because of what she had found. "Even if she hadn't actively ignored your mom's distress, if she had done her rounds, she would have seen the problem sooner, probably while your mom was still asleep."

Mom and I both knew for sure that we would not be going back there for future procedures, so when Mom developed congestive heart failure a few months later and her pulmonologist and cardiologists recommended a pacemaker, we insisted she be sent somewhere else. That ended up being a big hospital in Newark. It wasn't in the safest of neighborhoods, but it had an excellent reputation.

The procedure went off without a hitch and she was healing. She was breathing better than I'd seen in months. She had color in her cheeks, and there was a smile on her face. We were crammed in her room, five of us. Her two oldest grandchildren, Daniel and Laura, were perched on the end of her hospital bed. Phil sat in the corner, while Tom and I were on either side of her. Photos of Laura's high school graduation were being passed around. I was glad she had brought them. Mom was heartbroken she had missed the graduation, but her congestive heart failure had put the kibosh on that.

It was perhaps one of the hardest and saddest points in all of this. Laura had been the first grandchild and had spent so much of her growing up at her grandma's side. Mom loved each of her grandchildren in the way she felt each needed. She observed them, nurtured their interests and their strengths. But Laura was the first and had that special place a first can claim.

~

Now Laura was launching. Five years earlier Tom and I had promised to take Laura to Europe for her high school graduation, all she had to do was graduate. That evening we would board a jumbo jet to London and then on to Paris. This trip had been a long time coming. When we first started talking about it our intent was to expose our nieces and nephew to culture. If Mom and Dad were uncomfortable living by Phil, Tom and I would have been in pain. The place looked like most modern suburbs. Big housing developments built around swim clubs and golf courses. As you moved away from these attractions, the houses got smaller and definitely less grand. The people were all striving to move up.

My family were relocated Yankees in a town full of them. It seemed to us that most of the Yankees had tried hard to assimilate. When Tom and I would grab coffee and bagels on Sunday mornings and listen to the folks around us, we could hear these affected Southern accents complimenting each other, discussing their 4x4s, off-road vehicles, and plans for hunting season, while wives would wax on about their daughters' dresses for cotillion, the best recipes from church suppers, and kids' dance lessons.

We always wondered about the education the kids were getting. Confirmation of our deepest fears came during my niece's sophomore year of high school. We were visiting and had started talking about how close my niece's trip was getting. We asked Laura if she had given any thought to where she wanted to go.

After a lengthy and thoughtful pause, she asked, "Is Tahiti in Europe?"

I gulped, then responded, "No, sweetie, that's in the South Pacific, a long way from Europe. Is there something there you wanted to see?"

"I hear they have great beaches."

"Well, it's very far and probably too expensive. Besides, while this trip is going to be fun, we'd like to take you somewhere with history, art, and culture." Not that Tahiti doesn't have those things, but she was definitely looking for sun and surf and she'd gotten plenty of that growing up.

She looked at us kind of blankly and said, "I'll have to do some research. I'm not really sure what there is in Europe."

Now we were going. She had chosen London and Paris.

Laura loved London. We took in theater, which she mostly loved. We hit some art museums, the palaces. She even asked to go to some WWII-themed museums. This surprised and greatly pleased us. We made for good travelling companions. The only tension on the whole trip occurred one night when we were trying to pick a show to see. I was lobbying hard for *Mary Poppins*. Tom and Laura wanted *Billy Elliot*. Unfortunately, I won. They hated the show and I had to acknowledge I would have probably been happier with *Billy*, but *Mary* was a childhood favorite film of mine and I really had wanted to see the show.

She seemed enchanted by the youth culture of London, although she stuck firmly by our side. Once, she even asked to go to a gay bar with her uncles. Unfortunately, the one club we frequented on trips to London was not one where she would have felt welcome or comfortable and we really didn't know the others.

We were in London the week of the Proms: an annual event in London marked by concerts, both rock and classical, parties, and events. The streets were mobbed with kids at night. I would watch her eyes light up with excitement and a little fear as we would get pressed in the throngs.

Paris was a bit of a different story. She had taken some high school French but sought assurances before we left that she wouldn't be expected to use it. Our experience told us that if we made a bit of an effort most Parisians would easily and comfortably switch to English. In fact, while my vocabulary was impressive, my accent was so bad they usually asked me not to speak French.

We encouraged her to say *bonjour, oui, non, où est …*, the basics. When we checked into the hotel, however, I immediately started to speak with the clerk in French and we had a nice chat about the neighborhood and the weather. Laura turned to Tom and said, "I thought Uncle Mike said we didn't have to speak French?"

The clerk turned to her and said, "Don't worry, dear, you don't. We all speak English and will speak it with you."

I could tell she wasn't totally sold on it, but no more was said at the desk. The clerk pointed to the lift and stated it would take a few trips. It was an old hotel and the lift was designed to take two people at best. I volunteered to go up first with the bags.

Our reservation was clearly for three. Yet all I could see in the room was a full-size bed. I was used to snug accommodations in Paris, but this was a bit much. I was about to go downstairs and complain when Laura found her twin bed was a Murphy bed tucked into a wall of an alcove. It was actually quite comfy looking.

We wasted little time hitting the streets to start sightseeing, eating chocolate and pastries, and taking pictures. We saw all the majors: the Louvre, the Eiffel Tower, the Tuilleries, the Place de Concorde. We checked out a few stores and

Notre Dame. The whole time Laura spoke only English. As much as we encouraged her, she was reluctant to try. On our last day in Paris, she and I were enjoying a lunch on the Champs-Élysées. We had gone to see the Arc de Triomphe. Over lunch we discussed the trip. She could definitely say she preferred London. I suspected it was the language thing, but she focused on the youth we saw. The highlight had been a London Punk, covered in tattoos, hair two feet up in a Mohawk, full leather and chains. She spent some time talking to him and then asked if she could get a picture with him. That picture was a favorite of the trip and she told her parents he was her new boyfriend. It was a great souvenir and only cost me a pound.

At one point she asked me if I knew where the bathroom was. "No, but just ask the waitress."

"I don't know how."

"Yes you do." I was sure she could ask in English, but I didn't volunteer that.

"Remind me."

"There are a few ways, but the quickest is *où est la toilette.*" She practiced it and headed off. While she was gone, there was a bit of excitement in the street, a truck, going a few kilometers more an hour down the Champs-Élysées than it should have, tried to enter an underground parking garage. There was a sharp scraping and sparks as the top of the truck peeled off and the truck slid into the entrance. By the time Laura returned the cops were swarming and she wanted to know what she had missed.

"I miss all the excitement."

"Go take a picture of it, no one will know you didn't really see it. And who knows, maybe they will want your pictures for a court case and will fly you back to Paris." A man can dream, no?

~

While we were enjoying ourselves across the pond, Mom was having a trip of her own. Phil had agreed to stay and help with Mom while we were away with his daughter. Mom got out of the hospital the day after we left. Phil, his son, Daniel, and Mom spent the week together.

It was hard for me to trust anyone but myself to take adequate care of Mom. I left very explicit instructions explaining medication regimens, setting out pills for the week, doctors' visits, and so on. I wanted to be able to forget about care-taking for just a week.

That Friday was a very blustery day in New Jersey. The weather reports were warning about gale-force winds with possible tree damage. It was the kind of day I don't think I would have taken my mother out in unless we had a definite destination: a doctor's visit or a prearranged social outing. Mom, however, wanted to go out to dinner.

They headed to one of Mom's favorite restaurants, which was literally down the road from her development. They had not remembered her handicap hangtag and so they had to park about twenty yards from the entrance. They enjoyed their dinner.

As they made their way to the door, Phil reported, they could see some dust and papers flying around the parking lot but there were no nearby trees to suggest the strength of the gusts. Mom walked out on Phil's arm and they headed for the car. Suddenly a gust of wind grabbed Phil's glasses off his face and blew them onto the pavement. They started to blow away as if they had a life of their own.

He let go of Mom's arm and started to dive for his glasses. Another gust blew up and Mom seemed to lift off the ground. I wish I had seen it. My childhood dream of having Mary Poppins as my nanny would have come close to being. Phil, of course, panicked and reached to grab her. As he did so his glasses whipped farther across the parking lot. He attempted to rush her to the car but there was no rushing Mom. He was helping Mom into the car and watched his glasses blow farther away. A car blew by them and was heading for Phil's glasses. He tried to signal but it was futile, without letting go of Mom.

When she was finally seated, Phil closed the door and headed out to find his glasses. He looked where he last saw them and didn't see his glasses or even pieces of them. Of course, without his glasses on it must have looked somewhat comical. When he found them, they were scratched and perched on the edge of the drain. He grabbed them in time to prevent them from falling in.

When Tom and I returned home, Mom delighted in telling us about her flying adventure. I told her I'd call her Mary Poppins, or even Sister Bertrille (The Flying Nun).

14

AURORA IN CHAINS

Mom was back in the Newark hospital for an angioplasty and had complications during the procedure. I swung by for a visit after work. When I got off the elevator onto the cardiac wing, I heard a little strangled voice calling, "Help me! Help me!" I recognized it immediately as Mom's. I ran down the hall, past the nurses' station where the new shift was busy getting coffee and the exiting shift was finishing their notes.

I turned into her room and found her collapsed into the fold where the back of the bed met the bottom when it was in the up position. She wasn't stuck as much as lacking the strength to pull herself into an upright position. I hit the button to lower the back some and pulled Mom into a sitting, or rather lounging, angle.

"I need a bedpan, quick!" she squeaked.

I ran to the bathroom and grabbed the nearest one. It felt like seconds, it was definitely less than a minute and it was full. "I need another one, quick," she cried. I grabbed her roommate's. Thankfully, it was clean and the roommate was sleeping, so she wouldn't need it right away.

It did not take but a few grunts for it to be full. *Mom must be reacting to some medication, again*, I thought.

"Quick, I need another." I went to run down the hall when I heard, "No, there's no time for that. I need another."

I yelled down the hall since no one had answered the call button in all this time, "Please, come quick … and bring a goddamn bedpan."

There was no response. I looked around the room and grabbed the garbage can. I tilted the bed to support my mom and positioned her on top of it. Once she was settled, I ran down to the nurses' station.

"Please, come quick, my mom can't stop shitting herself … And bring a bedpan."

"We're in report," came the response. "She'll have to wait."

"She can't wait, that's the problem. At least tell me where I can get another bedpan."

"Sir, go back to her room and we'll be there as soon as we finish report."

"Could you at least send an orderly with a bedpan?"

"When we're done."

I must've gone back and forth three time before Aurora took over. She stormed back towards Mom's room screaming, "Christ, a simple bedpan, this is not a joke, it's an emergency. Who the hell do I have to fuck to get a bedpan for my mother?!"

Mom was still on the trash can, shitting and crying. "Mom, it's gonna be all right." I found a second trash can and positioned it under my mom. I turned around and there in the doorway were two fully uniformed police officers.

"Sir, please step out," said one of the officers.

"I will as soon as one of the nurses gets over here to help my mother. She can't stop shitting and no one will help her."

"Sir, if you don't step out, we'll have no option but to arrest you."

I was about to make a snide comment about hospital security not being able to arrest me when I noticed their guns and Newark Police Department badges. *Shit*, I thought to myself, *they really are cops.*

"Sir, as soon as a nurse is here to assist my mother, I will step out and follow whatever instructions you have for me, until then, could you please go to another room and grab me a bedpan or garbage can?"

"Excuse me, I am a police officer, not an orderly, and I have asked you to step out!"

"Sir, I can tell you are a police officer. If the uniform didn't give it away, I am sure the nightstick in your hand or the gun in your holster would have. In fact, when I was eight, one of your brothers in blue came to my classroom to tell us about a policeman's job. He really emphasized that most of his job was not like on TV, but was spent helping people in distress. Now would be a good time to prove him right, which is why I asked you to get another receptacle for my mother's uncontrollable diarrhea."

"Wise ass, are you?" the other cop said.

"No sir," I said, tears starting to roll down my face.

"You need to step out of the room!"

"As soon as there is a nurse here to help my mother, I will step out of the room. Until then, I am not trying to cause trouble, I am trying to get a dying woman some help. What would you do if it was your mother?"

"My mother is not the problem here, you are. You are causing a commotion."

"Sir, do you see a commotion? Where is it? I am just doing what I need to do to get someone to pay attention to my mother."

A nurse came into the room. She, of course, did not have a bedpan or anything in her hands. "What do we have here?" she said in her little nursey, condescending tone. "Looks like a mess."

"Not sure why you're so surprised," I said. "I've been trying to get someone to attend to her for over twenty minutes and all you bothered to do was call the police."

"Now, now, Mr. Keren, surely you're exaggerating."

"Well then, you can explain to the Director of Nursing why my mother had time to fill two bedpans and two garbage pans with shit in the interim … and, it's not Mr. Keren, it's Dr. Keren!"

I walked out of the room and into the grip of one of the policemen. He threw my hands against the wall and began to frisk me.

"What are you doing?" I screamed. "You have no right to do this to me. I'm merely trying to get some help for my mother."

As he pulled my one arm behind my back, I saw the flash of silver that was the handcuffs in his hand. Simultaneously, I heard, "What's going on here, that's my patient's son." As if by a miracle my mother's doctor appeared. Luckily, he was decked out in all his doctor regalia, white coat, stethoscope, and hospital ID.

The cop stopped short of closing the handcuffs. "This guy has been creating a scene. When we responded to the nurse's call, he refused to leave the patient's room."

"I told you the patient is his mother. Dr. Keren, were you making a commotion?"

"I suppose you could say it became that. I got off the elevator and I heard my mother's desperate calls for help. I ran down here, past the nurses' desk where the new nurses were getting coffee and the ones getting off were writing notes.

Mom has awful diarrhea. She filled two bedpans and I was calling for help and asking for another. No one came. They just kept telling me they would come when report was done … Not one nurse from the previous shift, no tech, nobody would respond, so I got loud. I had to seat my mom on some garbage pails to catch it all."

"Officer, it sounds like the hospital just might avoid a lawsuit if you stop trying to put those cuffs on him. Let me ask, officer, did either of you offer to help him out?"

A quick glance down the hall showed there were people hanging out of every doorway in the hall.

"Well, no. We were called here to take care of the disturbance," one of the cops said.

"Seems to me you could have done that just as easily by finding him another garbage can or getting the nurses to hustle!"

The officer returned the cuffs to his holster but blocked me from going into my mother's room. "Dr. Keren, I'll check on your mom. You go wait for me in the empty room at the beginning of the hall," Mom's doctor told me as he took a pad out of his pocket. "Officers, before I go to attend to my patient, I'll need to write down your names."

I turned to go to the room he directed. As I began to walk down the corridor, a chorus of claps greeted me from every room. I smiled. I felt vindicated. Clearly, I was not the only one struggling with the deficiencies of the nursing care. I recognized that nurses are busy and they were probably chronically understaffed, but this had been neglect and rudeness.

I sat down on a chair in the empty room. I didn't know whether to laugh or cry. I really liked this doctor. Even before he rescued me from the Newark Police, I had felt he was a good doctor who was going to care for my mother. We had met so many doctors over the last few years. They probably all believed they cared. Some had really conveyed it. This doctor had shown, time and again, he was as concerned about the patient as he was with the problem. He was skilled with the high-tech equipment the hospital put at his disposal, but he excelled at the personal connection that should be at the heart of medicine.

Even though Mom and I first met him in the prep area of the procedure room, he felt different. He treated us both with the utmost respect. He laughed at my jokes (an important test for me). He had told me to expect the procedure to last an hour to an hour and a half. He would send word if there was an issue. At the two-hour mark, I hadn't heard a thing and wondered if I had misjudged him. I asked the receptionist in the waiting area if she could find something out for me. She said, "Oh, when you were in the bathroom about forty-five minutes ago, he sent a note out for you with a nurse." She searched around her nearly empty desk and found it under her copy of *People*.

When he came out of the procedure, still in his scrubs, he asked me to join him in a consultation room. He asked me if I needed a drink. I didn't, but told him he must be thirsty and feel free to get himself one. He flicked on the computer and brought up the recording of my mom's procedure. It was an angioplasty. I was a bit excited to see video. "I just want to show you one part, but before I do, here's what you are going to see. During the procedure, your mom threw a clot, had another heart attack. Because we were in there at the time, we were able to address it immediately, dissolve the clot, and probably prevented any damage." He ran a four- or five-minute section of tape where you could see exactly what he had just described to me. "This is probably an artifact of the angio procedure, the wires or the dye disturbed some plaque and threw off the material that caused the clot. I think you realize your mom's heart is not in the best of shape, so she's had such incidents multiple times."

"I know. Sometimes I find it miraculous that she is till walking around with all those stents in her."

"I don't know about miracles, but she certainly has had her life extended by modern medicine." We chatted a bit more about my mom's condition, her care, and my caretaking.

~

I don't know how he found me, but Tom walked in the room while I was waiting for the doctor. I got up and collapsed in his arms, tears streaming down my face.

"What's going on? The whole floor feels so tense."

"You missed it. I was in handcuffs." I exaggerated a bit, but I felt Aurora would approve.

"What?"

"Long story, but I got a little loud trying to get Mom some help and they called the police on me. Doctor took care of it. Probably no record at all."

"Glad you can be so glib. What did you say?"

"Well, say is putting it mildly. I yelled, at the top of my lungs, 'Who the hell do I have to fuck to get a bedpan around here?'"

We looked at each other and spontaneously burst out laughing. "Why we sitting in here?" he asked.

"Doc is examining my mom and the cops had blocked me from entering the room. You can probably go down and say hi, let her know I'm okay."

He was gone for five or ten minutes, I lost track of time. He returned with the doctor. While he was gone, the hospital page system had played a few stanzas of Brahms Lullaby three times. Funny, if it worked as a lullaby, people would have been dropping off to sleep all over the facility. It was the hospital's way of announcing new arrivals on the maternity unit. The tune had been in my head the whole day.

"So Doc, how's my mom and why the shits? She does have a lot of drug sensitivities and that is the result. In fact, this is what happens to her on statins. You didn't put her on one, by chance?"

"Of course not. I read your extensive history and wouldn't have dreamed of it. I think it may be from the dye used in the angio, but it could be C-diff so we are going to run a test."

"Thanks, Doc. Sorry for asking, but you'd be surprised."

"Actually, I wouldn't. I'm not offended. Unfortunately, the runs have weakened your mom even more than the procedure. I'm going to move her to the Cardiac Intensive Care Unit if there is a bed."

I expressed my relief. My exhaustion was oozing out all over. He suggested we go down and visit with Mom while he arranged the transfer.

"One last question, Doc. Tell me about your practice, is it general cardiac or do you primarily focus on surgery?" I was already fantasizing moving Mom's care to him.

"More general cardiac. I do some procedures. Angios, stenting, pacemaker implantations but send my patients elsewhere if they need bypasses or valve replacements."

"Where's your office?" My heart sank when he told me. It would never work. It was closer to my office than to her apartment. A cab there would cost her cost more than a hundred dollars. And forget public transportation.

When we got to her room, Mom was smiling, clearly wiped out, but smiling just the same. "So there's my hoodlum." She laughed. "Glad you're okay."

"Hoodlum, huh? What, do you think I stole the year's supply of bedpans you ordered?"

She started to laugh and it turned into a cough.

"Take it easy," I said. "Don't need you dying from a laughing fit after all I went through to save you today."

"I know, but where did you learn such behavior?"

"Well, Mom, the woman who raised me used to love to tell a story about trying to get attention from the sales help in Alexander's. When she was repeatedly ignored, she walked up to a table of clothes that had just been folded, screamed some profanities, and threw everything in the air. Do you remember that? Hmm?"

"Well, I could avoid going back to Alexander's, but today I'm stuck here and have to deal with these nurses."

"You're not stuck, they're moving you to the CICU where you'll get better care and more attention. You should know by now I would not leave you in a den of wolves."

"I'm so lucky. Thanks."

I gave her a big kiss and tried to hug her in her bed. The Brahms went off again. Tom said, "Is that a message for the patients to go to sleep and visitors to leave or something?"

"Can't be," my mom said. "I've been hearing it all day."

"They play that every time someone pops out a baby in the delivery room. At first I thought it was sweet, but I'm having second thoughts. Why do the babies get special attention? How about those at the other end? Shouldn't they play taps or a requiem when a patient dies? And down in psych, when someone gets manic they could play 'Happy Days are Here Again!' The list is endless."

"Sometimes, I'm not sure you are my child. You are so twisted," my mom said.

"You don't know the half of it," Tom added.

"Actually, the twist is all genetic, I've seen the helix," I said.

The doctor returned. "Okay, I got you a bed in the CICU. They should be here to move you shortly. Hopefully, I can keep you there for most of your stay, we'll see how it goes."

"Thanks," the three of us said at once.

The orderlies arrived quickly and Mom was transferred. We introduced ourselves to the nurses, left them our numbers, and tucked Mom in for the night.

Walking back to the garage, Tom asked if I wanted to get some dinner. I said only if it's fast food because I was more interested in collapsing in front of the TV or in our bed. Sitting in Wendy's I started to laugh, nervously.

"Something wrong with your chili?" Tom asked.

"No, I was just thinking."

"What about?"

I didn't have an answer.

"You're just tired and have had a really upsetting day. What was it like to almost be in handcuffs?"

"A little exciting, actually. Never thought I'd ever see that happen. I'm a bad boy!"

Tom started to laugh. "Wish I had seen it. Bet it was hot."

We were both laughing now. Aurora and I were so lucky to have Tom as our partner.

15

A FUNERAL

After almost four years, three bouts of cancer, a mastectomy, a full hysterectomy, and numerous chemotherapy treatments, Joan's death still seemed to be sneaking up on us. She was so alive and vibrant that February when she excitedly got to cast her vote for Hillary Clinton in the New York primary. Her widowhood had shown her the power of her gender and now she was casting her vote to make one her president.

That April her house finally sold and she found an apartment in the same complex as my mother. She began saying her goodbyes to her neighbors and friends. One of her last tasks was a follow-up with her doctor for a checkup on her recovery from breast cancer and uterine cancer. It was going to be routine. Blood work, referrals to New Jersey follow-up physicians, and a grateful goodbye.

But the blood work was not okay. After a few more tests and a visit to a rheumatologist, the diagnosis was in: acute myeloid leukemia.

Within the week, Joan moved into her new home, met her new oncologist, and began chemotherapy. The prognosis was not good and the chemotherapy was a last-chance effort to forestall the inevitable. Joan was brave and maintained a good front.

Unfortunately, both Mom and Joan were too sick to walk across their parking lot to have a visit. There was no dropping by to gossip, watch old movies, or just share a sandwich, unless Tom or I came by and drove one to the other.

Joan was always optimistic. Despite the pronouncements that recovery was unlikely, she maintained her spirits and held onto her belief that she would recover. One day, Tom had arrived to pick Joan up from her chemotherapy appointment and heard her talking to another woman who was hooked up to IVs.

"That's my daughter. She's so good to me. Leaves work to get me to appointments, leaves the kids at home to pick me up. I'm so lucky to have a daughter," the neighbor told Joan.

"Daughters are nice. She seems very special. But I wouldn't trade my gay sons for anyone. They've been there for me through all these illnesses; but even before, I could always count on them. I feel bad for people who don't have at least one," Joan opined. It was such a change from the years when I first joined the family.

Joan developed a fever during one of her chemo appointments in mid-June. Considering how immuno-compromised she was, between the leukemia and the chemotherapy, the doctor immediately hospitalized her in an isolation room. A few days into the stay, the doctor announced the chemotherapy was not working. Joan was out of options. She considered what this meant and, in discussions with Tom and me, decided to go to hospice.

Her first day or two there was uncomfortable. Joan was attempting to keep a brave front. She had trouble sleeping and refused her pain medications. Hospice is all about making someone comfortable, and Joan didn't totally grasp the concept. She was concerned that they weren't giving her the diabetes meds she had taken so compliantly for several years.

Tom arranged for the resident priest to pay her a visit. When he came to her bedside, Tom reported to me that his eyes had rolled further back in his head than he thought humanly possible. Here was the priest—wearing a stained top that was slovenly untucked in several places, his collar slightly askew. His eye contact was limited and was complicated by numerous facial tics. Tom invoked his Irish family's response to fear, "Jesus, Mary, and Joseph!"

Despite this priest's appearance, a thirty-minute conversation with Joan about his own experiences witnessing death and his thoughts about what comes after provided her more relief than all the Xanax in the world. When he left, she rang for the nurses and began to accept the morphine being offered.

Two days later, the phone rang as I was getting out of the shower. I quickly wrapped a towel around myself and grabbed it on the third ring.

"Hello, is Thomas Johnson there?"

"This is his partner. He's not here right now. Can I help you, or take a message?"

"This is Haven Hospice. We were trying to reach him to speak with him about his mother."

"Well, I'm listed as someone you can talk to. What's going on?"

"I really need to speak with him."

"Okay. He's on his way there. You should see him in a few minutes."

I hung up the phone trying not to focus on being annoyed or hurt by the exclusion. It was hard sometimes. My first reaction was always that if we were a straight couple, they would have told me. But the hospice staff had been great to us. But still ... it wasn't my mother; it wasn't all about me!

I wondered what was so important. We had been at the hospice less than twelve hours before. We had gone by with two of Tom's friends who knew Joan really well. One of them had worked extensively in nursing homes and knew death well. She had taken in the scene and opined that Joan had a good two to three days left.

I threw on my clothes and jumped in the car. All the way there I wondered what the hospice was calling about. Recognizing that I was very hungry, I picked up my cell phone and dialed Tom.

"Hey, do I have time to stop and pick up a bagel on the way over? I haven't had breakfast."

"Of course."

"I'll get one for you too."

"See you shortly."

I was feeling more relaxed. Obviously, this call had not been that death was imminent. If I had time to get a bagel, I guessed I could breathe a bit easier.

As I walked into Joan's room I was still smiling and anxious to greet her Long Island friends who had driven out that morning to see her, and sadly, to say their goodbyes. They were all chatting quietly in the little conversation area on the side of the room opposite the bed. I handed Tom his bagel, distributed kisses all around, and walked over to Joan's bed. As I leaned over to kiss her, I noted that you couldn't hear or see her respirations. She must have been close to the end. Then I put my lips to her cheek and realized she wasn't in her body anymore. I looked over at Tom.

He looked back at me. "What?"

"She's gone."

"You didn't know? That's why they were calling me. She passed before I got here. Oh, I'm so sorry."

"No. No, I'm so sorry. It's just that when you said I had time to go get breakfast, I figured she was still hanging on, but it was close." I bent back down and hugged Joan hard. I said to her, "Be at peace. This is better than the pain you've had. We'll miss you always."

Tom came to my side; we hugged and held onto each other, hard.

~

It was a busy day. Phone calls, funeral arrangements, and flowers. We talked about tributes. Over lunch we finally reached Joan's brother. He told Tom that he wouldn't come up for the funeral and something broke open in Tom. Despite Joan's idealization of her brother, he had absented himself from the two prolonged years of her illnesses. He had finally arrived the day before she died, to say goodbye, and wouldn't be back.

"I can't believe Uncle Bill. So selfish. He's always been the prince, even as a kid. But he'll swear up and down how much he loves her." Tom let it out, all the frustration, resentment he was feeling for what he perceived as his uncle's lack of concern.

I could play the devil's advocate, but it was a minefield. Instead, I just held Tom's hand, let him vent, and occasionally peppered my agreement with reminders of the good memories he had with his uncle. As we finished up our hot dogs and root beer, we headed out for the one more task we had that day.

~

While waiting for the ambulance that was to transfer Joan from the cancer ward to the hospice, she had ventured into a conversation about her funeral. She let Tom know that she would like to have the service at her old church; no flowers, find a place to make a donation; a two-day wake; specific hymns and music for the ceremony; and finally, this:

"Tom, please go to Lord and Taylor and buy me a gown to be laid out in. I don't like anything in my closet."

"Are you sure, Mom? I was thinking one of your dancing outfits. Maybe those tight black pants with a sparkly 'Sexy Mama' quote across the front."

"Tom, stop that. This is a funeral. Be respectful."

"I am, Mom. You are that woman in the dancing outfit. Why not be her wherever you are going next?"

"Because it's just not done. Now promise me, or I'll ask Mike to do it. He knows how to respect a dying wish."

Tom laughed. He knew that no matter how I was disposed of, the last thing I would want is to be dressed up. I had often said, jeans, T-shirt, no underwear and no shoes or socks. He also knew I would have championed the dancing outfit; that it would have been my favorite thing about the funeral. But we were to have a different adventure.

We found ourselves in the local Lord & Taylor that Saturday afternoon. Two men wandering through the women's formal wear department in a high-end department store do not easily get waited on. We searched the racks for twenty or so minutes without once being approached by sales help.

"I don't think we're going to find anything here," I said to Tom. "Are there any other stores your mom would be okay with?" I realized I was speaking as if she was still there. It felt like she was.

"Well, she did offer Macy's as a second choice."

As we searched the racks of Macy's, I did notice the sales help was looking at us from behind the busy cash register. Tom was over at a wall looking at some long dresses in a floral print.

"I think it's perfect," I said. "If it has to be a gown, let it show her lust for life, the lust she discovered during her ten years of widowhood. When Jim died she came alive, discovered her own brand of feminism. She should not be buried in a staid, formal gown."

"You think so? You don't think it's too loud to be buried in?"

"What the hell is too loud to be buried in?" I asked.

We searched the rack for her size ten. They had a twelve and an eight. I grabbed the twelve and marched over to the sales desk while Tom continued to search.

The saleswoman looked up from the sale she was ringing and asked me to wait a moment.

"Can I help you?" she said.

"Yes, do you have this in a size ten? I have found an eight and a twelve, but no ten."

"If this is for you, I don't think you'll fit in a ten."

"It's not for me, it's for my mother-in-law. She just died and she had some very specific requests about wanting a new dress to be laid out in."

"Let me get this last sale and then I'll help you. I'll be fast."

Tom came over to my side. "What's up?"

"She's going to go look for a size ten."

Before she could finish her sale the other saleswoman behind the desk finished up hers and offered to go look in the back. "I think that is so sweet that you guys are willing to do this for your wives while they are grieving."

We looked at each other and burst out laughing. "What's so funny?" she asked.

"It's my mother who died. We're with each other and have taken care of her all along. This isn't new to us."

"Oh, I'm so sorry. My brother's gay and you'd think I wouldn't make so many assumptions. Let me go back and look."

Not only did she go back and look, but suddenly we had four saleswomen assisting us. They were all so impressed with us; they were enjoying (if that could be the right word) helping us out. When a ten couldn't be found they all offered their own takes on dresses they thought would suit her. You would have thought we were at Kleinfeld's looking at wedding dresses for the party atmosphere.

When all was said and done, we took the dress in a twelve and figured the undertaker could work some magic in arranging it.

~

I'll never get used to wakes. I love a good Shiva; the good food, sharing memories, catching up. But as a Jew, hanging out with a corpse in a box still feels too strange. Open caskets only add to the discomfort. Of course, the first funeral I ever went to was for a Jew and featured an open casket, but it was, as my mother said, "planned by a shiksa (a non-Jew, in this case his wife) so we shouldn't be judgmental."

Preparing for Joan's wake and funeral was interesting. Although she would have liked two days, we decided on one with a longer visitation and a memorial service. We brought the gown to the undertaker and she asked us about makeup. Tom loved that his mom had a female undertaker. Tom and I always hated that blue eye shadow, so we made an executive decision not to have her put it on her. We asked her to give some special attention to her hair. Going to the beauty parlor was a fight Joan and Jim had for much of their marriage. Jim believed "all those processes would just make your hair fall out." Deep down Joan always knew it was more about money, but she limited her visits. But she loved getting gussied up, and after his death she would get her hair and nails done whenever she wanted.

When the undertaker asked us if we had anything we'd like to include in the casket, Tom and I pondered hard. We decided on her favorite Rosary beads, pictures of the three of us from our trip to Ireland, a picture of her and Jim, and a picture of our dogs. I also advocated for the lap blanket.

~

Joan was always cold. When she'd visit our house, she would turn our heat up to eighty. We'd buy fleeces for her, sweatshirts, blankets, but she'd still ask for the heat to be turned up. I had taken up knitting and had decided to knit her an afghan. I had been working on it for weeks and when she decided to go to hospice I was in a panic because it wasn't done. I ran to my teacher and asked her if she'd finish it overnight for me. Understanding the urgency, she agreed.

The next day I brought it to the hospice. Tom was already there. "Mom, you have to see what Mike made for you."

Joan lifted her head and stared at the blanket. "It's beautiful ... for me?"

"I wanted you to be warm. I had hoped you'd get more use out of it, but It's here now."

She smiled.

Tom and I spread it over her. "It's gorgeous," Tom said.

"Too hot," Joan said weakly. "Take it off."

We folded it to the bottom of the bed and Joan grabbed my hand. There was a tear on her face. "Thank you!"

I hugged her, held her.

"Sorry," she said.

"Don't worry. Maybe later you'll be cold. It'll be right here."

She squeezed my hand; I squeezed back.

~

Tom was against burying it with her.

I persisted. "She was always cold and may be again."

"But it's a waste."

"It's not a waste. It was for her and I want her to have it."

Tom stopped arguing. We left it with the undertaker and went to make more calls.

The next afternoon, when we got to the funeral home, we were given time alone with Joan. I held Tom as we approached the coffin. The dress was perfect; she would have really been pleased. The blanket covered her to her waist, and her hands, clutching the beads, rested on top. As we looked at her face, we both choked back tears but had the same thought at the same time. We made a mistake. Without the eye shadow she didn't look like herself.

People came in and out that evening. Our friends, her family, even a few of her new neighbors. Those who knew her best commented on two things: how beautiful the blanket was and the missing eye shadow.

Tom and I both addressed what a loving woman she had been and commented on the grace with which she had approached her illnesses. As I shared my recollections, I was impressed at how unpredictable life was. Twenty-five years earlier I would never have been able to extol my mother-in-law so, and now I was reduced to tears.

The next morning Tom and I met a few family members at the funeral home for a last goodbye and to close the coffin for the trip to Long Island. Joan's cousin Karen spoke up. "That blanket is so beautiful, and you worked so hard on it. Take it home and remember her by it."

Tom echoed her sentiments. "We'll think of her whenever we're nestled under it."

"Okay. Take it," I said, unconvinced but too exhausted to fight.

Just before the undertaker closed the casket, Karen said, "One last thing!" She walked up to the casket, took some blue eye shadow out of her purse, and applied it to Joan's eyelids. "Now she looks like Joan." Tom smiled, nodding his head.

That day was clear, and thankfully not too hot for the first of July. My brother Phil had come up to pay his respects and I asked him if he would take the responsibility to drive Mom and our friend Anne to the funeral. Anne, a former coworker of both Tom and mine, knew our mothers quite well. Age-wise she sat squarely between our parents and us and mingled easily in both age groups. She had begun having difficulty with arthritis and would appreciate not having to make the long drive herself.

Since Joan was laid out in New Jersey, we started the procession to the church on Long Island. Tom and I shared the limousine with a few of Joan's cousins.

The ceremony was the most alienating of all. Although this had been Joan's parish for most of the fifty years she lived on Long Island, her illness had kept her from being active the three or so years prior. I was appalled that in all the time she was absent, no priest or lay representative from the church had ever called on her to check on her or offer her Communion. She got her Mass from the TV.

A young Filipino priest was the officiate at the Mass. He had never talked to us about Joan. He had come to the parish after she was no longer able to attend Mass and so knew nothing of her except for what he had been told by the lay staff member who had briefly spoken with Tom in setting up the ceremony.

From the first time he mentioned her by name, "our dear sister, Joanne," I was upset. I finally said to Tom, in a not-too-quiet whisper, "Who is he talking about, her name is Joan." I know the priest heard me, and yet he made no effort to change what he was saying. Other family tried to excuse the affront as due to his accent, although all the Filipinos I know dismissed that quickly and commented on his ignorance.

After the ceremony, we received the guests. As we were getting ready to get in the cars, Phil approached me.

"Hey, can Mom and Anne go in the limousine with you? While I'm out here I want to go visit some friends."

I glared at him with major contempt. Unfortunately, subtlety is lost on him. "Oh, I thought you had come out to help us out. Well, I don't want to get in your way. Have fun." That last part was added with just the right amount of sarcasm, which of course was wasted yet again.

A burial in the national military cemeteries is a unique experience. World War II veterans are dying at the rate of seven hundred a day. This cemetery instituted an assembly line–type system that feels impersonal and rushed to accommodate the need. A funeral procession enters the cemetery and the driver or funeral director goes into an office to announce your arrival while the others remain in the car. When he returns you wait for your signal that you are cleared to proceed to the chapel that has been designated for your event. There are several. They are very simple structures, open on both ends. The casket is placed on a bier and everyone enters. There is traditionally an honor guard of two soldiers who stand by and a priest or other officiate. A few simple words are said, an audiotape of "Taps" is played, and the honor guard folds the flag draping the coffin and offers it to the bereaved. Spouses' funerals are handled the same way. Henry Ford would be proud of the precision.

With the second impersonal ceremony of the day wrapped up, I began to help others back to their cars and direct them to the restaurant for the repast. At one moment I turned around and noticed Mom was wandering off, and not in the direction of the car. As I turned to go after her, I was grabbed by one of Joan's cousins, who said, "Don't you think you should go and help Tom?"

I turned around and there was Tom, draped over his mother's coffin, wailing, "I'm sorry, I'm sorry, no, no, no."

She was right; my place was by him. But the cemetery covers more than a thousand acres. Mom seemed determined to wander them all. I quickly called for Anne and asked her to go after my mother, retrieve her, and take her to the car. Anne, whose mobility was limited by her arthritic knees. Just for a moment I felt the earth falling out from under me. I thought I was going to drop to my knees and scream and cry. But then I remembered this wasn't about me. Sure, I might have to have the U.S. military mobilized to find my mother in this place. Of course, my brother had once again been a selfish prick, leaving me to attend to the guests at the funeral, support my grieving husband, care for my mother, and find a moment to tend to my own grief. I took a deep breath, waited for the earth to meet my feet, then hustled back to the bier and tried to console Tom.

He didn't really want consoling. He pushed me away and told me to leave him alone. I did what I could, which wasn't much. I rubbed his back. I tried to say it would be okay. I had seen displays like this only in the movies. I thought to myself we were lucky we were not graveside or Tom might have thrown himself in the grave. We had joked the day before that we should dress in black crepe with tall mantillas, carry lace handkerchiefs, and hide behind veils. I thought we were only joking, but I felt as though this was that very movie we were picturing the day before, minus the costumes.

My family doesn't do big emotional displays. Tom's family was always different. If they had a feeling, they talked about it or expressed it. This was definitely a *Steel Magnolias* moment, although, unlike M'Lynn, Tom didn't need any prompting to get the feelings out.

~

That evening, Tom and I drove Mom home. When she was firmly settled in her apartment, we went to leave. She grabbed Tom and gave him a big hug. "I'm so sorry for you, Tom. She was such a sweet woman and she loved you so much. I'm going to miss her."

"I know, Gloria. It was so great for us that you and she liked each other, a lot. That we could all do things together, have fun, enjoy each other's company. I'm going to miss that."

"I know it's not the same but anything you need from me ..."

Tom gave her a kiss and a big hug. "Just promise me you'll stay alive for another year. I don't think I could do this again so soon."

"I can't promise that ... I don't think I can keep it."

The chill went straight down my spine.

PART THREE

16

THE WAITING ROOM

There were many doctors' waiting rooms in the years after Dad died. The one we knew best was Mom's cardiologists'. While the two doctors shared a last name, they were partners in business only. I had been using one of them for my own healthcare for years, so when Mom decided she didn't like the doctor who had attended her when she first came back north and she learned her original cardiologist from her bypass was no longer in practice, it seemed natural for her to see my doctor.

Neither one was very punctual and the office ran on anything but clockwork. It was not atypical to sit in their waiting room for an hour and a half. Once in an examining room, a nurse would check Mom's vitals and then make us wait again. The upside was the appointment was never rushed. You could get questions answered, and I always had a few. Waiting in the examining room on so many occasions, I had memorized the content of all the posters in the room by heart.

One particular visit stood out. Dad had been gone about a year and a half. In the waiting room Mom and I had glanced at the magazines in our vicinity; most we had seen on previous visits and neither of us had much interest in the sports magazines. After staring at the news on TV for a few minutes and being bombarded with the latest blunders, missteps, and foreign policy insults of George Bush, Mom and I started to chat.

"Mom, do you ever miss Dad?"

"Sometimes."

Deep conversations were a rarity in the family. Mom would shut them down with her negativity, Dad with an outburst of anger if pushed. I was a rule breaker and I pushed on. "Like when?" I asked.

"When I need a ride," she replied, without missing as much as a beat.

Silence hung in the air between us. The silence was so loud it drowned out the TV, it drowned out the big-haired Jersey women with their husbands and the elderly couples yelling loud enough to hear each other without their hearing aids. Mom turned back to the TV and stared at the news while I kicked myself. What had I expected? Had I really believed that my mother was missing her husband of forty-nine years somewhere in her heart? Even if she did, she would never admit it. It was easier to turn to her practical needs as she did in life, creating the image that she was using Dad for what he could provide. I had, of course, inherited her skill at avoiding emotions.

I thought about the adage in psychology that we become psychologists to cure our mothers. I do believe it was true; also, when I realized I couldn't do it, I lost interest in the field. I recognized that even in death I couldn't fix my parents' relationship; Mom would never loosen her rigid positions. I once asked her why she married Dad. She told me that she had been dating three men. Her family was pressuring her to get married and my father was the one her family liked the least, so she chose him to spite them.

I sat there wishing that for just once she would tell me that she loved him, that she missed him for emotional reasons. She was content, if not happy, with the story she created of her life, a story that denied her much happiness.

I looked at her hard. "Really! Really, Mom, that's the only time you miss him?" She stared at me somewhat blankly. "So are you enjoying your time without him?"

"Not really. I kept wishing I would have some time to myself to enjoy life and do the things I wanted to do. Maybe travel; I still want to see Mexico and Japan. But I'm too sick to do it."

"I'm sorry for that."

"You've got nothing to be sorry for. You and Tom make my time more enjoyable. I live my life through your travels. You share your friends. You include me, and you take such good care of me."

"Still, I'm sorry that you made choices for the wrong reasons and felt stuck; that you stayed with Daddy if you didn't want to. I wish you had gotten to see the places you wanted to see."

"But I'm also sorry you only miss Daddy when you need a ride. That you didn't feel he was company, good company. Even if you didn't have passion, I wish you had had the company you enjoyed."

My mother didn't respond. I could feel her discomfort. I fought the urge to say something to make it better. For all her complaints, I couldn't believe my mother didn't get something from their companionship. They both loved to visit museums, try new restaurants; they even shared books they loved. And they both loved us children. I wanted to believe I was conceived in passion. I once counted back on a calendar from my birth, trying to figure out when I was conceived. It seems very likely I was conceived on the day of JFK's inaugural. This is a very satisfying thought to this avowed liberal. When I asked Mom, all she would say was "possibly, I don't remember." In my mind they were giddy with excitement over the election and looking forward to the possibilities. A little champagne and a little more ... nine months later ...

Mom's name was called and we were shown into one of the exam rooms. It was a good excuse to put the conversation on hold. Of course, unless I pursued the topic, it would not come up again.

The doctor came in and started to listen to Mom's chest. He stared at the chart. He asked if anything was new. Mom started to tell a story about one of the grandchildren and he said, "I meant with your health."

"What could be new? I sit home, I take my meds, and I wait to die."

"Gloria, have you noticed anything different in the way you feel? Any reactions to any of the meds?"

"I'm tired all the time, but that's not new. I'm not very hungry, ever."

My mom's appetite was not a finite thing. If we went somewhere she liked the food, she could eat her meal. If I brought her Pepperidge Farms, she'd find room for the forbidden cookie, but she had stopped really cooking for herself and had begun to live on frozen meals and leftovers. I wouldn't have much of an appetite for that either.

"I was going to ask you because you've dropped five more pounds since I last saw you and that's not good."

Mom, like myself, had always struggled with her weight. We both loved to eat and we both became Weight Watchers Lifetime members in the early 1970s. Of course, she was forty at the time and I was eleven. No one had ever said to me that dropping five pounds was not good, and it was probably the first time it had been said to her. I think I giggled.

"Well, I just don't feel like eating."

"Would you at least drink an Ensure?"

I knew that would go nowhere, asking Mom to drink something that was like drinking a glass of milk was a waste of time.

"Maybe you should take an appetite booster. I can give you a prescription."

"Another pill. I'd rather just waste away."

I was sort of glad the doctor was seeing and hearing this side of my mother. She usually presented as such a good and cooperative patient. I don't think she had ever revealed her death wish to him before.

"Well, Gloria, then you just have to eat more and make it healthy choices."

"Okay, will do," she said, with absolutely no intention to remember the admonition when she got home.

Before we left the office, the doctor offered Mom a flu shot and the pneumonia vaccine. Mom said, "I don't know. Maybe I should skip the shot and just get pneumonia and die."

"She'll take the shot," I said. I wasn't going to play that game. "But Doc, should we be talking about hospice? I mean, the way Mom is talking it sounds like she is ready to die and quit taking all these meds and stuff."

"No, of course not. Your mom is nowhere near ready for hospice. She still has plenty of life left in her. Why would you ask that?"

"Well, you heard her. She is just waiting to die. Hospice seems the place to do that."

The doctor stared at me with a look that said disbelief.

"Doc, for years I've listened to my mother plan to die if she ever got too sick to enjoy life or was suffering."

"Gloria, is that true? Do you want to die?"

"No."

"Doc, that's the wrong question. Ask her if she wants to live."

The doctor looked at her. "Well?"

"Well what?" Mom smirked.

"Do you want to live?"

"I don't really care one way or the other."

"Gloria, are you going to do anything to yourself to try to end it?"

"I don't have any plans right now."

"Of course not, you're having too much fun torturing the doctor and me."

She just smiled. He let it go. He gave her the prescription for the appetite booster. It was a powder she could mix with juice or water, but she never used it.

Mom asked me if we could go to dinner after the appointment. I guess we had to eat, although I really expected it would be an awkwardly silent meal and was surprised she was asking. I agreed and we went to one of her favorite local places.

Over dinner we started to talk. "So Mom, were you upset with me at the doctor's?"

"No, why would I be upset?"

I wondered if maybe I had just dreamed the whole episode after falling asleep in the waiting room, but the prescriptions in my pocket told me that wasn't so.

"Well, I sought of tipped the doctor off to your plans to do yourself in and your general dissatisfaction with life," I said.

"Oh, well, it was uncomfortable for a minute, but I knew he wouldn't do anything. You were just being a psychologist."

"What the hell do you mean by that?"

"You know, you always worry about feelings and stuff like that. The doctors never do. They don't want to hear it."

I knew she was right. Worrying about her mental state would just make their job harder; ignoring it allowed them to place the resistance they met from patients right back on their patients.

"But Mom, do you still think killing yourself is an option?"

"I really haven't thought about it. I guess I'm just fine the way things are going. If I die, I die; if not, not."

"So why do you sometimes tell me you would like to OD on your insulin?"

"'Cause you listen. 'Cause I need to know it's an option."

"You know it upsets me?"

"I'm sorry, should I stop?"

"Mom, you know how you used to tell me about when your mother was dying, when she was in so much pain she would beg you to push her wheelchair out into traffic. She would cry to you. How did you feel then?"

"I was miserable. I wanted to make her pain go away, but I wanted her to stop asking me to do that. I couldn't have. I used to cry myself to sleep at night."

"Did you ever ask her to stop asking you that?"

"No. She needed to express it and I had to hear what she needed to say."

"So no, Mom, I don't want you to stop telling me those things, but just, could you be less flippant about it?"

We sat there in silence and finished our fish.

17

ONE CRACK, TWO BAM, NINETEEN

Her doctor's appointment three months later went on in much the same vein. I discussed mom's growing isolation with the doctor, and he had started to recommend assisted living to us. Even more upsetting was a comment Mom had made about not being able to follow her mahjong games any longer. As the evening wore on it was becoming one of those nights where I was jealous of Tom's patients. He would get home as I was ready for bed. Although I would force myself to stay awake, he would be tired, both physically and tired of listening to the problems of others. I knew he would take the time to listen to me, to empathize and to comfort, but I would always feel like I was a burden at those times. Perhaps it was guilt. There were times when Tom's dedication to his patients felt like "an affair" I had to compete with.

When he walked in the door, Max, our dog, was quick to greet him. I followed Max to the door but knew I couldn't compete with his wet kisses and wagging tail since I was feeling so scared and anxious. Tom picked up on it immediately.

"What's wrong?" he asked.

"Plenty, but take your coat off and get comfortable and then we can chat."

Tom went upstairs to change and then offered me his undivided attention. "I think Mom may be more demented than we ever imagined."

"What? What happened?"

"At the doctor's, we were discussing her social isolation and the possibility of assisted living. I mentioned that we could find a facility where there were mahjong games. She told me she hasn't been playing; that she can't really follow the game and has been throwing hands that don't match the game she's playing."

~

Mahjong was such an essential piece of who Mom was. She always had at least one regular game a week. When I was a kid, Wednesday nights were Mom's mahjong night. When it was in our home, I knew there would be good cake, which I would never turn down. But the part I loved the most was the sound of the game.

The tiles all had a distinctive clack as they were spread out on the table or passed around. As the women were making their hands, they would call out certain tiles. "One crack, two bam, three soap, Mahjong!" I didn't know what it all meant, it was just an intriguing night for the ears.

~

"Did you do a Folstein?" Tom asked. The Folstein is a neuropsychological examination designed to give you a quick but fairly accurate assessment of a person's level of cognitive functioning.

"Right, like I'm just going to start asking her to remember words and count backwards. If she is getting demented, that may change our whole trajectory."

"Should we take her for a COPSA workup?" COPSA was the geropsychiatric mental health program where Tom had worked. Dementia assessments and caregiver support were their strengths.

I gave it some consideration. I needed some time to process it all. The slow loss of my physical mother I'd been coping with, but the possibility of losing her while she was still alive was knocking me for a loop. Sadly, I knew all too well what that would hold for me. Would she forget who I was?

We had gotten Mom to agree to start looking at assisted living centers. I scheduled two visits for a Saturday afternoon in October. It was to be one of the most trying days of the whole caregiving venture.

The first place we looked at was the one the doctor had recommended. I parked in the lot and went around to open the car door for Mom.

"It's not very pretty," she said.

"Let's see what's on the inside before we get too critical."

"I'm just saying, from the outside, it doesn't say much."

Actually, the facility was quite pleasant to look at; not institutional looking at all. It looked like a larger version of the seaside Victorian home I'd always dreamed of (without the sea or ocean views). The grounds were nicely landscaped and the wrap-around porch was decked with pots of colorful mums.

We climbed the four steps to the porch and the front door. "You would think they wouldn't have steps in a place like this."

"Mom, we could have taken the ramp if you wanted."

"What, I was just saying!"

I had a feeling she'd be "just saying" through the whole visit. I only prayed she'd keep it to a minimum with the social worker who was to give us a tour and do an intake interview. I suspected the intake interview might be more of a sales pitch but would probably also ask health related questions and about Mom's social and recreational interests.

We stopped by the reception desk and asked for Mrs. Wasserman, the social worker we were scheduled to see. She came so quickly Mom didn't have a chance to even test out the wing chairs that dotted the lobby. She extended her hand to Mom and introduced herself. Mom gave it a shake. Mrs. Wasserman then turned to me. "You must be Dr. Keren. Nice to meet you in person."

I took her hand. "Likewise, but please call me Mike, everyone does."

"Okay, Mike, you can call me Roberta, you too, Mrs. Keren. Now come with me, we'll sit and talk in my office for a while and then I'll take you on the tour."

Her office was pleasant enough: Ethan Allen classic colonial with a floral print upholstery and a smaller floral print on the wallpaper. Mrs. Wasserman looked to be about late forties, dressed in a Hillary Clinton pantsuit, and had her dyed red hair pulled to the back in a tight bun. When she left the room, briefly, Mom turned to me and whispered, "I think she's trying to pass as a WASP." I had briefly had the same thought, but since this facility catered to a largely Jewish population, I couldn't see the wisdom of this.

She returned to the office carrying two folders of information on the facility for us. "So, Mrs. Keren, may I call you Gloria? Your son tells me you're a mahjong player."

"You can call me Mrs. Keren. My son should've told you I *was* a mahjong player. I can't play well anymore, so why play at all?"

"Well, maybe you could just play for fun?"

"It is fun, if you play well. If you play with the speed of a turtle it's dull and pointless, so I don't play anymore."

Mom was not going to give this woman a break, but she was undeterred. "Well then, what do you enjoy doing?"

"Sitting in my apartment watching TV, or going out to dinner with my children."

"Certainly, you can do both of those here, although maybe you will meet some people you enjoy and decide to participate in some of our activities."

"Maybe. I used to love to roller-skate. Do you have a rink here?"

"No, we don't have much call for it."

"Do you have outings? Do they ever go to the rink?" Mom had not been on skates in probably fifty-five years; she was being a ballbuster with this nice woman.

"Mrs. Keren, many of our outings revolve around shopping: the grocery store, the mall, the outlets. Occasionally we'll arrange trips to local theaters for a play or a museum. And of course, you're always welcome to go out with family, friends, and your neighbors from here. Some of our residents are still driving."

"Oh great, bet that makes for a safe time in the parking lots." It was clear Mom had made up her mind on this facility, but I wanted to take the tour, to have a comparison when we saw other places.

"Mrs. Keren, we've never had a resident involved in anything more than a fender bender. We insist their driving skills be thoroughly evaluated on a regular basis if they are going to keep driving." She had an answer for everything and seemed very nonplussed by my mother's recalcitrance, so while I was feeling embarrassed, she seemed quite used to it. Obviously, Mom was not their first hostile potential resident. "Why don't we go take a look at the facility?"

As we made our way through the different available living arrangements they offered, I was thoroughly charmed. Most of the apartments were tight of living space but had plenty of windows and natural light. Of course, Mom usually kept her shades drawn these days, but who knew when I might need this place.

The second facility on the list was connected with the hospital and was located right across the street. Mom had no comments on the outer appearance as we were entering the building. My own reaction was that it looked like my childhood elementary school, laid out in corridors on a single floor. Entering the building did little to dispel this feeling. The wall opposite the front door was covered by pictures obviously sent in by some first- or second-grade class to "cheer up" the old people. There were no Renoirs, Rembrandts, or even Picassos in the bunch. This facility had us met by an "admission's rep." Her actual title should have been sales manager. She started us on a tour, moved at a fast pace, and seemed to have little concern with Mom's ability to keep the pace. The facility was set up to have several levels of care from independent living to assisted living through full nursing care. One thing I did appreciate was that this facility had a "memory unit"; the euphemism for a locked unit dedicated to advanced Alzheimer's patients. We didn't go see it.

As we neared the end of the tour and the rep was going to take us into her office, Mom made her first and only statement in this facility. "So, now we get to see if I can afford to have my son lock me away here." And then she smiled broadly.

I thanked our guide profusely but just wanted to get out of there and away from Mom. She had really hurt me with that comment. The admission's rep tried to convince us to stay and hear her sales pitch. It was clear Mom didn't like the place, and I wasn't going to spend any more time here.

Sunday was a new day. Tom was joining us for a tour. That might help keep Mom on better behavior; we could never be sure. We fortified ourselves with brunch at our favorite breakfast spot, a place where we were on first-name basis with all the waitresses, and they treated Mom like a queen because she was our mother. Over breakfast Tom asked Mom what she thought of the places we had seen the day before. She pinched her lips and gave Tom the raspberries.

"That was succinct," I said. "What would you like to find in a place that would make it comfortable for you, Mom?"

"Well, no condescending staff, for one." I couldn't blame her there; we certainly had dealt with plenty in our travels through hospitals and rehab centers. "No bingo. If you want me to play a game, let it have some skill or at least make me think."

This took me back a bit, not the bingo part but the "make me think" part. Whenever Tom and I wanted to take her out to the movies she would ask the same question, "It's not a message movie, is it? You know I hate message movies." And she meant it. She liked flics that were romances or adventures. She'd get out of her sickbed for a new Indiana Jones movie. She also loved her detective films. "So what games would you still want to play?"

"I think I could still handle Monopoly. Maybe Chinese Checkers or Boggle." Boggle had been the family game. Mom was merciless when she would play with us, but we always kept playing, kept trying. I hadn't played with her in a million years, but I think I could beat her only because her speed was so much slower than it had been, not because I'd grown smarter than she was.

"Okay, so we'll have to ask about that here."

In the parking lot I was surprised there were no cracks from Mom. It was a converted apartment building in a formerly working-class town, and that was exactly what it looked like. There were no pretty flower gardens, there were no gardens at all. She just seemed to stand and take it all in. The building and absent landscaping seemed to mirror Mom's depression and boredom.

When we entered the door there was a flurry of activity going on. It was hard to tell who were staff and who were residents, except for those who were very old. I went up to what looked like a reception desk and told them I had an admissions appointment. Val came out to meet us. Val was about ten years younger than me, had mousy brown hair, and wore a dowdy white blouse with a long bow down the front and a blue skirt and blazer. The blazer could not hide the fact that she was a healthy woman, and I prayed Mom didn't let out a comment about that.

"Welcome Dr. Keren, you must be Mrs. Keren."

"What gave it away?"

"I could see the family resemblance. It's clear in the face, except your skin looks so much younger." This was a point of pride for Mom. Without fail her nurses, therapists, and other hospital staffers would comment on what beautiful skin she had. My mom had maintained a loyalty to the same skin cream for most of her adult life. She credited the product. The biggest problem was that in the last year or so the company had discontinued it. She was trying to find a new product that worked as well, but with very disheartening results.

"Thank you," Mom said, throwing me a glare that said, "Ha! Ha!" I didn't care because if this woman won Mom over it would bode well for the whole endeavor. Val then turned to Tom and shook his hand as he introduced himself.

As we toured the facility I was impressed. It was clean and didn't smell like old people, that nursing home scent that is one part urine, one part talcum powder, and one part Jean Nate'. Val explained medications were handled by a nurse, centrally. Mom frowned at that one. Meals were offered communally. Each unit had a little kitchen with a microwave and a small refrigerator and freezer. It would be plenty for Mom, although I hoped she would join communal meals.

As the tour continued through the halls of residences, I became quite turned around. My first thought was, *Geesh, if I'm getting lost with a tour guide, how's Mom going to find her way around?*

Val anticipated my reaction. "The layout is a bit confusing but once a resident is settled in, they will usually navigate only a small part of the place; from their apartment to the dining hall or med room, or maybe to the recreation hall. As you can see each section has a central public space where most of the residents in the area will hang out. It's pretty empty today because it is Sunday and people are out with their family." It was partially comforting.

"Val, you mentioned the social hall, and I looked at the schedule of recreational programming available. Are things well attended?"

"Most programs are. The residents can suggest programs the staff can arrange. We have some residents who do a good deal of crafting and they will sometimes offer lessons to other residents. There are resident-run book clubs, card games, mahjong games, bridge tournaments. It's a very active place."

"If there are residents who tend to isolate, does the staff make any effort to get them to participate in activities? Mom has been pretty isolative lately; we were really hoping this would help to bring her out of her room a bit."

"Actually, the answer to that is usually, no. Unlike in a nursing home, our residents are independent but may need help with some activities. They can still decide on what they want or don't want to do. Early on, if it is felt a resident is having a difficult transition, the staff will offer some encouragement, maybe get the family in to try to help."

"Can I have a cat?" Mom asked.

"Unfortunately, we do not allow pets to live in the facility. They can visit, however, so if your son has a cat, he can bring the cat to visit."

"Well, Mom, I guess you're going to have to keep settling for Max," Tom added.

"Who's Max?" Val asked.

"He's our dog. Mom loves him, but she wishes he was a cat. Mom, when Stuart comes to visit, I'll tell him to bring one of his with him, and then they can bring him over here for you to play with," I said, making a big concession because that meant I would have to have a cat stay at my house.

We ended the tour in Val's office. Mom seemed to like this place, maybe because she sensed I was not overly enthusiastic about it. Mom wanted their one-bedroom unit. I said we could run the numbers and see how it would work out, but Val let us know there were not any one bedrooms open, but one was expected to be open the end of January, and then it takes two or so weeks to get the place ready. We could reserve it if we left a deposit that day.

"Just write us a check. We won't even cash it unless your mom moves in."

I looked at Tom and I looked at Mom. Neither seemed to have any objection. "Mom, you're not saying much, do you think I should write the check?"

"I wouldn't move in till February, it's only late October. I could be dead by then."

"Mom, writing this check today is not a commitment in a major way. If you change your mind you can get your money back; if you die, I'll get your money back. If you think this place is okay, that you could live here and not hate it, let's hold the room for you."

"Okay, hold the room. I probably won't make it till February anyway."

Val looked at me with a concerned look, and I said, "So now you're meeting the real Gloria Keren. So cheerful and optimistic."

"Well, Mrs. Keren, I hope you do make it and come join us. I love the residents who still have spirit, piss and vinegar."

~

The car ride back to Mom's apartment was fairly quiet until I put in the combo for the gate. "Oh, I wanted to stop at the supermarket. I need stuff."

"It's just as well, Mom, it's getting chilly. We'll drop you off at home so you don't have to sit in the cold car. Tom and I will go get your groceries."

On the way to the market, Tom and I began discussing the place. "So what did you really think?" he asked me.

"Well, it wasn't as nice as the first place we looked at, but Mom seemed to like it more. The care seemed adequate. I have two concerns. First, I felt turned around walking the halls and wonder if Mom would get lost."

"I had that thought too. I know Val tried to address it, but I was still unsure. I think if she got lost once, she would never leave her room again. What was your second concern?"

"Well, if Mom isolates there it becomes a very expensive apartment. I think she needs some encouraging and they aren't going to provide it."

"Isn't it like that at all the assisted living facilities?"

"I didn't really ask at the others because it was clear Mom didn't want to go to them."

"So, why do you think your mom is isolating so much?"

"What is this, a quiz? Why do *you* think she's isolating so much?" Tom put his hand on my knee. He knew I was at a snapping point and he didn't want me to go there. I felt like I was confronting all my mother's limitations in one fell swoop, and I felt totally abandoned by my brothers. Of course, I hadn't really asked them for anything yet, but I predicted their response to be what it had been every time I tried to get input, "You're the one that's there, we don't want to step on your feet!" They just didn't get that I either needed them to enthusiastically support me or give me something to work against. Their response left me feeling alone. I knew Tom had insight and opinions but was holding back so as not to impose. I needed them.

"Really Tom, what were you thinking while we were there?"

"Well, in my experience it seemed like a well-run program with attentive staff. The setting is a bit depressing, but Mom responded well to that. I share both of your concerns. It is close to work, so I can stop by between patients and try to coax Mom out to activities, and you could go by at dinnertime."

"So, basically, we'll be doing even more if she moves there?"

"Maybe ..."

"I think it's time we get the COPSA evaluation. Perhaps they can help us figure out if Mom's apathy and social withdrawal is treatable. If not, then this plan is not really going to work."

"I'll pull strings, get us their next available appointment."

"Thanks. I love you, you know. You'll never know how important you are to me in all of this."

"I think I do. I know how much you were there for me with my mom. I can't believe that ended only five months ago."

It was a relief to pick through produce and choose Mom's lamb chops after that. Little tasks that were so easy sometimes served such a soothing purpose.

~

Tom's strings still reached pretty far and we managed to get Mom in for her evaluation in a week. It was a bit strange since we knew much of the staff, including the social worker who was going to manage Mom's case.

When the testing began it didn't take long for Tom and me to get involved. The first time Mom hit a question that she hesitated on, both of us butted in to coach her. Quickly, we were reminded we were really there to observe and confirm answers that needed outside verification. The second time it happened we were asked to leave. Not all together; actually, they suggested we meet briefly with the psychiatrist to give her some background. The psychiatrist was a resident. As she was asking us questions, I could see Tom formulating questions of his own, performing his own assessment on her. When he finally did ask his questions, I could see in his face he was satisfied with the answers he got and we could feel comfortable in this woman's assessment. She excused herself after a few minutes and went in to meet with Mom.

We were called back into the office about a half hour later. Mom was smiling, the social worker was smiling, and the doctor was scribbling notes in a chart. Mom's chart had grown impressively during the few hours we had been at the clinic.

I asked Mom if she needed anything: water, juice, a bathroom break. She didn't. "Do you know this guy, what's your name?" she said, pointing at the social worker, "used to work with Tom?"

"Gloria, that's why we picked this place. I used to work here so I know how good they are."

"They may be good but they're nosy. They asked me about my sex life."

"What did you tell them?" I asked, a bit reluctantly.

"What's to tell? Don't like sex, never did. If I could've had you without it, I would have... . But that one," pointing at the psychiatrist, "made me draw a clock at a certain time. I think she was thinking I can't tell time."

"You did okay, Mrs. Keren," the psychiatrist said, handing me Mom's clock drawing.

I took the drawing and tried to contain my reaction. The clock test is a simple test where the subject is asked to draw a clock. They are then asked to fill in the numbers and finally to arrange the hands of the clock so it reads 2:10. On a gross level it does test for time-telling ability, but more importantly it is testing visual acuity, field neglect, and concrete versus more fluid thinking. Mom had drawn half of a clock, the right side. She had squeezed all twelve numbers around the outside and placed the hands with the small hand on the two and the big hand on the ten. This was not good.

The doctor went on to discuss Mom's performance on the Folstein Mini-Mental Status. Even with our earlier coaching, Mom had gone on to score a 19. Most people would easily score a 27 to 30 on this assessment. It is designed to test long- and short-term memory and a few other skills related to cognitive processing. Even with normal cognitive decline in aging, it is unlikely you'd fall much below a 25. A 20 is considered the cutoff for dementia. Tom and I looked at each other. We knew what this was.

"We also received some records from the hospital regarding CT scans and EEGs. You didn't tell me your mom had had a stroke," the psychiatrist said.

"*What?* I've never been told that. When, what?" I was upset and running through all of her hospitalizations in my mind. "When did this supposedly happen?"

The doctor gave me a date. I rifled through my mind. It had been almost a year before. I think it was the hospitalization when she first got diagnosed with congestive heart failure or maybe it was the second bout. There was some cognitive confusion at the time and they were unclear if it was from oxygen deprivation or a stroke. I vaguely remembered a brain CT scan being one of her tests; there had been so many through the hospitalizations that it was hard to keep them all sorted.

The doctor passed me the CT results, which I glanced at while I casually passed the clock picture to Tom. It was right there, in black and white. They called it a minor event, but later in the report the word stroke was used; not a Transient Ischemic Attack, or TIA, but a stroke. My mind couldn't process anymore, and for a long time after I wished I had asked for a copy.

The psychiatrist continued. "So, I believe your mom has both vascular and Alzheimer's dementia. I'll send my findings on to her doctor; you may want to consider trying one of the few medications out there that at least help to preserve or slow down memory loss."

"But, Doctor, will I be able to play mahjong again?" Mom asked.

"Do you play now?" she asked her.

"Well not much, I feel so slow.

"Well then, you can keep playing, clearly it won't harm you," the psychiatrist said, clearly not getting the significance of this question. "Is there anything you'd like to ask, Mr. Keren?"

I ignored the Mr. and said, "I guess I'm feeling a bit surprised. I'm recognizing how much we've been covering; all we haven't seen because of all we do for her."

"That's quite common." She cut me off before I could get out what I was trying to say. "Steve (the social worker) can give you the schedule of our caregivers group."

"What I was going to say was that our main concern has been her social withdrawal. We've been considering having Mom move to assisted living to help with her socialization, but they take a pretty hands-off approach to getting residents involved in programs. Do you think the social isolation is from the dementia or something else?"

"I can't really say, but if you need placement information, again, Steve can help you."

I asked no more. I felt the psychiatrist was not comfortable delivering the news and was anxious to get it over with. Not sure I blamed her, but she really needed help to make it less obvious. Her attitude was testing my patience.

We spent a few more minutes with Steve. He was helpful in terms of suggestions of assisted living facilities to check out. He and Tom reminisced a bit and traded news of recent sightings of folks with whom they had both worked. It was casual and relaxed and Mom's head was nodding with sleepiness.

After dropping Mom at home, Tom and I began to chat in the car.

"How you doing?" he asked, putting a reassuring hand on my knee as I drove.

"Not sure. Kind of shocked how badly she did. That clock …"

He tightened his grip. "Yeah, that was a shocker. We've really been covering so much for her."

"I feel like if we move her to assisted living, she'll just be occupying a more expensive apartment. What's the point?"

"Well, she'll be fed and get her meds. Someone will see her regularly …"

"I'm tired. I need a nap. Let's go home."

"Okay."

"Her place isn't available until February. I really don't need to think a lot about it right now."

18

THE POWER OF ADVERTISING

The months after Joan died were busy. It was fairly easy to close the apartment as she had barely moved in and most of her belongings were still in boxes. As predicted, much of the content of her house recluttered our attic. Still, it was sad and there were things to be done.

Mom was more out of the hospital than in it during this time period, but her decline was growing obvious. She barely ever left the apartment. If Tom or I went by to take her out to eat she would. She never came over to the house as she felt the stairs were too much for her. Phil would come visit. Stu had plans to bring the girls out over Thanksgiving. We would do Chanukah at the same time.

Tom and I needed a vacation and began to plan a trip to Costa Rica. It was exciting. We had never been to Central or South America. Feeling flush from his inheritance from Joan, Tom decided we should splurge and travel in luxury. We'd divide our time between two first-class resorts and build in some escorted nature trips. It was good to have something to look forward to. We would go in mid-January.

As summer became fall the buzz was all about the election. It seemed fairly clear that America was about to elect their first Black president. Working for a public hospital, I would have off on Election Day, so I volunteered at the Democratic Party office to drive people to the polls in the afternoon.

The day dawned and was filled with sunshine. The plan was for me to vote in Plainfield then head over to Mom's to take her and any of her friends who needed a ride to the polls. I didn't have to wait long to vote, but it was unusual to have to wait at all. Anticipating that by the time I got Mom to her polling place there might be crowds, I threw some water in a cooler and a few beach chairs in the trunk.

Good planning. The lines snaked through the gym. Mom looked at it and said, "Forget this. I can't stand for that long."

"Mom, I got you covered. You wait here, on line. I'll be right back."

When I returned from the car the woman behind Mom said to her, "Boy, he takes good care of you."

After I set up Mom's chair, I offered the other to her neighbor. At first she refused, asking, "What will you sit on?"

"How about we take turns? If I get tired I'll ask you for the chair back."

She smiled and sat herself down.

Looking around I could see there were dozens of other older folks who could use a chair. There were a few folding chairs around the periphery and I dragged a few over for those who really looked like they needed it. Then I had an idea. I told Mom to sit tight and I went to explore. Poking my head outside the gym door, I saw what I was looking for. A janitor was pushing his broom.

He startled when I addressed him. "It's pretty busy in there."

"Never seen an election day so crowded," he said.

"Most aren't this historic, this exciting."

"You can say that again."

We chatted some more about his excitement over voting for a Black man this morning. "Took my children to see me press those buttons." He was so proud and I remembered being a child and accompanying my mother into the voting booth.

I returned the conversation to the crowds inside and the people who wanted to wait but probably couldn't stand that long. He told me to wait there. He was gone about five minutes when he returned with a colleague. They were pushing a cart piled high with folding chairs.

"Could you help us set these up?" he asked me. Together we set out about forty chairs for people to get off their feet for a bit.

~

"Where you been? I thought you left me."

"Nah, no such luck. I was just getting some more chairs for your neighbors." She turned around and saw the crowd sitting around the gym.

"I can't remember crowds like this since Kennedy."

"I have to take your word for that, Mom. At least the lines are moving."

It looked like there were eight or nine people in front of us. When we finally got to the booth, Mom asked me to come in with her. "It's all computers now. You have to show me what to do."

Actually, we still had levers, but I wasn't sure Mom could reach them anymore. I walked into the booth with her.

"I'm sorry sir, you can't go in there." A poll worker had grabbed me by my arm.

"It's okay," I said, twisting my arm out of her grip. "This is my mom, she asked me to help her."

"Oh, that's what I'm here for. That way her ballot will remain secret."

Mom was smiling. She knew this poll worker was going to rue the day she tried to stop me. "Well, how will that be secret? You, an absolute stranger to her, pulling her levers to vote. Seems it should be her choice who helps her out."

"Sir, them's the rules. I didn't make them."

"Who did?"

She looked so confused. I felt a little sorry for her.

"Who did what?" she asked.

"Who made the rules?"

She was stumped and was signaling to someone who seemed to be a supervisor.

"Is there a problem?" she asked my mother.

"Well, I want my son to help me in the booth, but this woman won't let him."

"Oh, that's why we have poll workers."

I spoke up. "Ma'am, when I was little, my mom used to take me into the booth with her every time she voted. Not once did anyone ever get concerned about it. She taught me how to vote. How important it was. Since I've turned eighteen, I have voted in every election I was eligible to vote in. Now it's time for me to go back in the booth with Mom and return the favor.

"This is highly unusual, but if you insist."

I wanted to question her about what was unusual. Throw her a dig about her children not being helpful to her, but we had won the argument so I let it go.

Inside the booth we made our way down the list of candidates. Mom usually voted straight Democratic and I figured reading the list to her was just a formality.

"Obama/McCain."

"Obama!"

"Lautenberg/Zimmer?"

"Lautenberg."

"Stender/Lance? Which one for Congress?"

"Oh, that Linda Stender is a big, fat spender!"

"But Mom, she's the Democrat."

"Yeah, but she's a big fat spender."

Mom lived in a district with a heavily contested seat that year. The Dems had put up Linda Stender, a member of the New Jersey State Assembly, to run against the incumbent. Unfortunately for her, she was married to a man whose name lent itself to this cursed rhyme. All fall the TV had rung out ads ending with the phrase "Linda Stender is a big fat spender." Clearly it worked, especially among the slightly cognitively impaired elderly. I pulled Mom's lever for Lance.

We made our way down the ballot and the initiatives. I asked Mom if she was sure it was all correct. I kept staring at that Stender lever. I could change it and Mom would never know, or remember.

I stared at the Stender lever one last time before I pulled the big lever to reopen the curtain. The poll worker was standing, waiting for us to exit.

"Thank you," I said to her. "If you're still uncomfortable in the morning, feel free to call McCain and let him know how my mom cost him the election."

~

Well, Obama won the election. As I watched the returns with Tom that night, I recounted the story. We both had a good laugh. Of course, more sobering was my wonder if Mom would see the inaugural. Tom and I would miss it as that was when we were going to Costa Rica.

In December Tom and I threw Mom a party for her seventy-ninth birthday. I had invited her friends from the development and a few of our friends Mom knew. It was a fun night. I liked Mom's friends. I loved that my friends liked Mom and her friends. We had insisted there be no gifts, but that didn't stop anyone form bringing her a trinket.

After we dropped everyone at home, I helped Mom into her apartment.

"Thank you for tonight. I had a good time."

"I'm glad. You seemed a bit quiet."

"It's hard for me to keep up when there are so many people talking at once. But I enjoyed being in their company. And the food there was really good."

"Glad you enjoyed it."

"Yeah, not bad for the last birthday party I'll probably ever have."

It wasn't that I hadn't had the thought, or at least wondered if this were to be the last one, but hearing her say it was disquieting.

"Mom, if it is, I'm glad it was memorable. If it's not, we'll just have to top it next year."

~

Christmas was somber. The first without Joan, but I did my best to make it good for Tom. New Year's passed in a blur, and by Martin Luther King weekend we were flying off to Costa Rica.

Phil had agreed to come up and help Mom out for a few of the days. The days that weren't covered by him, I had enlisted friends to check in with her. I also purchased an international cell plan so I could be reached in an emergency.

We had a wonderful, relaxing escape. I barely thought about Mom. I even had an experience of caretaking by some very empathic new friends. Costa Rica is known for its ceviche. Being that I was avoiding drinking the water and eating raw foods washed in it, ceviche felt like a risky proposition. The night before we were to move from our volcano-based lodge in the center of the country to our oceanfront one, I let our tour guide talk me into indulging my love for the delicacy.

I was lucky. The cramps didn't hit while we were in the van for six hours the next day moving from one resort to the other. I even had a good night with a full meal of cooked fish before retiring to bed. Sometime, a few hours before sunrise, the pain woke me up. The rest of the evening was a repeating loop between a few moments of sleep and a trip to the bathroom. I imagined I had emptied out the contents of my entire digestive track, overloaded on an anti-diarrhea med, and managed about an hour of sleep before we were due to board the bus for our rain forest tour.

Approximately fifty yards into the park I realized I was not going to make it. I was probably dehydrated. I was running a fever and the cramps were coming back. The tour guide was very helpful. He pointed me to the path that would take me to a cabstand about half a mile outside the park. Tom wanted to come with me, but I insisted he stay. Two traits of mine drove that decision. I was cheap and wouldn't want both of our admissions to the tour to go to waste, and I hated hovering caretakers when I didn't feel well.

By some strong will I made it back to our bungalow at the resort. I didn't fall into an alligator-infested ravine, although crossing the bridge over it I thought it would be my destiny. I didn't have explosive diarrhea all over the cab, in fact, I managed to get into the bungalow and the bathroom before it began. As I sat there, moaning in pain and wishing for death, I realized I was being watched. At the window, which was open, there were three capuchin monkeys staring at me with the most intense looks of concern. Their chirps and cries, to me, sounded like expressions of concern. I felt taken care of and the screen on the window was just the space I needed to not feel crowded by their hovering. I wondered if I could get Tom to stay outside the window when he returned to administer to me.

I eventually fell into the bed, not bothering to even pull the drapes to our balcony. Before I fell into sleep, I noticed my capuchin friends had taken up sentry duty on the table on our balcony. They were there four hours later when Tom returned from the tour. They made great guards, as Tom had to get the resort personnel to chase them away when he returned. Sleep was what I needed. By dinnertime I was able to take in some broth and rice. The next day I was able to resume touring, and at the end of the week I returned to my caregiving duties with a new standard for quality care.

19

SAINT VALENTINE'S DAY MASSACRE

I could see it in my mind. For a moment, it would taste so good; it would feel so good, the burn in my throat, the fullness of my lungs. After all this time, I'd probably have to cough. It was all I wanted—a Parliament, a Marlboro Light. A year and a half without a cigarette would go down the tubes if I gave in, but who would blame me? Tom would be pissed, but I don't think he'd blame me. We were playing a waiting game. I predicted before we even left the hospital that we'd be back in the ER before the weekend was up.

I hated waiting. It's the most stressful feeling I know. When I was young and losing my baby teeth, I don't think a single one of them fell out naturally. I had twisted, yanked, and maneuvered each one out of my mouth before its time. I'd made half-baked muffins and cookies because that last minute and a half was too torturous to wait through. Each of Mom's procedures, the worst part was sitting in the waiting room, not knowing; wishing it was done. And there had been a lot of procedures since Dad died.

Mom had spent the past week and some days in the hospital with pneumonia. She had seemed to respond well to the antibiotics, but I had been surprised when the doctors said she could go home on Thursday. When she was admitted days before, they had many reservations if they could treat her at all. When Thursday came she was complaining she wasn't feeling right; she was too tired and asked for her oxygen back. The doctors agreed to keep her another night to watch her.

The social worker called me at work on Friday to tell me Mom was cleared for discharge, that I should come pick her up. When I got to the hospital, they had her dressed and sitting in the chair. She didn't look good—washed out, kind of gray, but the nurses insisted she was fine to go.

As she and I were waiting for Tom to bring the car around to the hospital exit, I asked her, "Are you hungry? I stopped at the store on my way over and picked up some fillets and potatoes to bake."

"Starved, but could we eat those some other night? I want to go out. Let's get fish."

Tom was pulling up. As I helped Mom into the car, I said, "To the Bonefish. Mom wants to go out."

"Then Bonefish it shall be. Nowhere's too good for m'lady!"

Mom attempted a laugh, but it came out more of a cough.

We all ordered our usual. Mom picked at hers but more pushed it around her plate. Tom ate heartily. I couldn't stop staring at Mom long enough to really eat. We had her meal and mine packed as doggy bags, but she wanted dessert so we ordered a piece of cake and three spoons.

When we had her back home, I laid out her meds, helped her with her shots, and helped her get ready for bed. She seemed so much frailer, and I couldn't shake the feeling she'd be back in the hospital before the weekend was over.

The next day was Valentine's Day. That morning I showed up around ten at Mom's apartment. The visiting nurse was coming to do Mom's intake assessment and I wanted to be there. Mom was still in bed. "Are you okay? It's not like you to be in bed at this time."

"Oh, I was up. Made a cup of tea. Took my medication. Just got tired out so I came in to lie down. Guess I fell asleep."

"The nurse will be here in thirty minutes so you should probably get up and washed."

~

I hated Valentine's Day. Why did I need a day to celebrate love; didn't we do that every day we wanted? What if I didn't want to do it on February fourteenth? I did it for Tom, because he loved card holidays. We were our mothers' sons. My mom scoffed at Valentine's, Mother's Day, Grandparent's Day; instead, we'd get heart-shaped love notes in our lunch bag whenever the whim hit her. We'd get a candy heart in April, as much because she loved us as because it was just cheaper to buy it then. Joan, Tom's mom, kept Hallmark in business. Not only did we get cards for every holiday, major to minor, but so did all of her nieces, nephews, grands and cousins, her neighbors and friends. Every card was a chance for her to pour out her glee with stickers. This would be our first Valentine's Day without cards from Joan.

Tom and I had decided to try a new restaurant for dinner that night. We had made a reservation and were a tiny bit excited to try somewhere new. First, however, there was the day to get through. The visiting nurse arrived. She wasn't too concerned with Mom's tiredness or her color. She took Mom's vitals, reviewed Mom's medications, and then took her leave. She was due back on Monday, two days later.

When I offered Mom lunch, she hemmed and hawed. "I'm not really hungry. Why do I have to eat?"

"The doctor said at least three meals a day. How about some chicken soup?"

"Nah! Unless it's homemade."

"Oh, coming right up! Just happened to whip some up in my free time between work, running to the hospital, and checking on your apartment."

"I can wish, can't I?"

"You sure can, and if I had had the time, I'd have made it for you. But I don't. So how about if I just run over to the Family Restaurant and pick some up for you? Noodles or matzah balls."

"Noodles."

~

After her lunch, Mom and I fell asleep in front of her TV. Tom came by around three and woke us up.

"If I knew you were coming, I would have baked you some cookies or a cake," Mom said. She would have, too. Besides her grandchildren, he was the only one for whom she would knock herself out anymore. He was not only her favorite child-in-law, he was a favorite among the extended family as well. Mom extolled his virtues everywhere.

"Oh, Gloria, a lovely thought, but you need to save your strength to get well."

Mom laughed. "What do I have to get well for?"

"Spring is coming, we'll take a trip."

"Oh, where? Timbuktu? Do I look like a lady who can travel? I'm lucky I can walk to the kitchen."

"Mom, you just have to get your strength back. You'll feel better. You'll have a visit from Stu and the kids at Passover, but you have to get your strength back."

"Why would they want to visit me? I'm just a sick, old lady to them."

Tom stayed for an hour and made small talk. Before we left, I showed Mom where I had put the spinach pie I had picked up for her dinner. She showed little enthusiasm for eating it.

"Mom, please eat. At least some of it. I want to enjoy myself, not worry about you all night."

"All right, all right. I will." I didn't believe her for a moment but I refused to worry about it. "Have a good Valentine's Day. Enjoy the dinner … Wait a minute." She got up from her seat and shuffled down to her bedroom. She came back with a fifty-dollar bill in her hands. "Dinner's on me."

"Thanks, Mom. I love you, you know!"

"Thanks, Glo. That's really sweet of you." Tom had taken to using the nickname my father had called her by most of my life.

When we finally found the restaurant, we were already ten minutes late. I hate being late for anything. If I'm not ten minutes early I believe I am late. So, somehow, I had married a man who if he was not a half hour late believed he was early. It could be lethal.

I hated the table. A tiny two top, in the dead center of the restaurant, with fawning heterosexuals surrounding us. Tom ordered his drink while we looked over the menu. It was an easy look as they had a special Valentine's Day prix fixe, which had not been mentioned on the reservations app we had used to book the table. Hard as I tried, the sweetbreads, featured so prominently in the menu online and extolled in the reviews, were not to be found on the special menu. Strike two for this night. They were the reason we had picked this restaurant over all the places we might have chosen. Since the day my mom introduced me to them when I was a young teen, I had ordered them everywhere I saw them on a menu. I know, I was a weird eater, a weird kid, but I had a sophisticated palate and ate what most kids fed to the dog when their moms weren't looking. I felt a hissy fit coming on. I tried to hold it back because Tom loved Valentine's Day and was trying so hard to make it special. I wanted it to be so for him.

I ordered the clam chowder and the surf and turf, shrimp not lobster; sat back and worked on not pouting. The breadbasket came. Unimpressive, limp-crusted, Italian bread with those little plastic pats of butter that had been refrigerated so long you could forget spreading it until a nuclear attack had come along to melt it. I had just dropped the rock of butter onto a slice of bread, folded it, and started its path to my teeth when the first one occurred.

Three tables to our right a young man, looking awkward in his blazer, as it seemed tight on his oh-so-large steroidal shoulders, dropped to his knees and popped the question to his girlfriend. She let out a squeal and screamed, "Yes, yes, of course …" as she struggled to get up and hug him in her too tight and too short black dress. The restaurant burst into applause. Not sure if she realized that while she was hugging him, he had reached down and popped another piece of bread in his mouth.

A variation of that scene would occur six times before we finished our desserts and left the restaurant. Another reason I detested Valentine's Day was the obvious way, at least in the suburbs, that it was not a holiday for us. 2009, we had domestic partnership in New Jersey, but they were still not ready to let us have the "real thing," and would not have applauded us, in this restaurant, if we had made a public spectacle of our love.

The food was edible. At least my steak was cooked to my liking. Dessert, a favorite for us both, was crème brûlée. As dessert was presented to each couple, the lady (that was from the menu, I cannot vouch for how many of the women might actually qualify for the term) was presented with a large, chocolate-covered strawberry. How would they handle us? Hopefully, we would both get one, as I could not understand why only the ladies got one. What, men don't like strawberries? Chocolate? Love? What a stupid division.

When the crème brûlée came there was no chocolate strawberry. Tom glanced at me and said, "Don't! Just eat and let's go."

I hated that about Tom. Sometimes, a scene was necessary and he knew it. Okay, maybe it wasn't necessary here, but I was angry. Not only was all this heterosexual privilege being celebrated all around me, but now I was being treated as a second-class citizen. I was not going to leave without my strawberry. The waiter came over to ask if Tom wanted more coffee and if we wanted anything else.

"Yes, I think you forgot to bring us a chocolate strawberry," I said in the softest voice I could muster.

"I'm sorry, but those are just for the ladies," he said.

"You're joking, right? You know it's against the law to discriminate based on sexual orientation in public accommodations in New Jersey," I said, getting just a little louder.

"Sir, it has nothing to do with your sexual orientation. They are only for the ladies."

"So, if we were a lesbian couple, you would have brought us both strawberries?"

He looked blank. "Maybe, we need to see the manager."

"Is there a problem?" the manager asked, as if I would look this angry and exasperated if I wanted to compliment his chef on the dinner.

"Yes," I said. "We are here celebrating Valentine's Day. It is quite clear to us that each of the meals on your menu comes with a chocolate-covered strawberry, but this gentleman is refusing to bring us one because he does not think we are ladies." The sarcasm function had been initiated; I could not know where this would end.

"Well, he's quite right. The strawberries are just for the ladies."

"So, why do I have to pay the same price for our meals as they do for theirs? We're not getting the same meal or treatment."

"Well, they're not really paying for the strawberries, that's our gift to them."

"Oh, and your gift to us is your check and your homophobia."

"No reason to get nasty."

"Oh, yes there is. There is a lot of reason to get nasty. You know darn well that your little policy is nicely discriminatory in so many ways. You have no problem taking my queer money, just like theirs. You have no problem jacking up that price of our meal, just like theirs. But just 'cause neither one of us possesses a vagina, you think it is perfectly all right to treat us like this."

"Mike, come on, let's just go."

"No, I'm sorry, but I won't just go. I want my strawberry!"

"Sir, you're disturbing the other patrons. I think you should leave."

"Sure, as soon as I get my strawberry." I glanced around. I had gotten most everyone's attention with my vagina comment. There were a good many folk glaring at me, but also enough folks giving me a thumb's-up to encourage me to continue.

"Sir, I'm sorry. We have just enough for the ladies. If we give you one, the rest of the gentlemen will want one, too."

"Well, why didn't you say so? That's understandable, totally."

He smiled and relaxed his guard just a bit.

"Except that when we made the reservation, we didn't identify ourselves as raging homosexuals. For all you knew we were a *normal* couple. Therefore, you should have a strawberry back there for us ... unless of course, our strawberry is in that little rotund gut of yours already." The manager turned bright pink, then white. "Now, either bring us a strawberry or comp us this meal."

He walked away. There was a smattering of applause, mostly of approval. Three women walked over and offered me their strawberries. I thanked them but told them to hold onto them, as I had a feeling we would be getting at least one, momentarily.

The waiter returned and left the check on the corner of the table. He turned to slink away, but Tom told him to wait. They had not comped us the check and had not brought us a strawberry. I wanted to walk out without paying. Tom wouldn't. He put the money in the folder and we left.

Our ride home was silent. I was mad Tom had paid the bill. I know that is who he is, but it still really irked me. The restaurant would not get away with it. I went online and wrote a few scathing reviews of the place to make myself feel better. Tomorrow, I would research how to file a complaint under the state's non-discrimination bill.

20

BETTER CALL THE TROOPS

I woke up to the day after. Somehow, I had actually slept fitfully. I threw on some clothes and walked the dog. I dialed Mom's phone when I came back in. It took a few rings, but eventually she answered, "Hello." The voice was soft, distant, and labored.

"Mom, it's me, are you okay?"

"Not really. I feel like something is sitting on my chest. I'm too weak to get out of bed. I can't even get to the bathroom."

"Mom, when I hang up, I want you to press your Life Alert button and have them send an ambulance. I'll be right there."

Tom had appeared by my side, in his sweats, having heard me say Life Alert.

"Okay. Hurry, I'm scared."

"I'm coming."

~

Arriving just as the ambulance did, I let them in. Mom was in bed. She was white as a ghost. I gave the EMTs her history and they went to work. Her EKG was not too bad, but her blood oxygen was critically low. They put an oxygen mask on her, then loaded her on the gurney and into the back of the ambulance.

Blood work, X-rays, and a whole lot of waiting later the doctor came back with confirmation her pneumonia had returned. Not only that, but it was now in three lobes instead of one. For once, I wished I wasn't so right. I texted my brothers the news. No messages came back in return.

Later that afternoon her doctor asked if she could speak with me. I liked this doctor. She worked with the Levines, Mom's regular doctors. I knew Mom was really not feeling well because she had not made a single disparaging comment about having a female doctor. Very old school, my mom did not trust any woman to be her doctor. It went even further: If she knew anyone who died under the care of a woman doctor, she would swear the person would have lived if she or he had only had a male doctor. It was another of my mother's enigmas. She certainly supported women in the workplace. She had worked most of her adult life. She didn't really believe women needed men. Given a choice, she was clear she'd have preferred to be a single mom. But, she rarely had nice things to say about women.

The doctor and I found an empty lounge. She offered me a coffee and took a seat next to me. "I want to be up front. Your mom is very sick. There is a good chance she will not make it. She is already weak from last week's hospital stay, her infection is much more extensive, and she does not tolerate many of these medications well."

"Is it time for me to call in the family?"

"How far away are they?"

"My one brother is in D.C. He can be here in three hours or so. The other is in Ohio, it's a short plane ride."

"Let's wait a day and see how she responds. She needs sleep now more than anything. I'm hoping I can get her a private room. For now, we are going to put her in a transition bed. It's a much smaller nursing ratio and tends to be quieter."

"Doc, thanks. You know she has a living will. No extraordinary measures. Do Not Resuscitate. It should be in her chart. I can bring another one if they can't find it."

"I'll have the nurses check. She has her own pulmonologist, right?"

"Yeah, she sees Dr. Henderson."

"I'm going to call him in. He may actually want to take over the case since it's more pulmonary than cardiac at this point." I was fine with that turn of events. Dr. Henderson was my own physician. I had met him when he did a consult on my mother when she first developed congestive heart failure. I had liked his bedside manner and confident way so much, I jumped at the chance when he mentioned he takes on patients as a primary provider.

"Good. She'll be comfortable with that."

I went back to her bedside. Mom was sleeping. Tom asked me what was up and I gave him a brief synopsis.

I encouraged Tom to go home and do what he needed to do. I knew that he had to teach in the morning, and that he would stay up half the night overpreparing if he didn't do it this afternoon. "Pick me up later for dinner. I'll call you if I need you." I kissed him goodbye and settled in with the newspaper.

Dr. Henderson poked his head through the curtain. "You all decent?"

I laughed, although Mom didn't stir from her sleep. "Well, I am, but who knows what's going on under her sheet. Come in, anyway."

I gave Mom a gentle nudge to rouse her. "Mom, Dr. Henderson is here. You want to open your eyes to talk to him?"

"I wasn't sleeping, was I?"

Dr. Henderson began to examine her and basically just concurred with what we already knew: Mom was very sick. There was pneumonia in three lobes of her lungs and she was very weak. She might not be able to fight the infection off. As he continued examining her, he turned to me and asked, "So your surgery should be soon. How are you feeling about it?"

Dr. Henderson was one of the very few people who knew I was scheduled for gastric banding surgery in a month's time. He knew because he had recently done my presurgery physical. I had decided to wait until after the surgery to tell Mom because she had basically been against bariatric surgery since its earliest introduction.

Mom perked up, and I saw her staring at me out of the corner of my eye. "Okay. Last I heard though they were waiting for your report. Do you know if the office sent it?"

"I'm sure they sent it out, but I will check for you."

"Okay. I'm working on what I last heard and that was at my last appointment, over a week ago."

As he put away his pen and rehung his stethoscope around his neck, he said to my mom, "I want you to sleep all you want, but try to eat."

"And no smoking," I added. Of course, she had never smoked a day in her life, and we looked at each other and laughed. It was the first real smile I had gotten from her all day.

I walked to the desk with Dr. Henderson. "What do you think? Should I call in my family? Is this the end?" It was so strange to ask that.

"I can't predict how she'll respond to the antibiotics, but she's very sick. Why don't you wait a day or two to get your brothers in?"

"Thank you, Dr. Henderson. I really appreciate your honesty." He put a reassuring hand on my shoulder. "Oh, one more thing, cat's out of the bag now, but Mom hadn't known about my surgery."

"Oh, I'm so sorry. I feel awful. I should never ..."

"It's okay. She's not going to yell at me now, and who knows how this will go? Maybe I won't be able to go forward with the surgery at all."

"Think positive." He squeezed my shoulder a bit firmer.

"I will. And thanks again."

I went back to Mom's curtain. "What was that all about? What surgery? What's the matter with you?"

"I'm fine, Mom." I hoped that would end it.

"If you're fine, what kind of surgery are you having?"

"I'm getting a lap-band. I can't stand this weight anymore, I can't stay on a diet, and I am feeling it in my legs, in my lungs, even the stress on my heart. I have to do something."

My weight had been a constant issue in my life and my life with my mom. She could be both supportive and destructive around it. On the one hand, she would encourage me. She took me to my first Weight Watchers meeting when I was eleven. It was my best attempt, having reached goal weight in six months, mostly by having a growth spurt of three inches in five months. I only lost eighteen pounds, but I had grown into a height more appropriate for my weight. I obtained lifetime membership by age twelve. There had been many diets since then, as every weight loss would be followed by a period of gaining it back and more. In my adolescence, when she would take me shopping, Mom would sing the old polka song, "Roll Out the Barrel." It was her warped way of expressing her disgust at my weight, her frustration with trying to help me, and her attempt to motivate me. Motivate me it did, mostly to soothe myself with Ring-Dings or Yodels.

Ten years before, I had lost 125 pounds through a combination of Fen-Phen, strict dieting, and personal training. I had even managed to keep most of it off for five years. But over the last five years it had been reemerging. I was up to 325. Everywhere I went, I huffed and puffed. My bones ached and my circulation was poor.

Mom just sort of stared. "When are you supposed to have it?" she asked.

"Mid-March."

"Well, I hope I am well enough by then to take care of you while you're recovering."

I smiled. There really wasn't going to be much of a recovery. The doctor was allowing me one to two weeks off from work, but that was mostly to adjust to life with the band and all the changes it would bring to my routine. But I heard in her response her support, her effort to return to me what I had been giving to her.

"You're not upset with me?"

"I don't love the idea of that surgery. It killed my cousin, but if you feel you have to do it for yourself, I can live with it."

"Thanks, Mom. And it is very different now than when your cousin had it. It is so much safer."

Perhaps waiting to tell her had been a good decision. With our roles reversed, my being her caretaker, and her being so vulnerable, she saw me as the adult I was and accepted my decision as to what was best for me.

She fell back asleep. The nurses let me know they expected her to get a room before midnight, but beyond that they couldn't predict it.

Monday came and Mom was still in the transition unit. It was less crowded and easier to move around. When one of the Levines came around to do rounds, he looked very grave.

"How are you feeling this morning, Gloria?"

"Yech!" was all she could muster.

"The nurses said you didn't eat your breakfast. You need your strength. You have to eat something."

"Fuck you!"

That one surprised even me. When I turned to look at her, I saw a tear in her eye. I took her hand and she squeezed mine. I felt so powerless at that moment. I had no idea what the options might even be.

"Well, if you can muster up that kind of response, I'm thinking you have some fight left in you. That's a good sign." It was the first positive prognosis we had heard.

When he left I asked Mom if she would try to eat a corn muffin. She agreed to try. When I brought one from the cafeteria, she looked at it and said, "It's so big."

I had to laugh. What a line. But I knew what she meant. My mom had a staple at breakfast, mini corn muffins. She always ate one, sometimes two. This muffin was as large as six of those.

"You don't have to eat the whole thing. Just have a few bites and I'll bring you some mini-muffins."

She ate a few bites with a few sips of tea. I kissed her goodbye and headed off to work, to my paying job.

21

Later

Tuesday. Work was a waste. I sat in meetings barely hearing what was being talked about. It's funny how when your feeling of not wanting to be somewhere echoes other's feelings of not wanting you there, you possess the power of invisibility. It had been three months since I had lost the battle in a staff meeting over their proposed policy that highlighted the hospital's lack of ethics. My staff still loved me, but my peers in the administrative team had all gotten the memo that I was to be excluded due to what I had done. I just had to be careful not to make a mistake that would give them a reason to get rid of me.

I had given up the financial consulting about a year before, having allowed myself to be sidetracked by all the caregiving. That early in one's career, building your "book" or client list should be the only thing you are focused on. Though I loved the work, I could not make it primary, and I had to admit I wasn't really good at it.

I had taken a job administrating a psychology department at a county hospital. It was not a good match. They didn't like me and the feeling was mutual. Today, I didn't care. I just couldn't focus.

Four o'clock came and all I had to do before leaving was lock my office door; there was nothing to straighten up because I had done nothing all day. When I got to the hospital, Mom was sound asleep. That was good; she needed rest. I sat down in the chair next to her and drifted in my thoughts. When the nurse came in to take Mom's blood pressure, Mom barely stirred. "She's really out," I said to the nurse.

"Good. About time. Maybe she'll stop complaining," she replied.

I looked at her questioningly, but she said no more. "Was there a problem?" I continued.

"No. She's just one of those who is never satisfied with anything."

"Maybe it's because she doesn't feel well." She certainly captured my mother in her sentiment, but she could be a bit more professional. She was talking about my mother, after all, and it wasn't like I was one of her colleagues in the back room of the nurses' station.

"She's been well enough to press the call button."

That wasn't like my mother. She would usually die before asking for help, like me. "Really. Anything serious?"

"A lot of requests for the bedpan. She barely ate and she's on a catheter so it was always empty, but all day long."

"Gee, she had the urge but she's on a catheter. Is the catheter working? Might she be getting a UTI?"

"Oh, you're a doctor?"

"Since 1991." I stretched the truth, but I certainly thought I could think more like one than she was. "Of course, you don't need an MD degree to recognize when something may be happening that doesn't meet the eye."

She gave me a "Hmmph," gathered her things, and left the room. I watched for her to go in another room and took myself over to the nurse manager's office.

"Hi. It's me again." Mom was on the cardiac telemetry wing and this woman knew me well from all of Mom's previous visits.

"Oh, I saw your mom is back. Is she doing okay? Comfortable?"

She never seemed irritated with my "interfering" in Mom's treatment and often encouraged my involvement. "Well, Mom's nurse today seems to feel Mom was a pain in the ass. I'm wondering if she might have a pain somewhere else." I explained my theory.

"Seems like a good call to me. I'll have her doctors order a test, although with all the antibiotics she's on for the pneumonia, they may already have a UTI covered."

"Well, at least we'll know and maybe she'll need a new catheter."

When I got to Mom's room, she was awake. She had spied my coat on the chair, so knew I had come in while she was sleeping. "So what trouble were you getting into now?" she asked, a slightly sheepish grin spreading across her face.

"Oh, I love you, too. I was just trying to arrange for Dr. Kevorkian to come do a consult."

"Finally. How long have I been asking for that?"

"As long as I've known you, Mom. Maybe I'll get you a consult for Mother's Day."

"If you loved me you would have gotten it for me for Valentine's."

"Caught me, Mom. I don't love you. Just doing all this caretaking so I can write a book someday. Besides, you hate Valentine's Day and never want anything. Now you're complaining 'cause I didn't get you the right thing. The nurse was right. You're a pain in the ass!"

"Oh, that bitch! I have to pee so bad and she complains every time she has to bring me the bedpan."

"But Mom, you're on a catheter."

"I am?"

"Yeah, in fact that's where I was. The nurse had said you had been asking for the pan a lot, so I was wondering if you're getting a UTI or a bladder infection."

"Are you sure I'm on a catheter?"

"Either that or they have hung someone else's bag of pee on the side of your bed."

"My son the doctor!"

Mom's dinner came and I was trying to coax her to eat a little soup when the doctor peeked in. It was the Levines' assistant, who we had met the night Mom was admitted this time. She checked her vitals and inquired about Mom's urinary issue. She had a great bedside manner, but I could tell Mom was irritated by her small talk. Mom would have been so engaged if this doctor was male, but she could not let go of her bias against female doctors.

Finally, the doctor told us that afternoon's X-ray still showed a significant amount of pneumonia, so it was not surprising Mom still felt so poorly. She also was going to order a urine test.

I followed her out to the desk while she wrote her orders. When she was done, she lifted her head and said, "I think you might want to encourage the family to come. She's really not responding to the antibiotics and if she does have this infection, it will only get harder."

I was shocked by the directness. I knew I would hear this at some point, I just thought Mom would have more control over it or it would come more suddenly, from a heart attack. Dying from pneumonia can be so long and drawn out.

I returned to Mom's room, suddenly sobered. She was sleeping again. I went to the cafeteria to get a burger, think, and maybe call my brothers. I called Tom. He was at work and I got his answering machine.

"Hey. Hope you're okay. I'm at the hospital. Doctors don't think she is responding to the antibiotics, so not doing well. See you at home."

I ate my burger and debated whom to call next. I dialed Stuart but got his answering machine, so I hung up. Would he come? When Dad was dying, he didn't feel the need. I would love to see him and Phil probably would come, so Stu could help me deal with him.

I called Phil. "Hey, what's up?" he answered.

"Well, I'm at the hospital. Mom is not getting better and the doctor suggested you might want to come up. This may be it."

"Right now?"

He had such a busy life, I thought to myself sarcastically. "Well, I don't think it'll be tomorrow, but I wouldn't wait too long."

There was silence on the other end.

"You figure out what you want to do. Let me know," I said and hung up. The last thing I wanted was to help him figure out his life.

Wednesday morning, Mom seemed worse. She again was refusing to eat. She was talking in a whisper. Nothing was to her satisfaction. I waited till her nurse left and I said, "What's the matter? Can I do anything for you?"

"Kill me. I can't stand this place anymore and I'm dying anyway, right?"

"Well Mom, the antibiotics are not working well, so you're not getting better."

"I'm getting worse. Stop lying to me."

"Mom, I'm not lying. They're not giving up hope, but things are grim."

"Thank you. I know how I feel, and all these Pollyannas around here, with their 'good mornings' and 'don't you look great' are driving me up the wall."

"Mom, you can't get out of bed, how could you drive?"

"Do I look like I'm laughing?"

"You don't really want to know what you look like. Now settle down or I'll get a mirror and give you a good scare."

"Idle threats," she said. "You wouldn't treat me like this if I wasn't in this bed!"

"'But you are, Blanche, you are!'"

"I never should have introduced you to the Million Dollar Movie. I ruined you for life."

"You're just pissed because I made you eat that parakeet."

That made her smile. Me too. *Whatever Happened to Baby Jane* was one of my all-time favorite movies. I had, in fact, discovered it first on the Million Dollar Movie, a 1960s and 1970s afternoon TV staple. Every day at four-thirty, channel 9 would broadcast a classic black-and-white picture. Before she rejoined the workforce, my mom and I often watched them together. Later, I would turn them on to keep me company on my long, friendless afternoons.

Magic was what it was. Others thought our humor crass, absurd, and inappropriate. It was our code and our secret weapon. When the world shit on us we could shake it off, shit on them, or just revel in it. Most people who were privy to it just shook their heads. Outsiders could think me cruel, but Mom came alive in it, even at death's door. It got us through some of the tough conversations, like this one, that she was going to die.

~

I reached Stuart from my cell phone while on my way to work.

"I was going to call you later," he said. "I'm on the road, doing my sign work." I really admired his drive to support his family. He had taken this piecemeal work on to supplement unemployment, living out of his car for much of his week.

He had been laid off and was having a really hard time finding work. He had a friend who had a franchise business applying advertising to ice machines and gas pumps, who had been throwing some work his way. It wasn't physically challenging, but he was driving far and living out of his car for days at a time. I worried about him.

"Mom is not doing well. She has pneumonia, again, and this time it's not responding to the antibiotics. The doctor is not hopeful and is suggesting I gather the troops. Do you want to come in? I'll buy the ticket with Mom's credit card."

"Do you need to know right now? I won't be back home till tomorrow night and I'll have to discuss it with Karen." Both of my brothers were married to Karens, so even with Phil's divorce there was still a Karen Keren.

"Okay. I don't think it's going to be today, probably not even tomorrow. But you never know."

"Well, if I don't make it, I'll understand … You okay?"

"Yeah." I didn't think I was, but I had to try to be productive so I just left it unexplored.

While I was on the phone with Stuart, a call from Phil had beeped in. I didn't feel like talking to him and didn't want to interrupt Stuart, so I had let it go to voicemail. As I parked my car, I played the message. "Hey. We're going to come up tomorrow. I'll work till noon and then we'll drive up. Can we stay with you?"

I didn't know who "we" was. I knew he had been dating via the internet since his last girlfriend had left him. That girlfriend, his second since the divorce, had been pretty serious. They had been talking marriage. She had two young adult children and had been previously based in California. She left my brother to go back to California to be nearer to her children. There hadn't been any talk of anyone serious and I wasn't sure that you really wanted to bring a new girlfriend to meet your mother while she was tied to tubes and oxygen, dying in a hospital bed. That was Philip.

At the hospital that evening there was little change. I was concerned I had yet to see Mom sitting in her chair. While the head of the bed was raised, doctors usually want pneumonia patients sitting upright as much as possible. The nurse told me Mom had been refusing to get out of bed.

Mom wasn't in the mood for conversation and neither was I. I told her Phil was coming in the next day.

"Why? What's he going to do?"

"Mom, he wants to see you. Do you not want company?"

"Now, I don't know. Is he coming to watch me die?"

"He's coming to cheer you up."

"That'll be a big help." She was being sarcastic and had a wicked grin.

That was not typical. Mom rarely spoke ill of Phil to me; she knew it would feed the flames. Only when she needed to complain about his church or his wife would she ever go there. Since the divorce and the way Karen had stepped up at the worst time, she would no longer complain about Karen.

"He'll probably pray for you too."

"Kill me now. If he brings Jesus here, I'll punch his lights out."

"Phil or Jesus?"

"Both."

She could barely laugh at her joke, but I did so heartily. As I was laughing, Tom rounded the corner to her room. He stopped dead in his tracks for a moment while he took in the sight.

"What's the matter?" Mom whispered. "Never seen a laughing corpse before?"

"What are you talking about Gloria, you look radiant," he said.

"You're such a bad liar … bigger bullshitter than the nurses around here."

"Mom, be nice or I'll make you share an urn with Daddy after you're gone."

She tried to throw a used tissue at me but it barely went a foot. Tom leaned in to give her a kiss.

"So what was all the laughing about?"

"Sorry, mother son joke," I said. "We could tell you but we'd have to kill you after. Better you not know for your own safety."

"Bullshit, we were laughing about Phil," my mother said.

"Oh?"

"Yeah, he's showing up tomorrow. Wants to watch me die."

"Mom, enough." Was she purposely making me defend him? Was it some devious, reverse psychology plan of hers or did she really not want him to come? I was worried she might actually say something to him; piss him off, so I would have to manage him as well as myself.

"How are you?" Mom managed to ask Tom. "You okay? How are the crazies?" That was Mom's way, today, of asking him about work. She wasn't really interested, just making conversation.

"I'm okay and they're about the same."

"Haven't you fixed them yet?" Mom had no use for psychotherapy. I think she found our work amusing in some way. But she was glad it kept us fed and housed.

"Well, as soon as I fix one, more come my way. Thank God … Enough about them, though, what did the doctors say today?"

"I can't remember that far back."

"They didn't have much new to tell us, just rest, meds, and fluids. We should go and stop wearing Mom out."

"Yeah, you trying to do me in or something?"

In the elevator I felt Tom's hand on my shoulder. I just shook my head.

"What's the matter?" he asked.

"I don't know. Aren't I supposed to be making her better, making 'it' better? I don't know what to do."

He put his arm all the way around my shoulders and hugged me tight. I just kept shaking my head.

"Are you all right to drive home?"

"Of course."

He walked me to my car. He hugged me and gave me a kiss as I got in the car. *Just have to keep moving forward*, I thought to myself.

I started the car but picked up the phone and decided to text Phil rather than call him. I didn't want to talk. "Of course, you can stay over. You have the key or you can meet me at the hospital after work." I drove home on autopilot. I have no memory of that car ride.

I was sure Mom had only days. I talked it over with Tom. I decided I should fly Laura, my niece, in. She was the closest to my mother of all her grandchildren, also the oldest. I had done my research and I could get her a flight right to Newark from Wilmington, where she was in school. It would be a cinch.

When I got to the hospital on Thursday morning, Mom's bed was empty. Of course, my first thought was that she had died during the night and they hadn't bothered to tell me. I got angry in anticipation. A hand on my shoulder startled me. It was the charge nurse. "If you're looking for your mom, Dr. Keren, she's down in X-ray."

I was relieved and confused. They had been taking Mom's daily X-rays with the portable machine, feeling she was too frail to move. "They took her down?"

"Yeah, the doctor feels you get a clearer picture. She was actually pleased to be getting to go on a trip."

I could imagine that was true. She came back while I was straightening up her tray table. "Morning, Mom."

"Really, what's good about it?"

"I didn't say Good Morning, just Morning."

"Morning."

"You have a good trip?"

"Oh yes, very exciting. Tomorrow, they're taking me to meet the queen."

"Well you better get your hair done."

It was brief banter, but it was something. She looked absolutely white. She fell asleep shortly after she got back in bed. I couldn't decide if I should stay or go. Maybe she was struggling with the same thoughts, though hers had far longer-lasting implications. As I was pulling on my coat, one of the Levines walked in.

"Good morning," he said. "How's she doing today?"

"Well, she had her X-ray. Seemed to tire her out. Fell right back to sleep."

"Yeah, that's not good," he muttered.

"So what's the plan?"

"I have to talk to Henderson (the pulmonologist), figure out if there is another med we could try. The lungs have barely cleared at all."

"Oh. If there isn't, how much time do you think she has left?"

"We're not at that point yet, don't even think like that."

"Well, your colleague told me the other day to call my family together. That it didn't look good ... She seems to be worse, not better."

"Well, I don't give up."

He wasn't making me feel any better. My mother wasn't a battle to be won, a mountain to be climbed, she was an old woman who had let him know several times her desire to go peacefully, not to be subjected to desperate measures to save her life.

"Remember, she doesn't want respirators and she's a DNR."

"Whatever."

"Not whatever, Doc. Those are her wishes and you need to follow them." Now, I felt even less comfortable leaving her here, but I had to get to work. "I have to go, but you need to remember that."

I stopped by the nurses' station on my way out to make sure Mom's living will was on the chart. It was. I told her nurse that she should be aware of it. That she was supposed to be a DNR if something happened, and she definitely did not want any respirators.

~

When I got to the hospital Thursday after work, I walked into Mom's room to find Phil sitting in the chair and his former girlfriend, Michelle, sitting on the end of the bed. I wasn't thrilled to see her. Michelle had been Phil's first girlfriend after his divorce. It had heated up very quickly. She was nice enough but had often seemed unstable. Being psychologists, Tom and I were very sensitive to people's strange behaviors. Michelle had a history of abusive relationships in the past and seemed to have struggled to free herself of her last one. She felt to us like a survivor of trauma who had not been well integrated. The relationship had gotten stormy and she left Phil as abruptly as it had heated up.

Mom appeared to be enjoying the visit but was clearly not feeling well. She was still without color. Her breathing seemed labored. I kissed her and grabbed the other chair in the room. She didn't have a roommate at this time and I was glad for that. We made small talk until Mom's food tray came. She took one look at it and pushed it away.

"Mom, at least eat the soup."

"Yech!"

"Try."

Michelle grabbed the napkin and began to tuck it under Mom's chin as a bib. I thought to myself that this would be a sight. Would Mom throw the soup at her or would she acquiesce, not wanting to be rude to someone she didn't know well?

To my surprise, she let Michelle feed her the soup. In my head I kept saying, *Here's the plane! Open the hangar!* the way Mom would feed us when we were young and being recalcitrant.

"How's the soup, Gloria?" Michelle asked.

"Not as good as mine," Mom answered.

My mother hadn't made her soup in seven years. Holidays were all in my house and the soup came from my kitchen. Of course, it was her recipe, but at this point, who followed recipes? I was pissed Michelle was calling Mom Gloria. She hadn't been back in the family five minutes. She should be calling her Mrs. Keren.

When she finished the soup, my mom actually took a few bites of the chicken before proclaiming she was too full. Michelle was careful to move the tray away from Mom, toss the napkin, and straighten the sheets.

"How was your day?" Michelle asked me.

"It was okay. Nothing special." Well, she was doing everything right. I'd have to give her a chance since she would be spending the weekend with us. Then I noticed her hand. There was an engagement ring on her finger. She saw me notice.

"Phil and I got engaged two weeks ago. Do you like it?" she asked, extending her hand so I could see it up close.

"Congratulations! When were you going to let us know, Phil? You never even told us Michelle was back in your life. Do the kids know?"

"Not yet. I want to tell them in person."

I thought to myself that was going to happen a lot sooner than he knew since I had bought Laura a plane ticket to fly up the next day. Mom was staring at the ring. I was really curious what she was thinking.

"So do you have a date for the wedding?" I asked.

"No, we haven't even thought that far ahead. I moved in with your brother just last month." I was trying to picture this. Two people living in that little one-room apartment that grew even more crowded when the kids came to visit.

"So we came to share the news with you," Phil announced. "And it's Michelle's birthday this weekend, so I thought we could all celebrate it."

"Gee, I don't think Mom is really up for a party."

"I know that. I meant you and Tom could celebrate with us."

"Oh." Ever thoughtful, my brother, so sure we didn't have other plans. It was just assumed we would entertain whoever came to visit Mom. At this point I didn't consider my brother a guest. My life was on hold enough with all the caretaking; I should be able to feel less burdened when he was here, not more.

Over dinner that evening I told him about Laura's arrival. "Oh, I know, she told me, but I changed her ticket for her. She is going to drive home to Cary and fly up together with Daniel."

I was seething inside. It wasn't that I felt Daniel wouldn't want to or need to say goodbye to Grandma, but how could Phil not even check with me? And why burden Laura with her brother? He was thirteen; he could fly by himself if he wanted to come up here. I grew sullen, holding my tongue to keep the peace.

In bed that night I whispered furiously to Tom about how I was feeling. I knew they were in the next room. They felt like intruders at this point, but I didn't want to make things more uncomfortable, especially with the kids coming the next day. Tom was patient and loving and said all the right things.

~

I stopped by the hospital to have a minute or two alone with Mom before the onslaught of visitors. "Morning, Sunshine! How ya feeling?"

I got a groan in response.

"I brought you some mini corn muffins. Wanna try one?"

Groan.

"Here." I put one on her tray and she picked at it. "So, any reactions to the news?"

"I won't live to see it. You're going to have to deal with it."

"Oh, you're so sure of that, are you? Well, I can't even think about the future beyond today. I have a birthday party to plan."

"Lucky you!" Finally, it was there. The eye roll was in her voice; she was as excited by the prospect of that relationship as I was, predicting disaster.

The X-ray tech rolled into the room with the portable machine and I had to step out. I bumped into Dr. Henderson.

"Hey, Doc."

"Oh, hey. How's the patient?"

"Not great. Seems worse today."

"Well, the X-ray should show if these new meds are working at all."

"Fingers crossed."

When the X-ray was done, I went in to say goodbye. "Mom, I'll see you later. I hope you have a good visit." We hadn't told her the kids were coming. I was hoping it would be a nice surprise and not overwhelm her fragile state.

"Have a good day. See you later."

~

When I got back to the hospital that afternoon, I got quite a shock. Mom was sitting up in a chair, eating dinner, and chatting away with the kids, who were sitting on her bed. Phil and Michelle were not there.

"Hello, Uncle Mike."

"Hey."

Both had jumped up and run to give me a hug and kiss.

Hugging them back, I said to Mom, "Look at you, like a queen with her subjects. Having a good time?"

"What a great surprise. You should have told me they were coming."

"What, and ruined it? Seems the surprise was the medicine you needed. You look well enough to go home."

"Let's not rush things, but I do feel better."

Was it the new medication or the power of love? I'll never know. I also didn't necessarily trust it: let's see if she got stronger or if this was a fluke. "So what's for dinner, there? You seem to be enjoying it."

"Meat loaf. It's all right."

I wondered how her stomach would handle it considering how little she had eaten the past week. "I think you and I are the only two people on Earth who look forward to meat loaf. What's wrong with us?"

"Nothing. We just know that if it's made well it's good. Tasty and hearty."

"Especially when we make it."

We spent the next hour or so catching up with the kids. Laura was loving college; she had so many friends to talk about and tales to tell. Daniel was quieter, giving yes and no answers to our questions about his new high school life. Phil and Michelle returned from taking a walk. The room was getting crowded. I wanted to leave, worried the crowd would tax Mom's strength, but I didn't want to miss Mom's time of being alert and involved. What if it didn't last?

~

That night we celebrated Michelle's birthday. Tom and I sprang for dinner and had bought her a little trinket. We were nothing but gracious and in return she was solicitous and friendly. Phil was smiling. I think he was looking at the scene and had visions of a happy home life to come. I wondered what the kids thought of her and this engagement. It was a lot for them to take in: that Michelle was back in his life, that they were living together and now engaged, that their beloved grandmother was sick again, that they were here to say goodbye. I longed to talk alone with them and hoped I would get the opportunity once we were back at the house.

The next day, I woke to find Michelle straightening up the kitchen and unloading the dishwasher. "Thanks, you didn't have to do that."

"Please, we are invading your home. It's the least I can do."

"Where's Phil?"

"He took the kids over to the hospital for a bit. He wants to take them into the city later today."

"Oh, okay. Do you know if you'll all be home for dinner?"

"I don't think so, but don't worry about us."

Mom's recovery lasted through the weekend. In fact, by Sunday she had taken a brief walk down the hallway with me. It tired her out, but it was a start.

By the end of the weekend, I was also feeling a bit hopeful Michelle had settled down and might, in fact, be a healthy choice for Phil. She had certainly made herself helpful this weekend. She was a bright participant in the hospital drama. She kept Phil happy and the kids didn't seem to mind her.

Phil, Michelle, and the kids left early Monday morning. Phil was going to drop the kids at the airport in Philadelphia on the way back to D.C. It seemed not only had he changed Laura's flight, he had changed the ticket from Newark to Philly to save money. So, Phil and Michele would drive up from D.C on Thursday, then three hours to Philly and back on Friday. Then when Laura and Daniel got home Laura would have to drive three more hours back to school. How inconvenient. He also asked me if Mom could send him a check for Daniel's plane fare. Nice of him to ask before spending her money.

I called work and told them I would be late and headed to the hospital. Mom was up and glad I had brought her a bagel with cream cheese, although after three bites she was finished. We chatted about the weekend.

"So, Michelle stepped up," I said. "I feel like she may be healthier than I thought."

"She was always nice to me, she just has a messed-up life."

"Well, I'm not sure it's a good idea for him to tie his life to hers, but it's his life."

"What's wrong with you, why can't you let your brother be happy?"

"Mom, it's not that at all. She has problems. He has problems. They could be the gasoline on each other's fire. I don't want to be the one to pick up the pieces."

"Why assume the worst? Let them live."

"Like you said, Mom, you're not going to be here to deal with it."

"Clearly, I'm not going to die as soon as we thought. I might leave here by my own two feet."

"From your mouth to God's ears."

"My mouth keeps praying for death … It's not God, it's the goddam doctors, have to keep saving me."

"It seems to me it was either the corn muffins Friday morning or the visit by Laura and Daniel that did it. So, do you want to blame them?"

"Of course not."

One of the Levines walked in. "Well, look at you. You look one hundred percent better. Ready to go home?"

"Are you fucking kidding? I'm lucky if I feel good a few hours a day."

He proceeded to talk as if Mom's recovery was all assured. He wanted Mom to go to a rehab to get her strength back but was arguing for one we didn't know. "We're affiliated there. We can keep watch over the treatment."

I didn't trust it and wondered if he had an ownership stake in the facility. I told him we'd think about it, but I wanted to go check it out first.

I followed him out of Mom's room. "So Doc, how are the X-rays? Is this rebound for real?"

"Absolutely."

"Well, I appreciate it. I thought we were losing her. She certainly was ready."

"I told you it was too soon to worry. That's for later."

22

AURORA'S LAST STAND?

Why is it so hard to make sure the patients have what they need? They do this all the time. No one ever puts her table where she could reach it. Whatever happened to customer service?

I had learned the phrase "the customer was always right" while training to scoop ice cream at Baskin and Robbins while I was in high school. Every sixteen- or seventeen-year-old who donned the pink and brown tunic had heard the phrase a million times.

What happened to that phrase? Does anyone know it, say it, and believe it anymore? I learned it well enough my senior year of high school, covered in all shades of ice cream. But certainly not the staff on Mom's unit. I had been calling Mom's phone for the better part of the afternoon without an answer. Her table had been moved from her bed to allow a nurse or doctor to examine her and it had not been replaced. I'd have to call someone, but why several times a day?

What happened to the days when the first staffer to pick up the phone would respond to your request, not leave you hanging in limbo listening to the hospital's advertising messages, and then accidentally disconnect your call or pass you on to some other person. No, the customer is rarely right anymore.

It was a busy day at work for me. I knew Mom was getting transferred to the rehab that day and I wanted to see how she was feeling. It had been two weeks since the Valentine's Day debacle and I wasn't taking chances. If she wasn't still progressing, then transfer be damned, I'd block it.

My phone rang and I could see it was Mom's social worker returning my call. "Hello, Dr. Keren. I got a message to call you, what's up?"

"I was wondering what time Mom was scheduled to be transferred."

"Probably around four-thirty. The doctors have to write her orders, and I believe they are planning to take one more chest X-ray."

"Okay. One more thing. Could you go by her room? I've been calling all day and nobody has answered. I'm guessing someone has moved the phone too far from her bed for her to reach it. Then if you could just call me back to tell me to call her again."

"No problem."

I liked that social worker. She always had a smile in her voice, but I couldn't hold that against her. She was very responsive. She had arranged for me to visit the rehab right after the doctor had suggested it. She had also shared some very good reviews they had gotten from other patients regarding the care there. I visited and was not as impressed by the physical plant, but the nurses seemed nice, the social worker competent, and the best thing I could report back to Mom was that they actually had an in-house therapy cat and therapy dog. Mom would be living with a cat again. It would ease the transition.

The social worker called back to say she had moved the phone back, and I called immediately before it had a chance to travel again. Mom picked up on the third ring. It was a faint voice. "Hello?"

"Mom, it's Mike. Are you okay?"

"I don't know. I don't think I feel well and I haven't been able to get out of bed."

Here we go again, a repeat of Valentine's weekend. Who should I call first? I was trembling so inside, I could hardly think. This was rage. Last time I was this pissed at the hospital I almost ended up in handcuffs.

Deep breaths ... I dialed the nurses' station. It rang for an eternity. Actually, five rings, but that was still an eternity. "Hello! Fifth-floor Telemetry Unit, how can I help you?"

"Hi, it's Dr. Keren, again. I need to speak with my mother's nurse. It's urgent!"

"Dr. Keren, she's busy. She'll need to call you back."

"No, I'll hold or you can connect me to the supervisor."

"Hold on!" Then there was dead air; no elevator music and no annoyingly pleasant voice announcing the awards and commendations received by each of the hospital departments, as if that would convince me to believe this was quality care. I had been disconnected. My rage was increasing. Deep breaths.

"Hello, Fifth-floor Telemetry Unit, how can I help you?"

"You cannot disconnect me again!"

"I'm sorry, who is this?"

"This is Dr. Keren. I am going to speak to my mother's nurse or the charge nurse or the Director of Nursing and you are not going to put me on hold and you are not going to disconnect me again!"

"Just a moment." That was it, no apology, and no explanation. I could hear the muffled talking as she covered the receiver with her hand.

"Dr. Keren, this is the charge nurse. How can I help you?"

"Hi. So my mom is scheduled to go to her rehab in an hour or so, but she just told me she is not feeling well, that she has not been out of bed all day, and she has not been able to eat. I really don't want her to be discharged too soon, even to rehab. You discharged her two weeks ago before she was ready and she ended up back there less than forty-eight hours later."

"Dr. Keren, I'm sure the doctors wouldn't discharge your mother if she wasn't better."

"Really, what makes you so sure?"

"Dr. Keren, they're very professional and have been at this for a long time."

"Yes, and they also answer to a hospital administration that wants to see turnover in their beds because of limited reimbursements. That's why she's back with you in the first place."

"Well, what would you like me to do?"

"I'd like you to have one of the Levines come examine her before she is transported."

"The doctors do their rounds in the morning."

"Well, then they will have to come special to see her, or send an associate, but I am not going to let my mother leave that place without her being seen by her doctors. I will cancel her transfer myself if I have to."

"Dr. Keren, please calm down. How about if I go check on your mother myself and call you back?"

I was steaming. The more she said, the worse this got. I wanted to have Mom seen by her doctors, not this nurse. When she asked me if her following up on Mom would help me feel better, I knew Aurora would be there soon.

"I feel fine," I said. "… Maybe a little aggravated that you're condescending to me, but fine."

"Sorry, that wasn't my intent. I'm just trying to clear this up for you."

"Okay, but please, call me back quickly. I want to leave work and be there at the transfer."

"Definitely, hang tight five minutes."

The phone rang six minutes and seventeen seconds later.

"I understand you've been trying to reach me."

"I'm sorry, who is this?"

"This is your mother's nurse from the hospital."

"Well, I was, but I gave up and was talking with your charge nurse. I was just waiting for her to call me back."

"Oh, I know, she told me you were upset and asked me to call you." If I squeezed the receiver any harder it would have burst in my hands. I was being passed around.

"Yeah?"

"Well, I just came from your mother's room. She's fine, she just wanted a corn muffin."

If this wasn't *Candid Camera* and Allen Funt wasn't waiting to surprise me, heads were going to roll.

"My mother is seventy-nine years old, she is college educated and has held responsible positions in the world of business. She knows the difference between not feeling well and wanting a corn muffin. I am coming over, will be there within forty-five minutes. I do not want her transferred until she has been seen by one of her doctors and until I get there. If she is gone when I get there, I will have your license. I promise you that."

"Sir, her ambulance will be here in fifteen minutes to take her to the rehab. I think you are being unreasonable."

"Unreasonable? … Try me."

In the car I dialed the rehab center and had an exchange with the social worker. I explained what I thought was happening.

"So, I think they are trying to dump her on you. We went through this two weeks ago; they discharged her despite her insistence she didn't feel right and she ended up in the hospital a day and a half later twice as sick as when she first went in. I don't want to see her get there and then not be able to do her rehab because she is too sick. I don't think she has all that many days of coverage left."

"Dr. Keren, I understand your concerns, but we are very well staffed and can take care of most anything that happens."

"It's nothing personal. If I didn't have confidence in your nursing staff, we would not be having this conversation. I'm looking forward to my mom working with you, but when she is well enough to benefit from it. Please, do not accept the transfer until you hear back from me."

"This is highly unusual."

"In what way? That my mother has an involved, aware, and caring son? That I am challenging the recommendation of the doctor who has not seen my mother in at least ten hours? In that I'm trying to give you the chance to avoid a problem? Or that as her medical proxy I am dictating quality care and treatment for her?"

"I'll await your call, Dr. Keren."

"Thank you."

That was only somewhat frustrating, I thought to myself. Thank God for cell phones. What would I do if I couldn't make these calls driving up the turnpike? It would be a year or two before talking on the phone would be outlawed in your car.

I tried Mom's room. The phone rang and rang. Either the idiots had moved her phone again, she was down for tests, or she was dead and they weren't trying to reach me. I would put my money on the first, but the last wasn't far from possible.

When I got to her room, Mom was lying in bed. The sheets were falling off the top corners and her pillows were all askew. I started to straighten out the pillows. "How are you feeling?"

"I told you before, I don't feel well at all."

"Has the doctor been in since we talked? I asked the nurse to call them to see you before you go to the rehab."

"No, I saw the nurse a while ago. She kept trying to feed me. Finally, I took a corn muffin from her, took a bite, and dropped the rest on the floor when she wasn't looking. I think it's still under the bed."

Mom's nurse came in the room. Mom introduced me to the nurse, who turned to me and said, "See, she's fine. I told you there was nothing to worry about."

"Does she look fine to you? Have you asked her how she feels? She is white as a ghost, has a fever, and is too weak to move a pillow. I'm sorry but you seem to be totally incompetent."

"Well, you think your mother is a joy to work with?" Clearly, she didn't recognize that Aurora was with me.

"Get out. Get away from me and from her." I was screaming at this point and glad this hospital only had security and not a police force. The nurse backed out of the room.

It took only seconds for the unit manager to be in the doorway. "Dr. Keren, please calm down, you're upsetting your mother."

"Just keep that nurse away from this room and get my mother's doctor here as I've been asking for two hours."

She closed the door. "This is the first I'm hearing of any problem. What's going on?"

I explained my daylong frustration of trying to reach my mother, the constant issue of the phone being moved out of her reach, and of the apparent repeat of the discharge disaster from two weeks ago. Then I went into the runaround I had gotten from Mom's nurse and the charge nurse and the preposterous story about my mother needing a muffin.

"I'm so sorry, Dr. Keren. Let me go to my office and see if I can reach one of the Levines and I'll send someone in to remake your mom's bed."

"Thank you. I appreciate that. Would you also send the director of nursing? I'd really like to speak with her."

"If you feel you must, I will. But do know that I will deal with today's nurses as well."

After she left, Mom turned to me and said, "Please don't make trouble for me. They're just doing their job."

"Mom, if they were doing their job, there would have been a doctor here an hour ago to check on you. I want to know you are all right and healthy enough to go to rehab."

"But you're getting so angry."

"Mom, do you know what your nurse said to me earlier, after we talked? She told me you were fine and just needed a corn muffin. A corn muffin."

"That's ridiculous!"

"Exactly! That's why my pal Aurora came to visit." Mom looked at me puzzled and I explained about Aurora.

Eventually, the Levines' associate came in. I was glad it was her; she was so much easier to talk to and seemed to respect my opinions. She listened to Mom's heart and lungs, then scanned the chart. "Could you excuse me a moment? I want to check her last X-ray and consult with Howard."

She returned about ten minutes later. "Okay. So we've cancelled the transfer, and in fact we are going to transfer your mom's care to her pulmonologist as this is really more of a pulmonary matter."

"Wait. In the ER you told me you wanted Dr. Henderson to manage the case, but then nothing happened. I mean he's been involved, but now you want to dump her?" I should've shut up since I trusted Dr. Henderson so much more.

"We're not dumping her, Dr. Keren, it's just that while she may be having a bit of a setback, her heart is fine and she doesn't need to stay on the telemetry unit. If we transfer her to a med-surg floor or to the pulmonary unit, she'll receive the care she needs and free this bed up for someone who needs telemetry. Of course, we will still do rounds on her every day."

"So, she's going to move to a different floor?"

"Yes. The nurses are checking on a bed and getting Dr. Henderson on the phone as we speak."

As her response was calming me down, I offered an apology. She, in turn, acknowledged I was concerned and was not upset that my care might make her job a bit less easy.

After she left, I looked at Mom. She had fallen asleep again. I ran to the candy machine to get some chips and bumped into Mom's endocrinologist. He seemed very surprised to see me.

"You're Gloria Keren's son, right?" he asked.

"You got it!" I really didn't feel like small talk just then.

"So what brings you to the hospital today?"

"Oh, I'm visiting my mom."

"What, no one told me she was here. How long? Whose service is she on?"

So, my mom had been in this hospital for two weeks and no one had bothered to fill in her endocrinologist. Considering the Levines had made the referral to him, I would have thought they would include him in her care.

I left him at the nurses' station checking her chart. Mom was awake when I got back. "Still here," I said.

"Well, I did go out to the movies while you were gone, but they only had message movies, so I didn't stay."

She was joking, but her tone said it was only half-hearted. "No, Mom, they're going to move you to another floor because you don't need to be constantly monitored. I was just referring to that."

"Oh. I thought I was leaving today."

She seemed confused. It was distressing to say the least. "Mom, you had said you didn't feel well. I had the doctor check you out and they have decided to let you stay."

"Oh, thanks." Another weak attempt at sarcasm. The endocrinologist popped his head in.

"Hi, Gloria. Mike told me you were here. Sorry I didn't know sooner, I would've come sooner. I was just reviewing your numbers and everything looks good." He smiled at Mom, turned, and left.

"Who was that?" Mom asked.

"Your diabetes doctor. You didn't recognize him?"

"Nah, they all blend together after a while."

I flipped on the TV. Mom and I watched the news for a bit. Nothing too exciting except for a possible snowstorm over the weekend. This had been a long February; that would just be the cherry on the sundae.

Tom popped in and I glanced at my watch. It was almost nine o'clock and still no word on when the move would happen. I had been here four hours.

Tom joined us in our TV staring. Nobody really talked. After an hour I just couldn't keep my eyes open. I walked over to the nurses' station. "Excuse me. Any word on when my mom is moving?"

"No, sorry."

"Well, I think I'm going to head home. Please, when she gets moved, call me at home. Leave me a message. Let me know she's moved and where to."

"Yeah. Yeah. Of course we will." I didn't trust her for a moment.

I walked back in the room. "Tom, you have a piece of paper and a marker or pen in your bag?"

"Yeah. Why?"

"Never mind why, just let me have it."

He handed me the paper. I started to write.

"PLEASE! NO MATTER WHAT TIME, CALL MRS. KEREN'S SON MICHAEL WHEN SHE IS MOVED. IT IS OK TO LEAVE A MESSAGE!" I signed it and added my phone number. I walked to the nurses' station, reached over, grabbed their tape, and requested they tape it to the front of my mother's chart. I watched as they did it.

"Thank you," I said.

"You're welcome."

Tom and I walked to our cars in silence.

23

Oatmeal

The alarm went off and I jumped from bed. I kept my clock on the other side of the room to prevent my hitting the snooze button or tearing it out of the wall. It being February the sun was not yet lightening the sky at six o'clock. Tom would not be getting up for two hours and I hated for my alarm to disturb his slumber. I turned on the shower to heat up and ran the razor over my face, not really caring if it had an effect or not. All I really cared about was that the phone had not rung all night. Had my mother been moved or not? Did they totally ignore my note and my wishes?

Drying off after my shower I checked the phone again; still no message. I threw some clothes on and went in the next room to call the unit. Funny, in the comfort of my own home, I felt the need to be dressed in order to speak on the phone.

They picked up on the fourth ring. "Hello, Fifth-floor Telemetry, can I help you?"

"Hi, this is Mike Keren, Mrs. Keren's son. When I left the unit last night there was a plan to move my mother to the fourth floor. I had left instructions in a note on her chart to call me when she was moved, no matter the time. I haven't heard anything. Was my mom moved?"

"Hold on, Mr. Keren, let me check." I was thankful I wasn't hearing the usual on-hold message with all the advertising and self-promoting gobbledy-gook, but the silence always left me wondering if I had been hung up on. It felt like an hour but was probably only ninety seconds until she came back on. "Mr. Keren, I'm seeing her listed in five eighty-two."

"Five eighty-two, that's not the fourth floor." I could feel the tension rising in my body like the line on a thermometer, and with it, the accompanying creeping irritation in my voice.

"Five eighty-two is an ICU bed. It seems she was moved about twelve-thirty last night to the fourth floor but was rushed to the ICU shortly after that."

"ICU, what happened, what's going on?"

"Sorry, Mr. Keren, I don't have that information."

"Well, who does? Can I speak to them?"

"Let me connect you to the fourth-floor nurses' station."

I was on hold before I could thank her. It was answered quickly. "Hello, fourth floor, Med-Surg, how can I help you?"

"Hi, this is Mike Keren, Gloria Keren's son. My mother was transferred to your unit last night and then was rushed to the ICU. I'm trying to find out what happened."

"I'm sorry but all the nurses are busy right now. Why don't you leave your number and I'll have them call you back when they are available?"

"Like they called me last night when my mother was moved? Like they called me when my mother was rushed to the ICU? Don't bother, let me just ask you one question. Is it hospital policy to not call a patient's next of kin or their medical proxy when there is an emergency and they are rushed to the ICU? Is it?"

"Of course not, Dr. Keren. I'm just coming on my shift so I can't tell you what happened, but I can understand why you're upset. If you want to hold on again, I can see what I can find out for you."

"No, thank you. I think I better get down there." I clicked off my cell phone and went into the bedroom to wake Tom.

"My mother's in the ICU. I have to run to the hospital."

"ICU, what happened?"

"Exactly what I want to know. Nobody seems to want to tell me."

"What do you … Never mind. You better get up there. Are you okay to drive?"

"If not, I'll just share an ICU room with Mom."

"Hold on, I'll get dressed."

"No. I'll be okay, just keep your cell phone handy."

Of course, I got behind every school bus between home and the hospital but it gave me time to rehearse my outrage. There was no telling how high it would go. I could feel it pressing on the inside of my skull and wondered if it was possible to really "blow one's top." As I searched for parking, I was trying to figure out where to go first—the ICU, the fourth floor, the Telemetry Unit? Everyone deserved a piece of this for their lack of communication. I gave up my search and handed my key to one of the valet parkers. "I don't know how long I'll be here."

I charged into the hospital, past the greeters and the information desk and banged on the elevator button. I knew I should go see Mom, but I had to dump some anger first. I got in the box and pressed four. I found the nurses' station quickly and demanded to see the nurse in charge.

"What happened to my mom and why did I have to call into her old unit to know she was in ICU?" I restrained myself from jumping across the counter.

"You're Mr. Keren, I presume?" she said, sounding rather smug.

"No, I'm Dr. Keren, so you presumed wrongly. Now it's my turn … you're the nurse in charge, I presume."

"Mr. Keren, your mom was transferred down here early in the morning. A short time later, while the nurse was doing rounds, she found your mother to be unresponsive. The doctors were called and the decision was made to move her to the ICU."

"Why was she unresponsive? What doctors? Why wasn't I called? When you say unresponsive, was she in a coma? Breathing?"

"My, you do have a lot of questions, don't you?"

She had to be kidding, was she really going to play these games? "Yes, I do. And since you apparently are not going to answer them for me, I guess I will have my lawyer get the answers."

"No need to get snippy!"

"I'm leaving now. Someone needs to be concerned about my mother and clearly it is too much to expect of you. Let me just say one thing … It is my only hope for you that someday you are in my shoes and someone condescends to you when you need them.'

~

I found the ICU and a helpful young man in scrubs directed me towards my mother's bed. I knew this ICU because it was where we had kept vigil over my father three years before, but this section was not familiar to me. It was a ward-like area with a bed in each corner and a large nurses' area to one side. I saw my mother lying in the far-right corner. As I approached her bed, I could see she had very little color in her face. She was wearing an oxygen mask and there were a myriad of wires and tubes running from her body to several monitors that were beeping away and collection bags filled with urine and other colorful fluids. She wasn't moving and her eyes were closed. I had seen her looking worse only one other time, when she had first come out of her triple bypass all those years ago. That time there were far more tubes and even more wires.

An attractive middle-aged woman in floral scrubs approached me. "Are you Mrs. Keren's son?" she asked. I nodded. She glanced around the room. "I hope you have a good lawyer."

I was stunned by her comment. Going from the callousness and procedure-ridden rigidity of the staffs on Telemetry and the fourth floor to a nurse making a statement to me that could cost her the job I could see she clearly loved, amazed me. While I might expect her comment would have riled me up, it actually relaxed me a bit. I was choking back tears. "So what happened?"

"The best I can tell your mom was given her insulin last night, about ten-thirty, before change of shift. She had both the long and short acting, as she gets each evening. I'm not sure what she had eaten that evening since they had stopped recording her input and output when she was removed from the monitors. For some reason, after the transfer, she received the same doses, again. When the nurses found her, she was probably in a state of insulin shock."

I knew well what that looked like. Nine years before Mom and Dad had travelled north for my fortieth birthday party. The night before the party my parents were having a fancy dinner for me with a few of my friends.

Mom hated taking her insulin in public so she took it before they left the hotel. But, it was rush hour and they got stuck in traffic. When they finally arrived and we were reading the menus, I saw Mom's head fall forward and her arm raise strangely up in the air. I charged into action: called the EMTs and asked them to come. Over the phone they suggested it might be due to the insulin and not a stroke. I fed her some juice while Tom fished her glucose tabs out of her purse. By the time the EMTs arrived, she was back among the living.

Since it wasn't a stroke and she seemed to have recovered, she didn't need to go to the hospital. We continued with dinner.

"That's it, we're going home tomorrow," my father said.

"You can go home tomorrow, but I'm staying to party!" Mom told him in no uncertain terms.

The next day the party went off without a hitch. Everyone had a great time and my parents had a new horror story with which to regale the masses. More than any other health crisis of my mother's, though, that evening seemed to be a dividing point between living with her diseases and dying from them.

The nurse continued, "She was showing a tremor and someone decided it was a seizure, so the doctor ordered Dilantin. Well, the Dilantin caused her already low blood pressure to plummet. It fell to forty-five over twenty-five. That's when they decided to move her here. We are stabilizing her blood pressure with saline solutions and her glucose with a glucose drip. Her heart is still strong and she's breathing fairly well on her own."

"Okay. Is she still unconscious, what's the status on that?"

"Well, consciousness is not an either/or proposition, but your mother is pretty far from alertness. But I think we'll be able to rouse her."

"Okay. You know she is a DNR and does not want a respirator, right?"

"Yes, Dr. Keren, well aware, but we're not in need of one at this point."

"Well, no desperate measures. She would never agree to tube feedings for life either. And by the way, *you* can call me Mike." I was impressed by this nurse's care and concern. I felt respected, informed, and included. Secretly, I was hoping she'd be my mom's nurse for the rest of time. "Is there anything else you need from me?"

"Dr. Keren, Mike, I think we have it all. That medical history in her chart is so thorough." I smiled to myself. Although my father had actually begun the document, I had been meticulously maintaining it and delivering it to doctors and Emergency Rooms across New Jersey through this whole ordeal. "I can't tell you how much we wish every patient came with something like that."

The nurse left me alone with Mom. I took her hand. Her hands were rarely warm so I made little of its coolness. I talked to her softly. "Mom, don't know if you can hear me." The Hollywood in me was watching for a sign—an eye blink, a squeeze of my hand, her getting up and doing the Charleston—but nothing. "I'm sorry. I'm sorry this is happening. If I had let you go to rehab yesterday … just maybe you'd be okay now. You'd be playing with the cat. Now, it's more hospitals, more tests. If you're done, it's okay to go. You can let go." I was lying, sort of. Of course, if she died I was going to be okay. But I was selfish, I wanted her to live, I wanted to keep taking care of her. What would I do without her, without that? She and it and my marriage were my life. Who would I be?

I gave her a kiss and stepped off the unit to the visitor's lounge. I took out my cell phone and dialed Stu. "Stu, it's Mike. Mom's in the ICU. They gave her too much medication last night and put her into a coma. I think you should come. Besides, I need you."

"Of course. Let me talk with Karen. I'll get back to you when I know more. Are you okay?"

"Yeah, a bit freaked out. Long story, I'll explain later. I'm glad you're going to come."

Stu hung up and I quickly dialed Phil. "Hey Mike, what's up?"

I could tell he was in the car. "Mom didn't get to rehab last night, she's in the ICU."

There was silence on the other end of the phone. "What happened?"

"It's a long story, medication mistake, I think you should get here, ASAP."

"All right. I'll turn around, go home to pack a bag and pick up Michelle. We should be there by one-thirty or two."

"Okay, don't speed. I don't think it's an any-moment thing. I'll talk to you later."

Looking around, I took in the scene. The waiting room was even shabbier than I remembered it from when my father was a patient on the ICU. The room could get busy as whole families camped out there for days. The rules of the ICU were two visitors at a time with a limit of fifteen minutes every two hours. I had no intention of following their rules. As far as I was concerned this place owed me. We were here because of their doing. I was not going to sit in this dreary room with worn, industrial-gray carpeting, butcher-block furniture in aging yellow and orange pleather, and a TV blaring FOX News twenty-four hours a day. I nodded to the Indian couple just spreading out their breakfast and walked back to the unit.

As I rounded the corner to the area where Mom was, I could see a nurse and an orderly over her bed. The nurse was gently shaking Mom's shoulder. As I got closer I could hear her. "Gloria, Gloria, come on, time to get up. Can you open your eyes? Gloria, if you hear me, open your eyes for me ..." and as I rounded the corner, "Look, here comes your son, Michael."

"Hi, Mom. Can you hear me? The nurse needs you to open your eyes now."

They had Mom's bed cranked up so her head was a bit elevated. Her face was somewhat responsive to what they were saying. "Mom, come on, you have a new room. I want you to see the view." Her eyes began to flutter.

"That's a good girl, Gloria, let's see you open them all the way," the nurse said.

Mom's eyes popped open and she stared hard for several seconds before they fluttered closed again. "That's it, Mom. Get angry. It'll make you feel better." The nurse gave me a quizzical look. "She didn't like you calling her 'good girl,' she hates being condescended to, tired of all the hospitals."

"So sorry, Gloria, just trying to bring you back among us. You've had a very difficult night."

Mom was much more alert now and her eyes were alternating between open and closed. She had even given me a smile.

"Mom, you're in Intensive Care. You had a problem with your insulin last night and then your blood sugar dropped. They brought you up here to monitor you closer ... do you understand what I'm saying?"

"I'm not stupid." It was slurred and quiet but it was Mom: angry, defensive, and sarcastic.

"We almost lost you," the nurse said.

"I wish had," Mom muttered. I noted the missing pronoun. "Enough."

"But Gloria, you're doing better, you have to eat something." The tech came back with a bowl of oatmeal. "Do you like anything in your oatmeal? Milk, sugar?"

Mom closed her eyes. This could be a struggle. "She doesn't like oatmeal, never has. I doubt she'll eat it."

"But Gloria, you have to eat. You need to get your strength back. Just open up." The tech meant well. She was doing her job and was probably too young and naïve to imagine that someone might not want to fight for their lives. She tried to spoon a spoonful of the mush into Mom's mouth. Mom clenched her lips.

Mom had a favorite story she would tell of her youth. It served to show how obstinate she could be, even as a child. Her mother used to make her hot cereal all the time. She enjoyed Wheatena, Cream of Wheat, even grits, but she detested oatmeal. One day, during the Depression, her mother was out of those and made a bowl of oatmeal for my mother. My mother refused to eat it. It was a game of wills as my grandmother told her that until she ate that bowl of oatmeal, she would get nothing else for any breakfast. For four days in a row Mom came to the table to find the now coagulated and hardening oatmeal reheated and sitting in a bowl at her place. On the fifth morning (sometimes Mom would claim it was starting to mold), she still refused to eat the oatmeal. Her frustrated mother picked up the bowl and dumped it on her head. Uneaten, my mom cleaned up the mess, cleaned herself off and never, ever found oatmeal at her place at the breakfast table again. Mom told the story as if she had won. If my grandmother had lived to tell it, I always wondered how it would go.

The tech had gotten a spoonful of oatmeal into my mom's mouth. She seemed proud of herself, but I could see the oatmeal was not being swallowed. As she started to scrape together another spoonful, my mother let the oatmeal fall from her mouth onto the sheet. She smiled at me. "Oh, Gloria, was that too big a spoonful? Let's try a smaller amount."

It was like watching a train wreck. How long should I let this young woman go on? "Maybe you should bring her something she does like. I bet you she would eat that."

"But this is what they sent up from the kitchen."

That sort of angered me because I knew the kitchen was very responsive and would send up a substitute quickly if requested. "Well, she'll never eat that. Cream of Wheat, maybe. Yogurt. Even some Jell-O or pudding, but not oatmeal."

"I'll keep trying. Now Gloria, open up." Mom let her put the oatmeal in her mouth and then did her best to spit it back. She was too weak to get much distance, but her message was clear. The orderly gave up and walked away, dejected.

I followed her. I felt bad because I had kind of enjoyed the struggle, but she was an earnest worker and wanted to make a difference. "Don't feel bad. You really tried and that's better than some of your colleagues. But you need to learn to listen to your patients, especially here. They don't all want to fight to get better. Some may be at the end of long or serious illnesses and may want to just be kept comfortable. Others just need to feel like they are still people."

"What do you mean?" she asked.

"For instance, you are very young; my mother is of a generation where one used titles of respect when there were generations separating you. Try calling her Mrs. Keren. She'll appreciate it and let you know if you can then call her Gloria."

"I'm sorry. I was just …"

"I know. And you were doing it well. Now just try being a person at the same time. It's not as hard as it seems. The patients will appreciate it." I smiled at her and she smiled back.

I ran down to the cafeteria and grabbed a cup of yogurt. I was glad it was a flavor Mom liked. I popped it open and began to offer her little spoonfuls. She took them in. I could see the tech eyeing us from her seat nearby. I nodded and she nodded back. Mom ate about a half of it before pushing it back towards me. I wiped her lips and rested the yogurt on her tray. She asked me for tea. I asked the nurse if it would be okay and got her approval to make a weak cup of tea.

Mom took a few sips. "Feeling a bit better?" I asked.

"Where am I?"

"Oh, Mom, don't you remember what I told you? You're in Intensive Care."

"How'd I get here?" Her voice was stronger than before, but a long way from what it had been even the day before when I was questioning if she should leave the hospital.

I was holding her hand and recounted the story. She started to cry. "Mom, why are you crying?"

"I'm just tired of putting you through this."

"Through what, Mom? I'm not complaining. What else was I going to do today?"

She laughed, but continued, "You have your job, your life. I'm done. I just can't die. I don't know why, it just won't happen."

"Maybe it's not your time yet. Maybe there is a God and he or she has a plan for you."

Mom snickered. She was a Jew when the Jews were threatened but she didn't believe in God, or feminism, so the snicker could have been about the idea of God in general or at the idea of a female God. I on the other hand did believe, and if God was gendered often argued that God must be male because if God were female things wouldn't be so messed up in the world.

"Yeah, his plan is to make me suffer from the age of three until I finally get to escape."

"Probably revenge for your comments back in Sunday school. Never fuck with a vengeful God."

I laughed to myself. I certainly knew she wasn't a happy camper, ever, but I know there were many things she had enjoyed. Even recently, her grandchildren, her time with Tom and me, there were plenty of smiles and laughs.

"Okay, so I know you're tired, and you can always refuse treatment, but let's wait and see what the tests say." I wasn't saying it but I was sure there had been further neurological damage in the last twelve hours. I could hear it in her language and see it in the way she was moving in the bed.

My phone rang and I saw it was Phil. I let it go to voicemail, but he rang back very quickly. I stepped away and took the call in the hallway. "What's the matter, Phil?"

"She's gone." He sounded panicked and crying. I couldn't remember ever hearing him cry.

"What? Who's gone? What's going on?"

"I stopped by work to let them know I'd be out and pick up some work I need to do and then I went home to pick up Michelle. She wasn't there. There was a note with the engagement ring I gave her. She left me." The tears were coming now. We had been right not to trust her. Her timing couldn't be worse.

"Did you guys have an argument?"

"No. I'm in shock. She just packed up all her stuff and left."

"That bitch. I knew she was crazy." He didn't respond. "I'm sorry, that probably wasn't helpful."

"I don't know what to do."

"Well, you don't sound like you're in shape to drive. Maybe you should stay put."

"But Mom. She needs us."

I assured him we could hold the fort until the next day. I was thinking to myself that I had enough on my hands; I didn't need him crying and moping on top of this unraveling catastrophe at the hospital. I didn't want to take care of him. But he was insistent he wanted to be with us.

"Okay, why don't you look into taking a train or flying up? You shouldn't be driving. Also, call a locksmith and change the locks at your place. You don't need her coming in and stealing your stuff."

"She wouldn't do that."

"No, she'd just dump you on what is probably one of the most difficult days in your life, with your mother dying in Intensive Care. Yeah, she wouldn't do that."

"Okay, see your point, I'll change the lock. I'll call you back with an update."

As soon as I hung up, my phone rang again. It was Stu.

"Wassup?"

"Karen and I are at the airport. There's storms out here and our plane is delayed a few hours, but I think we'll get there by tonight."

"Okay. She's doing a little better. She's alert. Not sure if there was permanent damage from last night though."

'Well, at least she's awake. Is she cooperating?"

"She's trying to be good."

Stu laughed at that. We both knew exactly what that meant. "I'll call you when we're boarding. Hang in there. Give Mom my love."

"Will do."

I got back by my mom's area. One of the Levines was there. "Hey, Mike. Was just trying to chat with your mom. We've got some labs back and we're trying to make sense of them. Good news is her kidneys are still working the way they're supposed to. Her blood sugar is coming back up and her blood pressure is stabilized at a workable place. There's a little problem with her clotting factor. Her blood doesn't seem to want to clot. I've asked for a consult with a blood guy. I have no idea what that might mean."

"No clue at all? What does it usually mean?"

"I don't have an answer and I don't want to speculate. Right now your mom is stable, but the fluids, tubes, and medications are what's keeping her there. We're going to run a few more tests."

"Doc, could you get a neurological consult while you're at it? I really feel her cognitive functioning is not where it was yesterday."

"Ever the psychologist, always worried about the brain."

"Well, Doc, someone has to." It was a subtle dig, not even sure he got it. Months before, Mom had a neurological incident that he and his partner had failed to let me know about.

"Mom is always concerned with her ability to live and function and if there was any damage from last night's incident, we'd want to make educated decisions about how much treatment to pursue."

"Right now, I'd like to start her on tube feedings. She needs more calories to get her strength up."

"Did she agree to that?" I looked her way. "What would that entail?"

She was shaking her head pretty vigorously. "We would put a tube down her nose and give her liquid nutrients several times a day." The pace of the head shaking was picking up. Did he not see it?

"Well, you might want to ask her about that, not sure she'd want that."

"Gloria? Don't say 'No!' I heard about the oatmeal. You have to eat something."

"Doctor, I'd have said no, too. Oatmeal is her least favorite food in the whole world. I brought her yogurt and she ate that. Give her food she likes and she'll eat it. If she is saying no to the tube, I'll support her with that."

Neither of the Levines appreciated my advocating for my mother. They could be cowboys who focused on the illness and not the person. I was making him feel threatened, and he suggested we were stupid not to take the feeding tube.

"Well, Doc, maybe you're right. It sounds kind of gross to me, but maybe it's really not a big deal. Why don't you insert one on yourself next time you come back and let her see how easy and comfortable it will be? That might help." He gave me a sneer as he was leaving the room. "Don't forget the neurological consult," I added.

Mom looked at me, smiled, and said, "Thank you."

I had to laugh. "I knew that fight was going to be a losing battle, so let's get some results back and see what's happening." Only after the doctor left the room did it strike me that the Levines seemed to still be running the show.

24

ANUBIS

Mom and I were sitting there quietly. Catty-corner to Mom's bed there was a woman who was on a respirator. She looked to be about five years older than Mom, in her mid-eighties. There was a respiratory team attending to her; apparently, they were trying to wean her off the respirator. I wondered if she knew in her unconsciousness how many staff were attending to her at that time. I watched as they disconnected the tube in her throat from the machine to allow her to breathe on her own. They watched their watches; within seconds one of her monitors began to beep. They reconnected her tube. Mission failed. I listened in to their conversations because I was nosy. They had been trying to do this twice a day for the last four days. At her age, did they expect this to work? Was this a life that would be lived if they did get her off the machines? I knew I was glad my wishes were clear to those who loved me: no machines.

Realizing I hadn't updated him since I left that morning, I sent a quick text to Tom. "Things stable. Come as soon as you're free, I could use your company." If he were with patients, he was more likely to see a text than answer the phone.

A few more doctors trickled by as the afternoon progressed. At four o'clock I heard from Stu that they were boarding a flight and should be in by six-thirty. They'd get a car at the airport. Phil decided to take a train and he would cab over from the station, which was nearby.

The other Levine came by mid-afternoon. He started again with tube feedings and Mom told him to get out. He suggested parenteral feedings. We both looked puzzled, so he described a process where a port was inserted into a vein through which my mother would receive her nutrition: lipids, protein, and vitamins. There was a high risk of infection, however, with parenteral feedings.

"I don't want it."

"Why not?" he asked Mom.

"If I can't chew my food or even taste it, what is the point? That is not living."

"But Gloria, I'm not saying it's permanent."

"So you're saying it won't be?"

He was silent for a bit as we waited for his answer. "We can't be sure."

Mom glazed over, tuning him out. I asked about test results and the neurological consult. Now he looked lost.

Mom squeezed my hand tight. She was telling me to take a deep breath before I spoke. "When your partner was in this morning, I mentioned she seemed to be having some cognitive problems. They haven't cleared all day, and I asked him to order a neurological consult to get a reading. It would really help us to make some decisions about treatment moving forward."

"Yeah, yeah, sure."

He stopped by the desk and I saw him jot in Mom's chart before he left.

I looked at Mom. She had fallen asleep, but you could see the trail of a tear that had run down her cheek.

I asked the nurse if the doctor had left an order for the neuro consult. She checked the book and confirmed what I already knew: he hadn't.

Mom was spent, not just by this episode but also by the last two years of hospitalizations, procedures, impersonal treatment, and her withdrawal from life. I knew she would have limited patience for testing and prodding, that if she was not going to go home, at some point she would probably stop all treatment and choose hospice. I would not bring it up without answers, and without input from my brothers. On the other hand, if I was just overpathologizing and Mom was functioning where she had been the day before, I'd stand with the doctors and encourage her to take her meds.

Tom came in and I brought him up to speed. He suggested we ask someone we trusted for an opinion about the feedings. Mom knew our gastroenterologist; we had called him in for Dad's treatment on the last hospitalization. We placed a call to Dr. Rosen. Luck was on our side. He was in the hospital and they would have him come by her room.

~

I had run home to walk the dog. When I returned about an hour and a half later, Stu and Karen were there sharing pictures of the kids with Mom's nurses. The shift must have changed because I didn't know any of the nurses. They didn't seem to mind that we were all there. There also was a new patient in the bed next to her. This new woman didn't speak English and the nurse was having a translator assist her in getting her settled. She had two people with her who I assumed were grown children or child-in-laws; they did not seem to want to be there.

When Phil arrived the party was complete. He got a good deal of sympathy from the nurses. I guess my telling the earlier shift the story of his getting dumped on this morning of all mornings had been passed along in report. If Mom was aware of what was being talked about, she didn't indicate it.

Mom was drifting in and out of sleep. I asked the nurse if she would order her some soft-scrambled eggs, I thought we could get her to eat them. Throw some broth and a tea in also. I was right. Mom ate about half of the eggs, drank some of the tea, and a few sips of broth under our coaching. Watching her eat I realized how hungry I was and suggested we all go get some dinner.

There was a lot of chatter over dinner. Most of it I didn't participate in as I was just trying to keep my head out of my plate. I was tired. Phil got the sympathy he needed from Stu and Karen while I threw in some venomous comments about Michelle. She was as good a target as any right then. I was glad we were all together. It felt right, somehow. I didn't feel angry with any of them. I wasn't even anticipating being disappointed by them if I asked them to do something while they were here.

After dinner we went back to the hospital. We were all sitting around Mom's bed and she was enjoying the company. I wasn't sure how much she was keeping up with the conversation. She just liked having us all there. In the opposite corner her neighbor on the ventilator was being visited by her son and daughter-in-law. Tom was sure he knew them, and he probably did. After twenty-three years with Tom, I was used to him seeing people he knew wherever we went: the theater, restaurants, Europe, even Disney World. At least he had not gone up to them to play the "Don't I know you game" as they were angrily engaged with the nurses. I listened to their complaints and I found them unreasonable. I felt indignant for the nurses. These were good nurses; they were bad family, neglectful. How dare they walk in here for a fifteen-minute visit and just start to complain? I hated them on the spot. I was being judgmental, but I felt entitled.

At one point Mom's eyes focused on the woman lying in that bed. She turned to me and said, "Why does that woman have a dog's head? It's ugly."

It was the loudest thing she had said all day, and of course I was sure they had heard it. To make matters worse, Stu, Karen, Tom, and Phil had all turned their view that way to see to what she was referring. Karen started to laugh, which of course became contagious. I wanted to crawl under my mother's bed and I shushed them. They all turned on me with scowls. I turned to Mom. "What do you mean? A dog's head?"

"Why are you whispering? She can't hear you. Look at her, she looks like she has the head of a dog."

Tom, ever helpful, chimed in. "You mean like Anubis, the Egyptian God?"

"Yeah. Like that, whatever you said."

"Mom, she has a lot of tubes and is on a ventilator. Trust me, she has a human head."

"Oh, so now I'm seeing things."

"Mom, stop. She doesn't have a dog's head."

"I know what I saw. She did have a dog's head. Not now, but she did."

Throughout this hospitalization, and forever after, the Kerens would always refer to this woman as Anubis. Interestingly, Anubis was the Egyptian God of the Underworld; he accompanied the dead to the other side. He was also present, in Egyptian myth, when the hearts of the deceased were weighed to determine their worth as humans and their appropriateness for the rewards of the hereafter. Could Mom have really seen Anubis in that bed?

25

CORNERS

I'd heard this story before, many times, but this time was different. This time we were standing right at the spot. In 1986, Mom and Dad had sold the house on Long Island right after Stuart graduated high school and moved to central New Jersey. Dad had six more years till retirement and Mom could get a job anywhere. Mom hoped that by moving here they would see more of her Pennsylvania-based family.

I had taken her to the market and we were loading the groceries into the trunk when she suddenly pointed to a two-family house across the street from us. "That's the house I lived in when I was teaching. It was where I brought your grandmother to die."

I looked at it. Except for the newish siding, you could see it was a place with an unimpressive history. It needed a new roof, and the wooden steps leading to the front door looked termite-eaten, or at least in desperate need of paint. "Is it hard to see it after all this time?"

"Why would it be hard? It's just another place I lived. Sometimes I miss the landlady. She was very nice to me; looked after me when I first started teaching."

She had told me many stories of this woman. "Does it make you remember your mom? Her illness?" I asked. "That seemed like such a difficult time for you."

"Not particularly. You know I don't dwell."

I didn't really know this. Mom could hold a grudge the way the Statue of Liberty held her torch, high and bright for everyone to see. It was moments of tenderness or caring that she didn't repeat often. Her life, as she told it, was one long succession of disappointments and injustices. And as her confidant, I had heard them all, in detail.

"Mom," I started, "were there stores here then? Was this road as busy?"

"There was a bit of a shop here, like a grocery-deli, but it was mostly open field. The trucks would still come off the highway to get to the factories and warehouses back there."

"So is that the corner that you always talk about?"

"That's it. That's the corner Mom would beg me to roll her chair out into so she'd get hit by a speeding truck. She'd cry, she'd beg me! I had to plead with her to stop. The nurse I hired would tell me to go out for a bit, but there was nowhere to go. I'd go out to that little store, or just wander in the field looking for interesting stones I could pick up and take to class."

I put my arm around her. "That sounds awful, Mom. I can't imagine it. She must have been in awful pain."

"Well, it didn't have to be. If she had let them give her a colostomy bag when she was first diagnosed, she might have lived, but she was too proud. Wouldn't hear a thing about it. They did what they could, but it just returned and metastasized."

"Well, at least she had you. You must have really loved her, just starting out yourself and bringing her here, where you were by yourself."

"Almost didn't happen. I had to fight your uncle Sidney over that. He wanted her to stay in Easton. Insisted they could take better care of her. He actually said he didn't think I could do it. I knew she didn't want to be with him. He was a bully."

I'd heard that story several times but I let her go on. Caretaking her mother always seemed an important part of her life, no need to cut that off. "Mom, do you think your mom really expected you to push her in the road? Did she know how much that was hurting you?"

"I don't know. Maybe she did. She would always remind me how lucky I had been to have her; how she took care of me when my father abandoned us. I couldn't have done it, though. I wouldn't have stopped her if she could do it herself. No one should suffer like that."

Eight years later, when Mom and Dad moved to North Carolina, Mom would stop having colonoscopies and mammograms. "If I get cancer, I wouldn't treat it. The treatment is worse than the disease. If it got bad and the pain was too bad, I'd just take an overdose of my insulin and be done with it."

Mom said this over and over again to me during her years in North Carolina. That, along with her living will and multiple discussions about her end-of-life wishes were always topics of conversation when we would visit her. A broken record, did she think we could ever forget? Gone, however, during those years, was her pointed message to us kids that had been repeated numerous times in earlier days, that she would never want to be a burden. Should she get too sick to care for herself, we shouldn't hesitate to put her in a nursing home.

~

Those memories of conversations past dominated my mind that second night I left my mom in the ICU. Things were not looking good. The neurologist (by nagging enough I finally got a consult for her) had confirmed my suspicion that whatever had happened had impacted her cognitively. The nurses were still pushing food on her and she didn't want to eat. Even more concerning was her doctor's announcement that her blood wasn't clotting properly and they had no idea why. She wasn't complaining about pain, just the endless tests and the discomfort of being in a hospital. Maybe we should talk about hospice. The hospital had an excellent hospice program. In fact, Tom's mother had passed away there just nine months before. Tom and I discussed it in the car on the way to the hospital.

"Tom, do you think we should propose for her to go to hospice? Is she going on for us or her?"

"Is there any harm in talking to her about it?"

"Well, she does romanticize her own death. She might just give up because she's tired. I don't want to encourage her, and I don't want to feel responsible."

"There's no way, when she's gone, you could feel guilty. You have been so attentive, so giving, and so loving. If you talk to her about this, you're doing so for her, not you. You'd go on forever if you had to."

"Thanks for saying that. I wish it were totally true, but part of me does want it to be over. I don't think that's why I'm thinking this. She's been so clear about not wanting to suffer, but then again, she has always said she would do it to herself if she reached that point ..." I was fighting tears and Tom reached over and gave my leg a rub. "I've half-expected to have gone to her place and found her dead, empty vials of her insulin surrounding her. When she'd be sleeping on my arrival, I always let out a sigh of relief when I saw her chest rise or heard a snore."

She had stopped talking about overdosing on her insulin when I had told her that my experience of hearing it so often was like what she went through with her mother wanting to be rolled into traffic. She had always accepted treatment. Even when the doctors suggested she get a pacemaker and internal defibrillator, she had accepted their advice. Her will to live was as strong as her desire to be dead. I got it and I didn't.

When we arrived at the ICU, Mom was being attended to by a nurse I hadn't met. She was a middle-aged Filipino woman with a rather stern disposition. "Oh, are you Mr. Keren? Your mother is refusing to eat. She won't get better if she doesn't eat."

"Well, what did you serve her?"

"I'm her nurse, not her dietician. Whatever was on her tray. Well, I'm going to tell her doctor to put her on a feeding tube."

"You do that. We'll see how that goes." Aurora was poking me in the ribs, aching for a fight.

Tom, sensing Aurora's imminence, put his arm around my shoulder. I noticed the nurse sneer.

"Well, she's got to get ready, she has an MRI of her brain at noon."

I looked at my watch. It was eight-thirty in the morning. "Oh damn, and she has nothing to wear, I'll have to run home and get her evening gown. Mom, are you up to wearing your pumps, or should I just bring the silver ballet slippers?" What does one do for three-and-a-half hours to get ready for an MRI?

"The black flats would probably be most comfortable," Mom said, laughing at the nurse.

"Mrs. Keren, I don't know why you're laughing, you're very sick and you have to eat. You didn't eat your breakfast."

"It was shit. Cold cream of wheat and weak tea."

"Mrs. Keren, such language!"

"What are you going to do, throw me out?"

The nurse stormed off.

"What am I getting an MRI for? I know what's wrong with me, this place!"

"Mom, they're worried that when you were unconscious there was a stroke or some ischemic incident."

"Yeah, so I'll just be more crazy."

Dr. Rosen came in, followed by Phil. "Good morning, Gloria, how are you feeling this morning?"

"Well, I've been better. All these tubes, I feel like my grandkids' Habitrail. And the catheter bag, I'll never find shoes to match."

Maybe she was getting better. She hadn't been this acerbic and witty in weeks.

"Gloria, you're going to need better material if you get out of here. That joke is way too old. Now, let's start again. Are you feeling any better this morning?"

"Better than what? I'm feeling better than Estelle Getty." How she pulled that one out of her memory bank, I'll never know. Our favorite Golden Girl had passed almost a year before. "Doc, just tell me, am I getting better?"

"Well, your sugar seems back on track, but the rest of you …"

"So, just bury me."

"Well, you're not quite there yet. I'd like to give you a feeding tube because you're not eating enough calories."

"Well, if the food was better …"

"With a feeding tube you don't have to taste it."

"Then what's the point of eating?"

"So no feeding tube, then?"

"Not for me! You can give it to that one over there," she said, pointing to Anubis. "Just bring me some food I like."

The doctor walked off to put a note on Mom's chart.

"Mom, why not just let the doctors do their job?" Phil said.

"He is, he asked me if I would accept a feeding tube and I said no! Now, butt out."

"Okay Mom, no feeding tubes," I said. She smiled at me. "I'm going to go speak to the doctor outside for a minute."

~

"Dr. Rosen, what are we looking at here? Prognosis? Options?"

"Well, the glucose drip is keeping her blood sugar up, for now. That was the problem in the first place. Her blood pressure is still all over the place and we're not sure why. There does seem to be some additional cognitive slippage. The MRI should tell us more about that, but doubtful we can do much if there is anything there. There is still the issue with her clotting problem and, of course, it's all moot if she doesn't start to eat."

"Can you give her a day? I'll bring her things she'll eat and we can see how she's doing?"

"I don't know if that's a good idea. Maybe a few hours."

We chatted some about the possibility of ending treatment. I knew where he stood from the conversation he and I had had at Dad's bedside. He expressed that Mom did still have a chance at recovery, but he could not guarantee she'd get off of any supported feedings once they started.

I asked him what would happen if she stopped treatment, and he described how death would come. He did not think she'd hang on for long, but it wouldn't be instant either.

"Doc, I'm going to speak with her about all this when my other brother arrives. I have a feeling she's going to choose to stop treatment, but we'll see. Could we hold off on the MRI, at least until this afternoon when she's had a chance to talk it over with us? Why put her through the discomfort?"

"That seems fair. I should be in the hospital till about noon. That gives you two and a half hours. I'll check in before I leave."

When I went back to Mom's bed, Karen and Stu were sitting there. I didn't know how they got by me without my seeing them. I was pleasantly surprised. They got up to give me a hug. "Don't get up, it's okay."

"We brought you a bagel." I looked over to where Tom and Phil were munching on theirs.

"Mom, where's yours?"

"We didn't know if she could have one," they said in unison.

"Mom, you want half of mine?"

"Can I eat them? Don't I have to eat Cream of Wheat or oatmeal?"

"Sure you can, Mom, if you want to try. You haven't eaten much in two or three days so it might be heavy in your stomach." I opened the bag with the bagel and pulled it out, separated the halves into open quarters and placed them on her tray.

She picked up a quarter, then put it down. "Maybe not."

I went to get Mom a yogurt. I was thankful for a minute to myself, anyway. When I returned they were all still munching bagels. There were a few cream cheese mustaches in view.

"Mom, so I want to review what the doctor told me with you while you eat. Okay?"

"Do I have a choice?"

"We can wait till you're finished eating."

"Okay, shoot."

"So, Mom, here's where things stand. That bag of glucose is keeping your blood sugar up. That bag of saline and some meds are barely managing your blood pressure. You seem to be having even more memory problems since Friday. And, there is an issue with your blood not being able to clot appropriately." I noticed her start to lose interest. "Even with your eating yogurt, you are not getting enough calories or nutrients to get better. The doctor would like you to consider parenteral feeding."

"What the hell is that?" she asked, seemingly having forgotten an explanation given her not too long before.

"Well, instead of food into your stomach through a tube in your nose, which we know you don't want, they'll put a catheter into a vein and give you nutrients through it."

"Is it all day long?"

"I believe so, but I'm not sure."

"Will I have it forever?"

"I didn't get that sense, but again, I'm not sure."

"Mom, what difference does it make? You need it to get better," Phil chimed in.

"I think it's Mom's choice. Maybe she doesn't want any more treatment," Stu added.

Phil seemed to favor trying more treatment. Phil had become a born-again Christian and nobody wanted to open a religious can of worms, so we tried to keep him quiet.

"What about your grandkids? You want to die and leave them?" Phil said, adding a touch of Jewish guilt he hadn't had washed away during his baptism.

"Phil, I'm sure if she felt well and had the energy she had when your kids were young to play and enjoy them, this wouldn't be a question, but she's been through so much and she has the right to decide if she's had enough," Karen said, quite forcefully.

"Thank you, Karen," said Mom. "I love the kids. I'd love to see Laura graduate college and get married; Daniel graduate high school and go to college; and be at Ani and Izzie's bas mitzvahs. But even if I get better from this, who knows if I'll be able to be at any of that stuff? I hope they remember me for what I was when I was with them."

"So, Mom, if you want, you could stop treatment all together," I said. "We could have you moved to a hospice, maybe there's a bed in the one right here. But that means that you're ready; that you know you are going to die without any treatment. Is that what you want?"

Silence hung in the air between us all. Any irreverence we had shared around Mom's bed the past few days was gone.

"What do you think I should do? You are the one who gets the brunt of all this, you and Tom."

"Gloria, don't worry about me," said Tom. "I'd love to have you around forever, but that won't happen. If we have you a bit longer, I'll be here, next to you and Michael. If you decide to go, I'll miss you but certainly will understand."

"Mom, I can't make this choice for you," I said. "I love you. I love helping you out, keeping you comfortable. But I can't be the one to decide when you've had enough. It's always been something you had to know for you."

I looked around at my siblings. Everyone looked so calm. I know I didn't feel that way, but I wondered if I looked that way. I looked over at the nurse, who just glared back at me over the chart she was writing in while eavesdropping on us. The room around me was so bright from the lights up above. Outside, however, the world looked gray.

At least the world grasped the somberness of the moment. Actually, the grayness was from a winter storm that was making its way up from the Gulf of Mexico. I was vaguely aware of the storm preparations swirling around me that morning as I was heading to the hospital. It was due to hit overnight, and they were predicting up to a foot of snow by morning. I knew Stu and Karen were feeling anxious about it as they were hoping to fly home that evening. I wasn't registering much of anything about it, except that primitive excitement I still felt as snow was approaching and the anticipation that school might get cancelled. A day off from work would mean a day less to worry about while spending my time at the hospital.

~

Time passed without our noticing, and Dr. Rosen appeared just before one o'clock as expected. "Gloria, you're still here!"

"Well, I had to wait for you. Couldn't leave without saying goodbye." Her sarcasm was getting thicker.

"Well, thanks for that. Did Michael share with you the things we talked about?"

"Only the parts that were appropriate for all ages." The doctor laughed and so did I. It was a good one.

"So he explained parenteral feedings to you?"

"He tried. I found it kind of dry and dull, like a Stanley Kubrick film."

"Well, did you have any questions about it?"

"Well, how long would I have to be on it?"

"That would depend upon you. If you got your strength back and were able to eat full meals again, we could take you off of it."

"And if I didn't?"

"Well, you can actually get these feedings at home as well as in the hospital. You could stay on it forever." I noticed Mom frowning over that option. She squeezed my hand, which she had been holding.

"Doc, what will happen if Mom doesn't have the feedings?" I asked.

"Well, with the amount of nutrition she's getting now, she might stabilize or might grow weaker. I can't really predict. She won't get much better though, she really needs the calories."

The doctor reiterated what I had shared with them. How there were no guarantees she'd be able to get off the feedings. What death would look like if she stopped treatment.

"Mom," I said, "are you following what he's telling you?"

"Yeah, I'm not deaf." I wished she hadn't been sarcastic. I felt this conversation was in need of gravity. I needed to know this was thought through, what she really wanted, not a decision made for effect or because contemplating it was too much work.

"What would you like to do? Do you want to stop treatment, go to hospice, call it quits?" I asked her quietly.

"Yeah, it's time."

"You're sure about this, Gloria?" asked the doctor.

"Yeah, probably should have done this months ago."

"All right, let me get the ball rolling."

~

Several hours had passed and we were still in the ICU. Mom was still on her IV and the nurse continued to take her vitals. About three o'clock the nurse came to give her some medications. "What meds are those?" I asked her.

"Her blood pressure meds, her BP was a bit elevated."

"What is taking so long for her hospice bed? No one's even come to see her."

"Oh, I haven't called on that. Your mom isn't ready for hospice."

"That isn't your call." I was getting angry. "She has reached this decision in consultation with her doctor and her family. You are not either of those."

She turned to my mother and in her singsong canter said, "Miss Gloria, you don't want tube? God wouldn't want you to give up, Miss Gloria."

She had the wrong one here. This was my mother, who bragged how she had gotten thrown out of her Sunday school because she announced she didn't believe her Bible stories. She flipped the nurse the bird.

"My mom does not want any more treatment and she wants to go to hospice. The doctor has left you orders to arrange that, has he not?"

She just stared at me. "Gloria, is this what you really want?"

Mom nodded. Who the hell was this nurse to question this decision? This didn't need to be this complicated.

This shouldn't have been a fight, but it was. The nurse, ostensibly a religious person, was refusing to call the social worker from the hospice or even call our doctor for us. I had to take matters into my own hands. Asking Tom to come with me, he and I went to the hospice unit and brought the intake worker to Mom's bedside.

"So, Gloria, I understand you feel you've had enough. You'd like to go to hospice," he said to her.

"Yeah, I want to go now."

"Why?"

"I'm tired of the poking and the prodding. I'm tired of the pills and the needles, the tubes, the nurses. I'm just tired. Can we just go, now?"

"Gloria, you realize if you go to hospice it means you are going to die?"

"Of course, I realize."

"Okay, some people don't understand that. If you go to hospice you will be stopping treatment. There will be no more tubes, no more tests, and the only pills or medicines we will give you will be to manage your pain."

"Yeah, yeah. Can I go now? It's time to die."

"Gloria." He kept repeating her name. I'm not sure why but that detail stuck with me. As if, by reinforcing whom she was in life she would make clearer decisions. "You seem in such an awful rush to go to hospice, to die. Why is that, Gloria?"

She pointed at me and said, "To get away from this one." She had a big smile on her face when she said it, but I wasn't amused. The intake worker looked puzzled. He didn't know me and didn't know our family.

"Mom, what if those are the last words you ever utter? How am I supposed to take that? Is that the legacy you want to leave me?"

She got visibly upset at my question and I was glad for it. "Of course not, you've been amazing and I'm eternally grateful. God, no, no I don't want you to ever feel bad about anything you've done in this process. Doctor, he has been the best caretaker anyone could ever imagine. I'm sorry, Michael, you know me."

"It's okay, Mom, I know it was just a stupid comment and that is not how you feel. But, if you're going to do this it has to be what you want, what you feel is right for you. And not because you're worried you are inconveniencing any of us."

"No, no. It's what I want. I've had enough."

Mom signed some forms and within the hour was in bed on the hospice unit.

It was a nice room. Her bed looked like it had been on the showroom floor at Ethan Allen only hours ago, except it had all the functionality of a hospital bed. There was a not uncomfortable couch across the room under a set of windows that stretched the entire length of the room. Unfortunately, her view was pretty dismal. The section of the hospital it looked out on was only a few stories high, so she looked out on the tar roof dotted with vents and steam pipes. There wasn't much else to look at beyond that. There was a full dresser and a TV console opposite the bed. The TV was a decent size and a very modern flat screen (this was 2009 and flat screens were an extravagance).

Of course, Tom and I were well acquainted with the unit. It had not been that many months since we had said goodbye to his mother. The room where Joan spent her final days was catty-corner to this one, separated only by the coveted corner room on the unit. Just like when Joan was admitted, there was a very old man in that room with a large family. I had to look twice. Of course, it wasn't the same man. He had passed the night Joan had been admitted. This man would pass that night as well.

As soon as Mom was settled, Stu and Karen said their goodbyes. They had managed to get on an earlier flight and were heading back home. They had decided to bring the girls back to say goodbye to Mom and would be back Tuesday afternoon, as long as they could get flights. The weather report was still calling for a large storm that night.

I was convinced if I went home something would happen at the hospice and they would be calling me to come say goodbye to Mom. I, of course, knew I would be stuck and wouldn't get there. I decided I would spend the night in Mom's room, on the pull-out couch. Let it snow, I would be safe and warm with my mommy.

26

HOSPICE

I woke up and checked my watch: six-thirty. The stiffness in my back reminded me I was on a pull-out couch, which in turn cued me where I was. I jumped up to see the promised snowstorm. Nothing! It wasn't snowing and there was nothing on the rooftop. I angled myself to get a better view and there was no snow to be seen on the grass, in the parking lots, or on the roads. I was seven years old again and feeling the disappointment of a failed weather prediction.

The nurse came in and asked if I would step out so they could "freshen" Mom up. I excused myself, took my bag into the bathroom, and prepared to meet the day. When I emerged ten minutes later, refreshed and clean, I was shocked to find a Levine sitting by my mom's bedside. I'd had little contact with them in two days.

"Good morning," I said.

"Good morning," he said. "Just stopped by to see if your mom was comfortable."

Strangely, I didn't want him to care. I didn't totally believe him either. I held the Levines responsible for the crisis that had ended with Mom choosing hospice at this time. "Oh, thanks. She's fallen back asleep, I see. Was she awake when you came in?"

"No. Has she been alert? What's she been like?"

"She seems at peace with her decision to stop treatment. She's really been fed up with being pushed and probed, not feeling herself. You know, she had always talked about her wish for one, big, dramatic heart attack or stroke that would finish her off, hopefully in her sleep. She feared a long, drawn-out death. Lately, she has felt constricted. No life, and too scared to burden friends with her health, so she was just sitting at home, by herself, waiting to die."

"I'm sorry to hear that. I really don't think it was her time."

I thought to myself that he didn't approve of Mom's decision. "No, you and your partner have been determined to keep her alive." By his smile, I think he heard it as a compliment, not the sarcastic retort I meant it to be.

He got up and began to gather his things. "I'll drop by every day to check in, but she's under the hospice doctor's care now."

Mom opened her eyes. "Is he gone?"

"Mom, you were faking it the whole time?"

"Most of it. I was hoping he would leave."

I just laughed. Even on her deathbed Mom was Mom. I went to kiss her and realized her feet were sticking out of the bottom of the blanket. I went to pull it down. As I brushed her foot it was stone cold. I felt a bit farther up and as I approached her ankle there was more warmth present.

Giving her a kiss, I said to her, "I'm off to work. Don't give them too hard a time. I'll be back around dinnertime."

"Very funny," she said. "You know I'm not eating anymore."

"Yes, but I am and I thought I'd come eat in front of you."

She stuck her tongue out at me as I walked out the door. Stopping by the nurses' station I mentioned my observation about her feet.

"That's death," the nurse said, "when it comes slowly. You'll feel that more and more depending on how long your mom holds on." It wasn't exactly comforting, but it was helpful in a strange way. They didn't pretty things up. They used real words. It helped me to accept that like the creeping cold I'd have to let the idea of Mom dying take hold of me.

~

When I got back to the hospital after work, Phil was sitting in the room. He and Mom were facing the TV; he staring intently, she just staring into space. "Hey, how you doing?" I said to either.

"Great!" Mom said. "Never better." Dying seemed to be making her happy.

"I'm doing okay," Phil said, looking up from the news. "I'm going to head back to D.C. for a day or two and will come back if you need me."

"Do what you have to, Phil. You have to keep your job. Are you driving tonight or in the morning?"

"Tonight. Just wanted to say goodbye to you."

You could have just called me, I thought to myself. "Thanks. Thanks for all your help. Please drive safe." What a relief that he had rented a car when he got up here. It would have been torturous if I had to have been his chauffeur on top of all this.

"I will. And of course I'm here to help." He hugged me and kissed Mom and walked out the door.

I actually think Mom's good mood was about Phil and me working together. It was such a rare occurrence. I was making an effort to hold my tongue and my sarcasm in relation to Phil. To say he and I were working together was an over-statement. There really wasn't that much work. I knew he was hurting from being dumped. He didn't need me to make him feel like shit.

"Did you have a good visit?" I asked Mom.

"Eh, nothing special. Mostly he watched TV and waited for something to happen. I did get to speak to the kids. Laura was crying."

"That must have been hard for both of you. Do you want me to fly them in again? I will if you want me to."

"For what, to watch me die? Let them remember me standing up, or at least sitting up."

"Okay. If you change your mind, let me know. How was Daniel?"

"Daniel was Daniel. Big kisses, not much to say." He was probably Mom's biggest worry, such a loving child but quirky. She was always worried he'd starve to death because he had such a limited diet.

I continued. "Isabelle and Ani should be here tomorrow. Stu and Karen are flying in with them."

"That's nice." It was a weird response from Mom, who lived to grandparent.

I sat by Mom's bedside and held her hand. "Mom, so what does it feel like, how do you feel?"

"I just feel tired. Not hungry, not even thirsty. Why is it taking so long to die?"

"Mom, they can't even give us an idea. The nurses didn't think you'd last this long. I keep thinking if only they would have turned off your pacemaker, as well as the internal defibrillator, it might go faster." When I had asked them to turn off the pacemaker, the doctors had insisted that her heart muscle was so weak the pacemaker wouldn't be able to keep the heart from stopping.

Mom squeezed my hand. "Don't be mad at the doctors. It's not worth being mad at anyone." These were funny words of wisdom from a woman who made being mad at people a career.

"I'm not really mad, Mom. I'm frustrated. How about you? Are you scared?"

"No. Why would I be?"

"I've heard you talk about spirits, like the mother of the woman who owned our childhood home who used to rock in the chair in my room, but I don't know what you believe comes next. Do you believe in heaven? An afterlife?"

"Oh, yeah. There's definitely a place beyond. I'll get to see those who went before."

"So who are you most looking forward to seeing when you get there? Your mother?" I asked. I thought it would be a no-brainer. I had heard her talk about her mom so many times. Most of her stories, except for maybe the oatmeal, were wonderful or at least admiring memories. She would always speak to how much like her mother I was, a loving woman who loved to have fun, with a real sarcastic rebellious streak.

We were really looking at each other. She smiled. "No, I really want to see all the cats I have lost. There really aren't any people I'd like to see."

I pulled back a bit, shocked. "Really, Mom? You always talked about your mom as if you missed her so much."

"I did. But she could be a pain. I don't want any stress when I get to the other side."

I mentioned Dad would probably be waiting for her.

"I know. I don't know how I'll handle that."

"Maybe he'll be different on the other side. He's been on his own for three years now."

"He's probably been with his mother the whole time." Even on her deathbed she had to get digs in. I hoped my father had moved on, found a celestial girl-friend, or been reincarnated already with a new shot at life. Personally, I don't believe in an afterlife and take great comfort in not believing. Once around this life is plenty for me.

~

When I got to Mom's room after work on Tuesday, I was greeted by Stu and his wife and kids. Ani, the youngest, who was seven at the time, was snuggled with

Mom on her bed. Mom was clearly enjoying her attention as she beamed from ear to ear. Isabelle, who was eight, was curled in a corner of the couch, on the other side of the room, reading a book and trying not to pay attention to what was happening around the bed.

Stu jumped up to give me a hug. "How was work?" he asked.

"Who worked? I locked myself in my office and stared at the wall most of the day."

"Ugh. I know those days, at least I remember them."

Karen gave me a hug and a kiss. "She's eating up Ani's attention."

"What's with the other one, over there in the corner? I said, nodding towards Isabelle.

"Who knows with her? We'll talk to her later. They're hungry, we waited for you for dinner, okay?"

"All right. Let me give Mom a kiss and check in with the staff. Then we can go."

Over Chinese food the girls chatted on about school, ballet, their friends, and all their pets. Isabelle just kept focusing on how she was "missing school for this."

"Isabelle, someday, you'll be very glad you came to say goodbye. She loves you girls very much and would love to have more time to see you dance and hear about your lives," I said.

"Oh, I love Grandma. She always likes to do things with us. She's fun," Ani stated.

"But I'm missing school!" Isabelle pouted.

We'd later learn Isabelle was afraid she'd catch death from Mom, like it was a virus, but she wouldn't tell her parents that until she was back home. For now, I was just aware of all the attention she was not paying to Mom.

When we got back to the hospice, the staff was rolling a new patient into the corner room. I couldn't see the patient in the bed, but I noticed the family. It was the old woman from the ICU they couldn't get off the respirator. Anubis had followed Mom to hospice.

The nurses peeked in and asked if we would step out so they could "freshen Mom up."

Stu said, "We have to get the girls home to bed."

I said to the nurse, "Can you give us a few minutes so the girls can say good night to their grandmother? Then we'll get out of your way."

As Stu and Karen were gathering their things and putting on their coats, Ani was busy squeezing Mom with hugs and covering her with kisses. "Careful, you don't want to break her," Karen said.

"Grandma, I'll come see you in the morning and give you some more kisses, okay?" Ani said. Over her shoulder I noticed Isabelle mockingly mouthing every word her sister said.

As I was walking them to the elevator, Tom was just getting off it. The girls were thrilled to see him. They adored him and loved to climb all over him. He's bald and they loved to pretend they were using his head as a canvas and would pretend to draw all over him.

When they left Tom and I took a seat in the family lounge. He gave me a big hug. "How you doing?"

I started laughing. "What's so funny? Where's this coming from?" he asked me.

"It's all so surreal that I just need to focus on those stupid, funny thoughts. Right now they are 'freshening up my mother.' Every time they say that I think of those little evergreen trees you hang in your car, but I see them changing one that they have hanging on my mother, near her naughty bits."

Now Tom was laughing hysterically. "You're wicked, Muriel!" he said to me, misquoting one of our favorite lines from the movie *Muriel's Wedding*.

"I mean how unfresh can she get in two hours? She's not drinking or eating; it can't be a diaper thing."

The juxtaposition was somehow delicious. The family room was a darkly paneled library of sorts. Lots of books, a few games for the kids. The few times I had looked in, the people using it talked in hushed tones. Here we were, laughing hysterically, in a hospice.

Our laughter was interrupted as the door to the lounge creaked open. It was Anubis's son. He picked a book up and took a seat on the far opposite side of the room. "Good evening," I said to him.

He replied with a nod of his head and returned his eyes to the book he was reading. Tom and I finished our conversation in a whisper, our giggly mood broken. "How was your visit with them?" he asked me.

"Blessedly short," I responded, filling him in on the dichotomous reactions of the two kids.

"They're not used to death. Will we see them again?" Tom's comment sent my thoughts drifting. Can one be used to death? I guess the staff here at the hospice could, they see it every day, yet they remain compassionate, attentive, incredibly caring.

"I doubt it," I said, returning to his question about seeing more of the kids, "Karen and the girls are heading out in the morning. Stu will be here till the end."

Mom had a smile on when we returned to her room. "So there you boys are. I thought you had left me."

"Nah, they just wanted to freshen you up."

"I get so much attention here, I feel spoiled. They may never get me to die."

I giggled to myself.

"Gloria," Tom said, "you should have been a stand-up. Even now you're still joking."

"Yeah, but I'm not standing. Maybe I could have been a lay-down comic." We had a chuckle. What an opening that could have been for a comedian, but even I resisted it.

Tom, Mom, and I sat in silence for a bit. I broke the silence. "It's strange, Mom, you seem much more alive tonight. In a good mood, joking, and so talkative."

She just shrugged as a response.

A few minutes of silence pursued. "Hey, Mom, it's Tuesday night, you wanna watch *American Idol*?"

"What's the sense of that? I won't be around to see the finale."

"You got a point there, Gloria," Tom said, "but we could always let you know the outcome when we meet in heaven."

"Assuming we all end up in the same place. You guys, of course, are guaranteed to go to heaven just for the care you've given me. You know how much I've appreciated it. If I could reach my ear, I'd tug it."

We both understood Mom's reference to Carol Burnett and "So glad we've had this time together ..." I think we felt the same way. The previous three years had been not only frustrating and scary, but also rich and rewarding. But was she saying goodbye?

We tucked Mom in and said our good nights. On the way to the elevator, I bumped into the hospice pastor. I introduced her to Tom and assured her I was doing okay.

"Okay if I give you a hug?" she asked.

"Sure," I said, even though I wasn't sure I really meant it. There had been a lot of feelings I didn't recognize or allow myself to experience over this enterprise.

"No one can predict how long the process will take, it just goes as it goes."

Tom and I knew that so well. As I thought that, I was glancing at the room two doors down from where Mom was, where Joan had left us months before.

"I think she's hours away. Tonight, she seemed to have a burst of life and she thanked Tom and me as if it was the end."

"She probably has nothing left to do."

I wasn't sure how to respond so I said my goodbye to her. I pondered the idea of having nothing left to do. Did I have anything left to do with her? Many times over the last few years I had sided with the part of my mother that wanted to die, the part that found life not worth dealing with, surviving. Sure, there were moments of fun, laughter, insight, but were they enough?

I'd love to let her know I wish she had taken better care of herself, avoided the long, slow death: but how would that change anything now? Did she know that part of me was angry? Of course, she knew. She saw it every time Aurora had emerged.

Walking past the nurses' station, the staff called out, "Good night!"

I called back, "Good night" but then turned and walked over. "I just want to say thanks. You are all so wonderful."

"Just doing our job, Dr. Keren."

"Well, you do it well … Mom was even talking about how comfortable she's been here."

"Well, thank you for letting us know. It's always nice to hear it."

"Don't I know it." We all laughed.

~

When I got to the hospice the next morning her room was crowded. The unit physician was by her side listening to her heart and lungs. A nurse was assisting him. The social worker popped in. There was no room for me at her bedside. The social worker asked me to stop by when I got a chance. I nodded to the hallway.

The quiet of the hallway contrasted with the activity in Mom's room.

"What's up? You sounded so serious."

"Well, today's day four. Medicare will not cover past today. Could you take her home?"

"What if I said no?"

"I'd ask you again."

I was wishing Tom were at my side. This was unexpected; I guess I was vaguely aware of the four-day limit on inpatient hospice, but since we assumed it would go faster I hadn't given it any thought. I felt panicked; I wasn't ready to move her.

"And then?" I asked.

"I'd get to work helping you set up whatever you needed to make it work."

I leaned against the wall. I needed something to support me. "If you asked me a few days ago, I would have said of course, but at this point it will just make her a lot less comfortable. She thinks the end is momentary, anyway."

"Well, the doctor doesn't think that's the case. He thinks it could be a few more days. He seems surprised by her resilience."

"And if we refused?"

"Well, you could do nursing home hospice."

"Is there any chance they'd let her stay?"

"Unless there's a medical reason, they will insist on her leaving inpatient hospice."

My head was spinning. I was angry, scared, frustrated, and lost. And now I was going to put on a smiling face to attend to Mom. If there were a target, I'm sure Aurora would have made an appearance, but the social worker had been a support. She tried to be comforting while delivering bad news.

Mom's room had emptied out except for a nurse's aide who was straightening Mom's sheets. The doctor had snuck out while I was with the social worker. "Hi, Mom," I said, taking up my place in the chair next to her bed. "So what did I miss?"

She shrugged, her usually animated face barely moving. It was such a stark contrast to the night before; more what I expected here at the hospice, but just a shock after the previous night.

I got up and took her hand. Staring at her face I realized she hadn't worn her wig since she got here. "Mom, I just realized you've had a lot more hair under your wig lately than you had in a long time. Quite a cruel joke, when you think how few people have seen you in the last few months." She smiled, not even a laugh. She tried to cough, but it was not a strong effort.

I wondered if she was experiencing excess fluid around her lungs, congestive heart failure. "Are you having a hard time breathing?" I asked.

The aide said that was to be expected. She would ask the nurse to give her something that would relax her and make it easier for her to breathe.

"Could she wait a bit on that? She is expecting her grandchildren shortly. They are coming by to say goodbye before they fly back home. I think she'd like to be awake for that, wouldn't you, Mom?"

Mom nodded her head, giving me a clear yes.

I didn't believe the doctor. I was certain today would be the day. This was the most drastic change I had seen in her over this whole period.

"Mom, you know, I have a slow day. I could call in and spend the day with you. Would you like that?"

She stared right at me and in a very hoarse voice she uttered the first sentence she had given me all day. "*Go to work!*" She couldn't have said it any clearer.

Was she telling me she wanted the peace to go off alone; or was she just pushing me off to work because she didn't want me to get in trouble for missing more work? It could have been that she didn't want to see the pain I was feeling.

"Okay, you don't have to tell me twice." I gave her a kiss and a big hug and walked out the door.

~

"*Go to work!*" would be her last words to me. When I got back to the hospital that afternoon, she was still alive, but she was lying in her bed, staring at the ceiling, pretty much unresponsive. Stu was sitting in a chair reading one of the sci-fi fantasy books he loved.

"Hey, how was your day?"

"Just another day at the office. How long has she been lying like that?"

"We got here about nine and she was basically unresponsive. She was able to put a little kiss on the kids' cheeks, but she didn't say anything and she hasn't moved. She can hear you. Can't you, Mom? Squeeze your hand in answer. But she hasn't used her words."

I let out a little laugh. I recognized the parenting phrase, "use your words," the phrase we taught parents to use with their tantruming children. I didn't think he thought this was a tantrum, and I imagined the phrase was as useful here as it was with kids. "Anyway, the social worker is looking for you. I think they solved the Medicare issue."

"I'll go find her and bring her back here. You're going to stay and help and Phil said he could be here by tomorrow evening."

"It sounds like that may not be necessary, but let's get her back here."

The social worker took a seat with us and explained. "So, when your mom was in the ICU they put a catheter in her upper thigh. Your mom's blood was not clotting properly so the doctor believes that if we try to remove the catheter she would bleed out. That would hasten death, which we can't do. Medicare will not allow her to go home with that catheter in her because it would lead to infection, which would hasten death, which we cannot do. I am fairly sure that by five o'clock we will have permission for your mom to stay with us until she passes. We will not need to set up home care. If they don't approve it, the hospice will absorb an uncovered day so we can get you set up at home. So, for now, you can relax."

I hugged her. I cried. Stu rubbed my back. I had to kiss her. Maureen, our social worker, was my hero.

~

That was Wednesday. Phil returned on Thursday. Mom would live through the weekend. One by one my brothers left. On Saturday afternoon, Stuart had gotten an urgent call from back home. Karen had been working at the temple, preparing lunch for the Hebrew school kids. Attempting to drain a large pot of hot dogs that had been boiling, she slipped and was being rushed to the hospital with some pretty major burns. Phil took him to the airport and sent him on his way.

Sunday morning, Phil was antsy. I had heard him on the phone and think he was getting some pressure from work. In the failing economy he had to take care of that. "Phil, there's not much going on here, why don't you say your goodbyes and go home? Save your job."

By mid-Sunday afternoon it was just Tom and me.

27

Rivka, My Darling

That Monday remains in my mind as if it is still occurring. I leave work and drive to the hospice. Checking in with the nurses and counselors behind the desk, I head to Mom's room. She lies there, much as she has for four days now. Her breathing is slower but still steady. I kiss her, adjust the sheet over her, and as I head to the other side of the bed to take the seat, I reach out and touch her foot. I've felt that cold for days now, but I am struck by how like ice it is feeling. I run my hand over her leg and realize that at least from the waist down, her body is feeling hard and cold.

I am reminded of being sixteen and my father opening his mother's casket so we can kiss her goodbye. My memories of my grandmother have forever carried that sense of her head being a cold, hard stone.

I grab her hand as I sit down. Not as cold as her legs, but it needed to draw from my warmth. Still holding her hand, I grab her room phone and call down to the cafeteria. One of the benefits of this hospice is that family is entitled to be served meals in their loved one's room, and goddamn it, I'm going to get what Medicare is paying for. Ordering the meat loaf, I turn to Mom and say, "We both love meat loaf, so if you want a bite …"

I know she is not conscious, but I know somewhere she is laughing at the irony, as I do. I start to wonder what others will think of this scene if I describe it in the future.

"Mom, anything you want to *watch*?" I ask, grabbing her remote from the bed stand. I know she won't answer but turn on a police procedural, as she would be doing if she were conscious. I am sitting there, meat loaf on a tray, holding her hand and watching *Law and Order*.

I begin to tell Mom about my day. I complain about the general disinterest in ethics, and even common sense, I find at work.

I know what she would say. "Common sense is a rare commodity in the world. Just be happy you got some from me." On the list of things Mom valued, common sense was very high. After twenty-three years with Tom, however, I came to realize the things and ways my mom called common sense were really just her well-entrenched ways of getting on in the world. Of course, many of them had also become mine.

As Mom and I "chatted" about family and friends who had been asking after her, the pastor came in to ask after my sister-in-law and then asked about me.

It surprised me how readily I had allowed this woman to take care of me over the past week. I usually have a distrust of religious of other denominations. She and I, however, had not even discussed religion, God, or any related topic. She just listened really well.

"You know you don't have to be fine. You've been everyone's rock, especially your mom's. Just for a little bit you could let someone, me perhaps, take over." She held my mom's hand on the other side of the bed.

I suggested we go out in the hall. We actually settled into the club chairs in the family lounge.

I began. "I just didn't think we'd still be sitting here … With no food or water, insulin or heart pills for over a week, with her blood pressure so low, her initial sugar so high, I thought this would be done in days."

She held my hand. "As much as your mom wanted to be done, she had something she needs to work through, or maybe it's just her body refusing to quit. There are no rules."

"I don't want her to die before she's done … Hell, I'm not sure how I'll even feel when it's over. Who I'll be."

She looked at me quizzically. "What do you mean by that?"

"My life has been organized around caring for her. Pretty much for three years or so I've built my life around taking care of others, of her, of my mother-in-law. I neglected my job and lost it; now I'm struggling to make sense of the job I have. I will need a new life."

"Is it really that big? It seems to me you have a great life with Tom. You'll set your sights on building a role at work. You'll carry her legacy for your nieces and nephew. They all look to you, even your brothers."

"I know, but sometimes I don't want to be that person. I want to be the person who gets taken care of, who gets to be …" I didn't even know what I was wanting right then. My eyes started to well up, a tear rolled down my cheek. She reached out and hugged me. It felt good. It stifled my tears. It was confusing.

"Thank you. I think I should get back to Mom right now."

"Of course. Anytime, even after."

I walked back into Mom's room, sat down, and grabbed her hand in both my hands and brought it to my lips. Kissing her hand, I thought, *God, just let her go easy, don't make her suffer. Her life's been hard enough.*

I held her hand to my forehead and just closed my eyes with thoughts of her for quite a while. I was jolted by the vibration in my pants and it took a moment to recognize it was my cell phone, but it was just one jolt so it was a text.

It was my friend Peter. I was a bit shocked as he rarely ever contacted me. He lived near Boston and we mostly only had contact at parties and the one week a year we were all on Cape Cod. I read his text. "Are you okay? Just had a sense I should contact you. Call me when you have a chance."

How odd. Mom believed in all kinds of different psychic phenomenon: messages from beyond, ghosts, visitations. Not me. But how could he have had that sense? We were not psychically connected to my knowledge. I made a mental note to call him later or tomorrow.

I resumed my meditation. I was jolted alert again by my cell phone. This time it was a call. I checked and it was Tom.

"Hi, Hon. I'm in the car and there's an accident on the road so I'll be a while."

"No problem, we're not going anywhere," I joked. "Did you eat? Mom and I had meat loaf, but the cafeteria will be closed so pick yourself up something to eat. You can share it with Mom."

The nurse came in. "Dr. Keren, Mike, I have to freshen up your mom and adjust her position. Do you mind stepping outside for a few minutes?"

I smiled to myself. It'd been nine days and I still had that evergreen image every time. I think Mom would have laughed at it too. That was, is, was her sense of humor. When someone is this close to his or her end, not conscious, is it present or past tense? We need a new tense, I decided, even though verb conjugation was always my downfall when learning languages.

I went and took a seat in the family lounge. Could someone really focus on a book here? They were mostly novels, and mostly pretty thick. Why start a novel you're not going to have time to finish? I opened up my cell phone and reread Peter's text. I decided to answer him.

I started to type, "Are you some kind of freakin' psychic? I'm sitting at my mom's bedside in a hospice. Have been here for nine days. It's almost over, but when? Thanks for thinking of me. I'll get back when I can."

I went back to Mom's room.

"Did you miss me? Good. You feel all fresh?" I looked at her lying in the bed. She didn't have a wig on. She never really wore makeup and had none on now. She still looked like my mother, definitely paler. I touched her cheek and her face was feeling cold. It couldn't be that long, could it? I knew something was happening, changing.

At that moment Tom walked in carrying a Caesar salad. "Really, a salad?" I said to him. "You know lettuce upsets her stomach."

He looked at me, then at my mother. "Sorry, Gloria, I wasn't thinking. I just thought it would be quick and I wanted to get over here to see you before I went home."

"We'll forgive you," I said.

When he finished eating, he moved his chair next to mine. I was holding her hand; he was rubbing her leg. He spoke softly. "Gloria, it's okay. You can go if you're ready. The cats are waiting for you. I'll take care of Michael. We'll take care of the others."

I started to hum and then sing:

Rivka my darling, Rivka my love,

Tom joined in.

Climb into my pushcart I'll take you home,
Friday night is Shabbos and gefilte fish,
Rivka, Rivka, you're my favorite dish!

Mom loved to sing that song. She taught it to Tom early on in our relationship. She would sing it to me when I was a baby, which of course I don't remember. But I do remember her singing it to Stuart. Even though Rivka was, and remains, such a mainstay in my family home, there does not seem to be any record of the song. Scholars in Jewish and Yiddish folk music have been unable to help me track down its origin.

Each night, before Stuart was put to bed, during his infancy and toddlerhood, she would sit with him on the black rocker in his room and sing to him. Looking back, some of the songs she chose might seem odd choices. Many of them were love songs from the Great American Songbook, like *Down By the Old Mill Stream* or *When You Wore a Tulip*. My seven-, eight- and nine-year-old self, I think, processed them as songs of a mother's recognition of her child, but, clearly that was not the original intent. I would always sit at her feet, listen, and sometimes join in. I would peer up at my baby brother, who I adored, and commit those songs to memory so I could sing them to my child. Mom would sing with gusto in her sweet, often off-key soprano.

Tom and I proceeded through Mom's litany of songs. We would probably have seemed a sight to anyone looking in. We both finished up with big jazz hands, turning each song into a production number. We were singing them as Mom did, which was usually the way Mitch Miller did.

Mitch Miller was a bandleader who led a chorus of wholesome-looking Middle Americans in song each week on television. Often, he would have the words to the songs on screen so America could sing along. My family watched him regularly. Mom and Dad had all his albums and their liner notes were some of my earliest reading materials.

So Mom lie there dying and we were singing to her. Singing the songs she had lulled us to sleep by. It felt profound; we were singing her to "the other side." At one point I changed the mood with my song choice, *Three Little Fishies*. This Kay Kyser hit from the 1930s, (lyrics by Saxie Dowell) both delighted and tortured us. The song, basically a ditty about a momma fish looking after her three, adventurous baby fishes who are swimming around in a pool. The nonsensical refrain went as follows:

Boop boop, dittem, dattem, whatem—Chu!(repeat)

We both wore wide grins and devious eyes as we began to sing it. As was the custom in our family the *boop boops* were accompanied by a swirling, flying index finger. On the final *Chu* the finger would come in for a tickle attack. We kids would scream with delight, despite our squirmy protestations while anticipating the tickle. Of course, both Tom and I engaged in a tickle to Mom's side, with a little less gusto.

Finally, we made our way to where Mom's gay sons were most comfortable, the Broadway song book. As we began Rodgers and Hammerstein's *Some Enchanted*

Evening from their 1958 musical *South Pacific*. The song is about the magical moment of recognizing one's love in a crowded room. I noticed Mom's breathing start to slow and I thought 'Where would I see Mom again? Would I recognize her? Could she or would she come back to me?'

The song continues to insists that there is a surety that if nowhere else, you will see your love or hear her laugh in your dreams. Between my sleep apnea and my insomnia, I rarely dreamed. Would she find a way to come to me?

I stopped questioning. There'd be plenty of time for philosophy in the months to come.

Our moms are our first true love and mine was leaving tonight. She had waited to create this moment for Tom and me; a moment we would have that defined our family. That was why she waited for nine days, for her other kids and grand-kids to leave. She had been setting up this moment since I was eight years old at her feet by the rocker.

Somewhere, in the last verse, Mom let go. I had been watching her intently as I was singing. The song felt right as the evening had an enchanted air, an air I would remember, always. I saw the last rise of Mom's chest, and then her last exhale. As we finished the song I got up, lifted her up, and hugged her to me. She felt light, lifeless.

Tom did not realize she had gone and had begun to sing *Sunrise, Sunset* to the little girl we had carried the last three years.

I laid Mom back down on the bed and turned to Tom. "She's gone. You can stop." I hugged him tight. He hugged me harder. We both ached. He went and hugged Mom. We both sat there for a while holding her hands. We were all silent.

Finally, Tom looked at me and said, "What do we do now?"

"I guess we should get the nurse." I went out to the nurses' station and told them my mother was gone. One of them returned to the room with me.

She explained, "I have to try three times to hear a heartbeat and feel a pulse before we can call the death." She listened and felt for a pulse; once, twice, three times. "She's gone. I'll leave you with her as long as you like. Let me know when you're ready. Do you know who is going to pick her up, or should she go to the morgue?"

"I've made arrangements for her cremation. They are waiting to hear from me to come and pick her up."

"Okay, then we will keep her here until they come." She turned and returned to the nurses' station.

The nurse gave us each a hug as we walked off the unit. There'd been good doctors and bad doctors; good nurses and bad nurses. Heroes of my tale had emerged in unexpected places. The hospice nurses were the all-stars.

On the way home, I got a call from the funeral director. When I hung up the phone, I felt very lost, empty. Each day for the last three or so years, some part of each day was spent doing for Mom. I sorted her pills, paid her bills, took her shopping, then did her shopping. I entertained, I cooked, I transported. I accompanied her to the doctor, to tests, to Emergency Rooms and rehab centers. I spoke to her, of her, and for her. Tom had been there, too, the best supporting player a man could ask for. We didn't have this moment with his mom months earlier, but we had had others. We had done it together.

Suddenly, I didn't know what the future held. I didn't know who I was, or who I was going to be now that I wasn't going to be her caretaker. I was anxious. I needed a joke and I couldn't find one.

As I put my head on my pillow and curled up next to Tom, I said a little prayer for her rest, but also I prayed she'd pay me a last visit in my dreams that night. She didn't. It was my first day as not a caregiver. My time was for me. I picked up the phone, dialed Caroline's, a New York City comedy club, and signed up for stand-up classes.

EPILOGUE

28

CREMAINS

That Chanukah twelve or thirteen years before, when I received the cremation card, also included a discussion of what to do with their remains, or rather what to do with Mom's remains.

"I don't want a service," Mom started. "I hate funerals. Just scatter my ashes in New York Harbor."

"Why New York Harbor?" I asked. She had never expressed much affinity for the harbor or its landmarks. I was very curious.

"It'll be easier for you that way. Just throw them off the Staten Island Ferry or something." That was always my mom; she'd go twenty miles out of her way to avoid sentiment.

Dad was very quiet. Of course, Mom wasn't exactly letting him get a word in. He did not have any preference for what we should do with his ashes. When pushed, he answered, "Whatever your mom wants. I just want you to know the cremations are paid for so you don't have to worry about that."

Even then I thought to myself, *What if I want to worry? What if I needed a funeral to say goodbye?*

~

That Tuesday morning after Mom had passed, Tom and I sat with the funeral director as I signed the forms authorizing Mom's cremation. "So, what are your plans for the cremains?"

I burst out laughing at the sounds of that word. Just as dried cranberries had usurped raisins and went on to be called Craisins, human ashes from cremation were no longer just remains, but cremains.

I learned a great deal about the laws regarding the disposal of "cremains." To honor my mom's wishes would take permits and the chartering of a boat. "Of course, what they don't know won't hurt them," the funeral director said in a hushed tone.

"Whatever you decide, don't throw the ashes directly off the boat. If they are not in a container, they usually blow back at you and get in your hair, your mouth, just everywhere." I had once heard a story of someone having to spit his mother out over the side of a boat because the ashes had blown into his open mouth. As a therapist, the implications of that still rolled around in my head.

"You also don't want to throw the box they are returned to you in directly overboard. If it washes ashore, they can trace the label and you'll get in big trouble."

"So, what are our options?"

In the end we bought two biodegradable packages, one for Mom and one for Dad, whose cremains had been sitting in the bottom of his dresser drawers since I took them out of the trunk of the car after his memorial service. The packages were designed to dissolve the moment they got wet, assuring that they would sink to their final resting place and scatter before there was any evidence of the crime. They were quite attractive.

As we left his office the day we picked the cremains up, the funeral director said, "Remember, don't let even a drop of water touch them. The containers will start to deteriorate and you'll have just a wet pile of gunk." Immediately, my mind went to the movie *Gremlins*, and I felt some relief that my parents' cremains would not reanimate as gremlins.

So I brought Mom and Dad home and put them on the dining room table, where everything that enters our house first gets deposited. I would have to find a dry place to keep them until we could get them in the harbor. Both my brothers informed me they wanted to be present when Mom and Dad were tossed overboard. I let them know the urgency of getting the cremains into the water and asked that they confer on some dates when they could both come to us to attend to the matter.

Of course, months passed. Both would ask me if the other had suggested any dates, but neither had actually talked with the other about it. Mom and Dad got moved to a place in the butler's pantry when the dining room table was needed for some entertaining function. The sink in there was turned off due to a leak and except for the rarely used coffeepot there was no other source of fluids in the space. I constantly reminded myself that I should wrap them in plastic until we got the deed done.

That Halloween Tom and I travelled to Mexico to observe their Day of the Dead festivities. The timing, six months after my mom's death and fourteen months after Tom's mom's, was unintentional. We had been planning this trip for years, but the timing added even more poignancy. Two days after our return, I was upstairs in my room and I could have sworn I heard water running in the house. Living in a hundred-year-old house, however, often renders one blasé about hearing things. After an hour I put down my book, got out from under the covers, and went to investigate. I checked both bathrooms on my floor—nothing. I went downstairs. Could it be another pipe over the living room? Nothing. I entered the kitchen. Sink was off. No water pouring out under the sink, but the noise was getting louder. The dog was getting insistent as well, so I got his leash and took him to the curb, where he quickly relieved himself, knowing a treat would await his return to the inside.

I stepped into the butler's pantry to get the treat and was greeted with my own Niagara Falls. Not only was water pouring from a bulging ceiling, it was cascading down the shelves of the glass-fronted cabinets, forming picturesque waterfalls as it bounced from plate to plate and wineglass to champagne flute as it quickly was inundating the small space. I panicked, but there in the middle of the mess lay Mom and Dad. Amazingly, they were dry. I quickly got the plastic bags, covered them, and got them out of the way of the tsunami. I don't know how they were spared. My urgency to get them into New York Harbor grew more pressing. After getting in the emergency plumber service and calling the insurance company, I composed a text to my brothers.

Hi, guys. We almost lost Mom and Dad, again, this morning. We have had a burst pipe in the butler's pantry. There is much devastation. Ceiling is hanging down and floors are warped. As a result we will not be able to host any of the holidays this year. Sorry. Miraculously, Mom and Dad are intact but I cannot emphasize how much we need to get their remains into the water. PLEASE decide between yourselves a date to meet here to do it. Further delay could bring tragedy. As a bit of encouragement, I have decided that if you guys do not come out, or at least provide me with a date, by Chanukah, I will be dividing up the ashes in two cardboard boxes and giving them to the grandchildren as jigsaw puzzles. Your loving brother.

It sounds crass, but I was desperate to motivate them. To me, my parents were not in those envelopes and the actual depositing was not causing me much emotion. I carried Mom and Dad internally and those were just piles of ashes. But, on the other hand, I wished to honor Mom's wishes.

No surprise that they called my bluff. The holidays came and went. No word, no mention from my brothers of any plans to take care of this. Winter turned to spring, and then summer, and Mom and Dad were now in a cabinet in the dining room. Sometimes I forgot they were there. Near summer's end I realized I needed to make another pitch, so I sent another text.

Guys. What do I have to do to get your attention on this matter? If you want to be present when Mom and Dad are tossed I really need to get some input from you guys. If I don't hear from you I will be taking matters into my own hands. I have decided to divide Mom and Dad's ashes into four piñatas and will be bringing one to each of the grandchildren's next birthday parties. DON'T LET THIS HAPPEN!

My little brother quickly replied: "Sorry we have been causing you such stress. I think the piñatas are a great idea, only instead of bringing them to the birthday parties let's put all the ashes in one piñata and leave it on the shelf at Wal-Mart."

I had to hand it to Stuart. The idea had brilliance. I had been outwitted. But, I still had Mom and Dad in the cabinet. I had to give in and plan "the deposit." I asked Stu if he would consider coming out for Thanksgiving and then we could do the deed the next day. Once he was on board, I firmed up plans with Phil. It was all set; we would do it the day after Thanksgiving. Over a year and a half would have passed since Mom's passing, almost five since Dad's. We had closed up the apartment, sold most of their possessions, and divvied up the rest. The estate had been distributed. We had celebrated Phil's engagement and marriage to his new wife. We had welcomed his new stepdaughter as a new niece. It was time to put this and them to rest.

~

That Friday morning was a bitterly cold day. We were going to get on the ferry on the Staten Island side and get off in Battery Park. Tom and I would join everyone for lunch, most likely in the Seaport, and then Tom and I would return home to prepare for our Chanukah dinner that evening. My brothers and their children would remain in the city for the day and get home in time for dinner. We didn't expect the cold.

I had grabbed two messenger bags and put Mom in one and Dad in the other. I had sat both brothers down the night before and explained how important it was that we not draw attention to ourselves while doing it, and that I preferred to exclude the kids from the process, not even letting them know it was going on as I feared they would let it slip and we would get caught dumping our parents overboard. I had the whole thing planned in my mind. We would leave the kids and go stand on the back platform of the ferry. As we crossed the harbor we would wait until we were nearer to the Statue of Liberty and then unceremoniously throw the packages overboard. I assumed we would do it over opposite sides of the boat, as Mom would not want to spend eternity in the same pile of seaweed as Dad. We would then return to the kids and proceed to the city, where over lunch we could tell or not tell the kids what had just gone on.

The boat was supercrowded that day. When we got on the boat, Phil informed me he was having his kids participate in the tossing. I figured this would be okay. We got my new sister-in-law seated with her daughter and the younger kids near the front of the boat and the rest of us headed to the back platform. It was as crowded as could be. None of us had ever ridden the ferry before. It moves pretty slowly, especially as it is pulling away from the dock. The first ten minutes of the ride are pretty dreary as you go through the shipyards of Staten Island Bay before hitting the harbor. Everyone around us was in a festive mood. None of us was near the edge. Inside I had a creeping anxiety that we would get caught. I thought I was alone in feeling this. We stood shoulder-to-shoulder and worked the straps on the shoulder bags, one on me the other on Tom.

I struck up a conversation with a woman standing by the rail with her young daughter. They were headed to New York to see the store windows. It was their tradition the day after Thanksgiving. I shared my mission with her. She was quite empathic, sharing her own recent losses and insisting I have the rail for my "important" task. I protested but she insisted. I felt like a heel but also didn't want to see my chance disappear. As I moved into place, Tom came up to my side.

"Quick, the cops!" he muttered.

"Don't panic, they're just making rounds on the boat." I was not alone in my anxiety.

The cop seemed to take up station on the opposite rail and was staring at the disappearing Staten Island coast and the Jersey shore in the distance. Tom's anxiety was noticeably rising.

"Don't worry, he won't stay there," I tried to reassure him.

"No, I'm going to do it now. We have to!"

I called the others over to confer when out of the corner of my eye I saw the package go overboard.

"He was going to come over here," Tom responded to my annoyed eye.

Phil added, "Quick, the other one before it's too late." He took it out of my bag and chucked it overboard.

I said a quick goodbye to whichever of my parents was now slowly sinking in Staten Island Bay; condemned by our anxiety to spend eternity floating around the shipyards of Staten Island.

I wondered if they knew, were they watching? Did they and could they care? Would they come back and haunt us?

I find solace in the idea that the end had provided a subject for Mom to kvetch about for all eternity.

"So, I'm in Staten Island Bay. I never liked Staten Island. It's the story of my life—now, my afterlife ... But they meant well."

Acknowledgments

When my book is released, it will be exactly ten years and two weeks since I first walked into Memoir I at the Gotham Writers Workshop in New York City. I had just marked one year of being cancer free from prostate cancer and believed that I was going to write about that experience. Instead, this book about being the caregiver to my parents and my husband's parents poured out. Along the way, there have been many loving and supportive people who have contributed to the journey. First of all, I need to acknowledge my very first teacher at Gotham, Ryan Britt, who helped me to believe not only that I could be a writer, but that I was a writer. Ryan also created an environment in that classroom that fostered the development of my very first writer's group, a group that stayed together for more than two years. Together we supported each other's writing, learned each other's stories, celebrated each other's joys, and mourned each other's losses. Thanks to Jose Rolon, Jeanine Boulay, Mandy Berman, Natalie Chomet, Mihae Kim, and Susan Katz. Three other Gotham peers have stood out from among others for their support and quality feedback, thanks to Christola Phoenix and to Darrin Pruitt and Connie Murray who eventually joined our writers group.

Every teacher I had at Gotham contributed something along the way and I thank them all. Mostly, though, I thank Kelly Caldwell. Kelly taught most of the semesters of Memoir that I participated in and along the way became a mentor and a friend. I always looked forward to her editorial suggestions, valued her praise, and never questioned her critiques. Kelly, you are an essential element of *Four Funerals, No Marriage*!

Five years ago, I received a mysterious invitation to come to a writer's retreat in the mountains of Vermont for a free 5-day stay. Raised to be skeptic, I asked a lot of questions before accepting an invitation to When Words Count Writer's

Retreat in Rochester, Vermont. I'm so glad I went. I found an amazing community of writers led by the director Steve Eisner. Steve has become a mentor in the business of publishing, the stick in many motivational equations, and most importantly a friend. I appreciate all you've done and contributed to "Four Funerals…" I want to thank the staff at WWC, especially, Amber Griffith, who made us comfortable and fed us so well so we writers could focus on the task at hand. WWC also sponsors a contest for writers to win a publishing deal they call "Pitch Week." I want to thank everyone who was involved in the Pitch Week I participated in; the judges Dede Cummings, publisher at Green Writer's Press and Steve Rohr, publicist, both who became friends as well as mentors. Among the group of writers I competed for the contract with were Shabnam Samuel, Christine Merriman, and Robyn Aversa, a wonderful group of women who have become writing colleagues and dear valued friends. Finally, from Pitch Week I need to thank Peggy Moran who served as my copyeditor (as well as partial story editor on the side) and Charita Brown who served as the coach for all of us competitors and has continued to serve as a cheerleader and support. Thank you to all.

There have been many others who I have come to know while writing in Vermont, too many to mention you all here. Those that stand out for an extra thanks include Mary Build, Jen Epstein, Diane Pomerantz, Paulette Woolf, Justine, Mira T. Lee (who has gone on to become my webmaster), Vanessa Kilmer (who was also a Beta reader of my manuscript) and Amy Klinger who has become a huge friend and support. If I left anybody out, I'm sorry and thank you. A very big thanks to my other beta readers: Angela Scalpello, Charles Foy, John Caminiti and Nina Williams.

Over the course of eight years of writing I accepted the invitations of several friends and family members who had beach and/or mountain retreats that became writing refuges where many chapters were first typed out. Thanks to Mary Alosio and Bo Joelson, to Shawn Sobkowski and Helene Schwarzbach, and to Sally and Peter Rudoy. Your retreat spaces were priceless comforts on my path to publication.

To the team at Woodhall Press, led by David LeGere, I offer a hearty thanks for the opportunity to bring my baby to life. To Ben Tanzer, you have become an invaluable asset in bringing "Four Funerals…" to the World. I feel a beautiful friendship forming that I hope continues long beyond the covers of the book.

To my countless friends who have listened to me talk about this journey, endlessly, I thank you for your support and love.

Finally, to my husband, Tom, who traveled the journey in the book and then of the book, always by my side, you deserve more than any thanks I can put on this page. You are and always have been a support, a guide, a source of nourishment and a generous heart who made room for me to try on all my hats. I love you so much more than my luggage.

About the Author

Mike Keren is trained as a clinical psychologist with advanced training in psychoanalysis and family therapy. He currently maintains a practice with adults and couples in central New Jersey, although in the past he has worked in a variety of community and correctional facilities.

Mike enjoys a challenge in his free time and has explored the world of competitive gay tournament bowling (several trophies and a bit of prize money), golf (bored to tears) as well as stand-up comedy. He worked the open mic and bar comedy scene for several years but decided to leave the stage to the younger folks. He decided then to channel his humor into creative writing. If you are reading this paragraph, you are holding his first book in your hands.

Mike is supported in his endeavors by his loving husband, Tom, and their two canine children, Carley and Clyde. They divide their time between central New Jersey and the Pocono Mountains of Pennsylvania.